# THE BORDER CROSSED US

## The Case for Opening the US-Mexico Border

Justin Akers Chacón

Haymarket Books
Chicago, Illinois

Published in 2021 by
Haymarket Books
P.O. Box 180165
Chicago, IL 60618
773-583-7884
www.haymarketbooks.org
info@haymarketbooks.org

ISBN: 978-1-64259-460-7

Distributed to the trade in the US through Consortium Book Sales and Distribution (www.cbsd.com) and internationally through Ingram Publisher Services International (www.ingramcontent.com).

This book was published with the generous support of Lannan Foundation and Wallace Action Fund.

Special discounts are available for bulk purchases by organizations and institutions. Please call 773-583-7884 or email info@haymarketbooks.org for more information.

Cover design by Rachel Cohen. Photograph of art on the US-Mexico border wall © Christopher Morris/Corbis via Getty Images

Printed in Canada by union labor.

Library of Congress Cataloging-in-Publication data is available.

10 9 8 7 6 5 4 3 2 1

# Praise for THE BORDER CROSSED US

"*The Border Crossed Us* is a meticulously researched manifesto on the US-Mexico border. Justin Akers Chacón masterfully exposes how capital mobility necessarily criminalizes the movement of labor, and, with radical and urgent clarity, he calls on all of us to strengthen the movement to open the border." —HARSHA WALIA, author of *Border and Rule: Global Migration, Capitalism, and the Rise of Racist Nationalism*

"At last, here is a book showing just how critical the demand for the freedom of workers' mobility is to the anticapitalist movement. Justin Akers Chacón makes the urgent case for a new internationalism, one that openly rejects the divisive, racist, and anti-worker politics upholding national borders. With a clear-eyed examination of how labor repression is the core of the migra-state, Chacón's call for cross-border—and anti-border—organizing is shown to be a necessary part of working-class politics everywhere." —NANDITA SHARMA, author of *Home Rule: National Sovereignty and the Separation of Natives and Migrants*

"This brilliant and timely book lays bare the violent extortion and extraction of working-class migrant labor by untangling the hydra of the North American model of capitalist accumulation. Justin Akers Chacón's incisive temporal and geographic analysis of US capitalist imperialism sets the stage for the urgent and immediate mobilization within labor, migrant, and union organizing across borders. As a scholar-activist, Justin Akers Chacón empowers us to sharpen our critique of the border paradox of open borders for capital and closed borders for people, to finally dismantle and abolish the migra-state, from free trade agreements to detention centers. Our communities depend on it." —LESLIE QUINTANILLA, cofounder of the Center for Interdisciplinary Environmental Justice and assistant professor of women and gender studies at San Francisco State University

"*The Border Crossed Us* provides a salutary antidote to the stale debate about whether immigration harms the working class. The book offers a convincing and comprehensive account of how the "half-closed border" between the United States and Mexico gives more power to employers and makes workers on both sides more exploitable. As US capital has inundated Mexico over the past century, increasing its hold on the Mexican economy in the era of free trade, the border has kept Mexican people impoverished and limited their rights and alternatives both at home and in the United States. This book cuts through the distorted nature of our current debates on immigration and makes the most coherent case I've seen for how opening the border will help all workers, on both sides, by giving them the right to organize and fight for a decent life. The border only serves to prevent workers from fighting effectively against capital that has long been transnational." —AVIVA CHOMSKY, author of *Undocumented: How Immigration Became Illegal*

"This book captures the current political moment perfectly. It takes a look at the past and how we arrived at this point, and the crises that have harmed workers on both sides of the border. It also sheds light on the emerging worker movements that have arisen to overcome the ongoing efforts by capitalist industries to prevent or break grassroots and independent worker organizing. The question of open borders is one that we as workers have to ask ourselves. The borders are already open to finance, products, capital, wealth, but remain closed for the people who create the wealth through our labor. Yet, it is more than just a labor issue. It is a human right to migrate, and to stay home as well. Our union congratulates Justin for writing a book that is asking the questions we have always had to contend with, while also discussing and proposing a better world for all workers." —EDGAR FRANKS, political director Familias Unidas por la Justicia

"If you want to understand why international borders are open for the corporate class, while slammed shut for migrant workers, this excellent, incisive, thoroughly researched, and thought-provoking book is for you. In *The Border Crossed Us,* Justin Akers Chacón addresses precisely what most discussions on open borders lack: how their enforcement is entrenched in capitalism and the free market system. He makes clear that there is no "security" or "protection" with militarized divisions, that borders need to be broken down for the sake of humanity's collective well-being, and that it is a working-class, cross-border solidarity movement that can lead us to justice." —TODD MILLER, author of *Empire of Borders: The Expansion of the US Border Around the World*

"In *The Border Crossed Us,* Justin Akers Chacón asks and answers the hard questions about how the corporate capitalist class has been using border militarization and violent immigration enforcement to squeeze every last bit of profit out of workers, casting aside their dignity and humanity along the way. Chacón does the necessary work of staring hard into the everyday reality of people trampled by the border machine. This is an essential addition to border studies, as convincing of the need to open borders as it is compelling." —JOHN WASHINGTON, author of *The Dispossessed: A Story of Asylum at the US-Mexican Border and Beyond*

# Contents

## Part III: Immigrant Workers: Unionization vs. Criminalization



## Part IV: Opening the Border through Class Struggle and Solidarity

# INTRODUCTION

# The Bordering of Capitalism

North American capitalism has been transformed into two overlapping yet starkly contradictory realities for capitalists and workers. Nowhere is this more apparent than through observation of what has taken place between the United States and Mexico over the last four decades.[1] Through the aegis of the state, its two major political parties, and in alliance with the capitalist class of Mexico, the US state has transformed the region into a singular borderless economy dedicated to facilitating the movement of capital.

Integration in this form has been accomplished through what is characterized as a "free-trade agreement" (FTA). For the purpose of this book, I define an FTA as a state-crafted legal mechanism that supersedes, and eventually eliminates, the concept of "national borders" for the free movement of money. Throughout this text, the movement of money will be referenced both as *capital*: accumulated wealth invested in ownership of the means of production, and as *profit*: wealth accumulated from existing investments through the exploitation of workers and the extraction of their surplus labor value.[2] The Marxist conception of surplus labor value refers to the *extra* amount of value produced by workers *beyond* what is necessary to meet their own material needs to sustain themselves.[3] This extra value passes into the hands of the capitalist in the form of capital or profit, depending on its role in the circuitry of capitalism. Therefore, FTAs are not the same thing as free exchange in an abstract economic sense, as they have been developed and made operational within a specific historical period and political context and rely on the exploitation of workers beyond borders and on an international scale.[4]

Emanating from rich nations within the contours of the increasing internationalization and financialization of capitalism since World War II, the FTA functions as an instrument of *neo-imperialist* policy. They have been implemented to unravel and overthrow protectionist trade regimes put in place in so-called developing nations (formerly colonized states and those underdeveloped by anterior modes of imperialism) to theoretically prevent or inhibit foreign capitalist domination. In the case of Mexico, the imposition of the FTA is the culmination of stages in the dismantling of the nationalist capitalist project that emerged victorious from the Mexican Revolution.

The birth of state-managed capitalism in Mexico was the result of a radical and impulsively nationalist uprising referred to as the Mexican Revolution of 1910. The revolutionary movement toppled the dictatorship of Porfirio Díaz, which represented against an alliance of oligarchic landowners, the Catholic Church, and a weak Mexican capitalist class subordinated to foreign capitalists and investors. As Adam David Morton describes "combined and uneven development" in the Mexican context in his work *Revolution and State in Modern Mexico,* postcolonial states formed amid a rapid global expansion of capitalism and in various ways replaced, incorporated, and coexisted with previous forms of social relations.[5]

The development of the economy under these conditions shaped the class character of the revolution and its aftermath. It took its self-styled, postrevolutionary national capitalist form only after successive stages of revolutionary class war, when an ascendant middle-class coterie was able to divide, defeat, and co-opt mass popular movements centered around the rural proletariat and crush a small but potent revolutionary socialist movement that vied for leadership over the urban working classes.[6] The consolidation of power around this new ruling class with aspirations toward "national development," which became dependent on the subordination of the laboring classes within a capitalist framework, determined the bourgeois character and limitations of the revolution.

The eventual defeat of the Mexican model of state-directed and state-managed capitalism, referred to hereafter as state capitalism, was carried out in the context of incessant US imperialist opposition and war of maneuver (ebbing and flowing in relation to world events and the balance of social forces inside Mexico) and the prolonged crisis of capitalism that overwhelmed and eventually collapsed the system. This also took place with the direct coordination among sections of the Mexican capitalist class itself, especially those who built and maintained transnational economic linkages with US capitalists and who aligned politically with the ideological and military operations of US imperialism across the region.

The defeat of state capitalism occurred quantitatively, through incremental changes in the direction toward "free trade" as the Mexican capitalist economy became increasingly coupled to that of the US and integrated into global financial markets. The final phase occurred more abruptly and reached its culmination in the full-blown global crisis of capitalism that began in the early 1970s. The Mexican debt crisis allowed the US state to move more aggressively to boost the aligned sectors of the Mexican capitalist class through financial bailouts and bury and pave over the residual features of the postrevolutionary state. This allowed for the return to the prerevolutionary state of affairs, in which the inviolable rights of US-based transnational capital and mobility were reinstated, and the unfettered implantation and dominance over Mexico's national economy were reestablished, a condition that will be described in this text as the reimposition of semicolonialism.

This took place through the elevation of the rights and mobility of capital embodied in the North American Free Trade Agreement (formerly NAFTA, now the US-Mexico-Canada Agreement, or USMCA). NAFTA was the culmination of a guided process of destructive reorganization of the Mexican state capitalism compelled by a profound crisis in the global capitalist system. The collapsing of state capitalism in Mexico and subsequent opening of the nation's economy to unfettered capital export was a watershed event in the advance of the emerging US model of neoliberal capitalism and its international export.

## From Neoliberalism to Neocolonialism

The post-Depression-era model saw the peak unionization and rising wages, state regulation of industry and finance, progressive taxation, and state investment in comprehensive social programs and services.[7] This model of the state coincided with the greatest expansion of US capitalism after World War II and its preeminence on a global scale. These two factors—economic growth alongside a rising standard of living for working-class people—could coexist as long as the capitalist class increased accumulation and reaped profits through international capital export. This formula also required unprecedented military expansion, as the US state squared off with the Soviet Union for global dominance.

By 1973, this model of capitalism sunk into crisis, driven by a declining rate of profit and rising European and Asian competition challenging North American primacy within international markets. The end of the Cold War changed military equations, as the US emerged unrivaled with military power deployed across every corner of the globe.

In response, the US state in alignment with the capitalist class began by reordering social relations at home. The method chosen to restore profitability from this decaying capitalist model required squeezing more from the working class and necessitated a rupture with the existing order and a fundamental shift in the balance of existing social wealth from the working class back to the owners of capital.

The two capitalist parties, the Democrats and the Republicans, agreed in principle with this project, leading it to be referred to as the "Washington Consensus." This effort, which should be understood by its real name—*class war*—took place on many fronts. This involved coordinated union-busting, the suppression of wages, gutting of welfare, slashing of progressive taxation, and privatization of public institutions and services. It also included the building up of the mass-incarceration system and the bloating and arming of police forces across the country. These methods of wealth transfer and repression remain institutionalized today.

Capital accumulated through this process—or the value transferred from labor to capitalists to reinvest to make more profit by exploiting *more* labor—needed new markets. The US state and capitalist class set their sights on Mexico. After the revolution of 1910, the Mexican state established an economic model that restricted the operations of foreign capital. As a means to resolve their own crisis, US policy makers sought to overturn Mexican state capitalism through the incremental imposition of free-market policies.

In their effort, they found partners in sections of the Mexican capitalist class also seeking new methods to expand their wealth. Both groups saw the exploitation of Mexico's vast working classes as the key to prosperity.

The intensification and expansion of labor exploitation coincided with the US-led financialization of capitalism. This refers to the spectacular rise of financial capital on an international scale, which functions differently from other forms of productive capital. *Finance capital* is speculative in nature. It is used to buy out existing productive capacity or to finance productive activity or to be lent in the form of interest received from distribution as credit or debt. It is only deployed on the assumption of a relatively quick rate of return in the form of profits or more capital. In the second volume of *Capital,* Karl Marx wrote:

> [To the possessor of money-capital] the production process appears simply as an unavoidable middle term, a necessary evil for the purpose of money-making. This explains why all nations characterized by the capitalist mode of production are periodically seized by fits of giddiness in which they try to accomplish the money-making without the mediation of the production process.[8]

The financialization of capitalism has allowed for the accumulation of astronomical fortunes and the rise of the billionaires within the capitalist classes internationally.

The growth of finance capital has grown in proportion to the expansion of free markets. This helps explain the impetus for opening restricted or protected markets, especially from within the richest nations. It also goes far in explaining how the richest finance capitalists have entered directly into government to administer state policies in their favor. Financialization has also linked capitalist classes between rich nations and postcolonial and poor nations through partnerships and alliances.

The neoliberal stage of capitalism emerged from the wreckage of the postwar model of capitalist accumulation. For the purpose of this text, neoliberalism is used as a concept to describe the state-led process of the intentional and aggressive dismantling of existing national and international barriers and inhibitors to unmitigated capital accumulation in the context of capitalist globalization and financialization. As conventional methods of capital mobility and accumulation have receded, stagnated, or been impeded, the rich capitalist states have turned inward and outward to aggressively restore the primacy of capital accumulation and replenish declining rates of profitability. This process of class warfare has had many faces and manifestations in the past four decades.

For the purpose of this book and the case of the neoliberalization of US-Mexico international relations, we will focus on how state action has been taken to internationalize capitalist mobility, force open once-protected national markets, and to otherwise eradicate the vestiges of previous revolutionary advances, social reforms, and policy structures that embodied the accumulated gains of past episodes of class struggle. The neoliberal transformation of the political economy in Mexico was largely complete by 1990. The opening of Mexico became a model that was subsequently exported and replicated across the globe by the next global recession in 2008.

The increased exploitation of labor, the singular process through which surplus value can be extracted from workers and repurposed into capital, is at the heart of the transitional character of North American capitalism. While exploitation primarily occurs through the maintenance of the wage system, it also takes place in the form of destroying the mechanisms and gains accrued by labor in previous periods that served to minimize, mitigate, or otherwise inhibit the aspirations of the capitalist class to exercise total control over workers. This explains why unconcealed class warfare has become a more integral feature of capitalist class rule, and how more overt and expansive forms of state control have emerged and been normalized.

In the neoliberal period, for instance, the capitalist class has taken direct and uncontested power in the electoral arena through its political representatives. Different factions of capital vie for power through the Democratic and Republican parties, but there is a general consensus to use the state as an instrument to advance their collective interests regardless of which party holds the governing reins. In the neoliberal period, one characterized by deepening cycles of capitalist crisis, skyrocketing social inequality, pandemic waves, and climate catastrophe, this ruling-class accordance has worked even more aggressively to shift the social costs of economic failure onto workers within and across the US-Mexico border.

Under the auspices of neoliberal restructuring, the US state has abrogated previous arrangements and social expectations. Workers labor more for less, the standard of living has decreased, and the social-welfare and public functions of the state have been defunded or eviscerated to the point of inadequacy, dysfunction, and dereliction. Wealth has been transferred on an unprecedented scale from the working classes to the capitalist class. For instance, in the United States, the top 1 percent owns nearly $30 trillion of assets while the bottom half owns less than nothing, meaning they have more debts than they have assets. A recent analysis found that "between 1989 and 2018, the top 1 percent increased its total net worth by $21 trillion. The bottom 50 percent actually saw its net worth decrease by $900 billion over the same period."[9]

This pattern is also playing out internationally, illustrated by a report showing that the wealth of the twenty-six richest people surpassed the amount that is collectively held by 3.8 billion people, or half of the global population. Furthermore, the arc of inequality is increasing more rapidly each year, with one new billionaire created globally every two days between 2017 and 2018 alone.[10]

For the working classes, the picture has been very different. Of the thirty-six richest countries in the Organization for Economic Cooperation and Development, the US had the highest number of impoverished workers per capita by 2016, reaching about 18% of the population (with Mexico close behind).[11] An even larger share of the US population hovers just above the poverty rate. That group has also seen their standard of living plummet in the last two decades. By 2019, an estimated 78 percent of workers lived paycheck-to-paycheck, while an estimated 28 percent of US adults have no emergency savings, and another 25 percent have only enough savings to cover living expenses for three months.[12] This was the reality for millions of workers on the *eve* of the 2020 economic crisis and pandemic.

Since the global economic crises if 2008 and 2020, the latter coinciding with a pandemic, inequality, poverty, and precarity have accelerated. In the first six months of the 2020 pandemic, the 634 United States billionaires added $845 billion, or 29 percent, to their accumulated wealth. The total net worth of the nation's billionaires rose from $2.95 trillion to

$3.8 trillion—equivalent to roughly 18 percent of total US gross domestic product (GDP).[13]

The functions of the state that had previously performed redistributive and regulatory services to file down the sharpest edges of class inequality and mitigate class antagonism have been whittled away. According to one comprehensive study of the condition of the "welfare state" over the last four decades,

> The public sector appears under siege across the globe. While there are variations across and within nations in how this plays out, the arms of the state that provide the social safety net and protect citizens' well-being are especially at risk. The erosion of the state as an institution can be seen in cuts to social programs and public sector jobs, underfunded infrastructure, the sale of public assets and other forms of privatization, along with the more general weakening of regulatory authority and diversion of resources to the private sector.[14]

Over the same period, meanwhile, the state functions that are essential to the processes of capital accumulation, such as the military, armed state agencies, and the carceral system—have become enormously bloated with endless budget increases. The border has become increasingly walled-off and militarized, while migration has been restricted and controlled by an ever-growing army of enforcers and expanding operations within and throughout communities across the nation and even across borders.

Neoliberalism has also driven a reordering of international relations, as it operates within an imperialist framework. This refers to perpetual competition, wars of maneuver, espionage, and inevitably open conflict between competing capitalist powers and their allies. The scramble to take a larger share of global markets to export capital, exploit labor, and extract natural resources plays out in trade wars, shifting alliances, and ongoing forms of direct and indirect warfare.

The operation of capitalism cannot function without military buildup, which fuels an arms race between competing powers. Furthermore, capitalist expansion into other nations is predicated on exploitation and wealth transfer—which justifiably provokes resistance and oppositional movements. Therefore, the imposition of free markets and their perpetuation cannot occur without the use or threat of military force.

## The North American Model of Bordered Capitalism

In the case of the United States and Mexico, the US state has taken neoliberal measures to dismantle postrevolutionary outcomes, which were a barrier to capital accumulation. These included the removal of restrictions on foreign capital investment, foreign ownership, tariffs, and other artifacts of *anti-yanqui* nationalism. The opening of Mexico was driven by the notion that capital has a right to cross borders to exploit Mexican labor, but Mexican workers do not have the right to migrate. For them, there is a wall and *la migra*. The grotesque architecture of this system of *free trade without free people* has been elaborated into what is now a first principle of US-led global capitalism: international capital can cross borders to increase the exploitation of Mexicans in Mexico or whichever other nation, while criminalization of economically displaced migrants allows for a secondary form of exploitation of their labor when they cross the border as migrants who are precluded from having basic legal rights and protections.

Rather than "free trade," the imposition of NAFTA in Mexico can be better understood as a means to allow capital to cross borders freely. These accords are the new constitutions of capitalism that sanctify transnational rights for multinational capital that supersede the rights of people. In essence, so-called free trade and free markets have eliminated all borders to its movement and barriers to its circulation, creating a supra-economy for capital that operates in opposite manner to the bordered and restricted world of labor.

Since the exploitation of labor on both sides of the border is central to the production that enables the most profitable form of trade across borders, the capitalist state cannot allow for the free movement of labor across borders, as this would inevitably lead to cross-border integration, unionization, and wage equalization. So, while money and goods now move unhindered between nations, workers have seen a commensurate increase in persecution for doing the same. Therefore, free-trade agreements like NAFTA are an unmasked form of class warfare, in which a new transnational architecture has been forged out of the intensification of imperialist extraction and labor exploitation in order to augment and extend methods of capital accumulation.

The restructuring process of neoliberal capitalism on an international scale, with its legitimization of mass theft, repression of resistance, and embodiment of totalitarian rights for capital, ensures that it can only operate antidemocratically.[15] "Democracy" under neoliberal capitalism means the total liberation of capital and the elevation of its superior rights, which requires the destruction of all obstructive vestiges of the past and the clearing of the lane for the rule of the investors.

Freedom in the form of democratic participation was conspicuously absent for the Mexican people when the components of NAFTA were dictated by the US government and International Monetary Fund (IMF) during the economic crisis of the 1980s. These outside entities provided international political support and financial backing for the Mexican capitalist class and the aligned sections of the ruling PRI (Institutional Revolutionary Party) eager to tear away the husk of the old order. International creditors coordinated a forceful guiding hand by providing emergency funding when the economy approached insolvency after 1982. These were no ordinary loans, though. The IMF packaged these loans into so-called structural adjustment programs, which required the signatories to dismantle all barriers to international capitalist investment, shred the revolutionary guarantees of the constitution, and surrender half a century's worth of accumulated state-controlled wealth to the richest men in Mexico. Mexico's economy became the most open in the world in terms of access for international capital, with more so-called free-trade agreements than any other country in the world.[16] The speed and scope of the liquidation of the Mexican model of state-led capitalism was comparable to the collapse of the Soviet Union and aligned Eastern European regimes, which were tumbling at about the same time. The end of the Cold War and withdrawal of Soviet troops and diplomatic missions from the different corners of the globe increased the confidence of the US-led capitalist governments internationally. They began to extend their power and influence in the ensuing vacuum—both militarily and economically.

The transition to the new economic model created a class of millionaires and billionaires, while wreaking havoc on the majority working classes. The outcome has been cycles of austerity, foreign economic recolonization of whole sectors of the economy, and the largest episodes of displacement and out-migration in modern history. By 2020, for instance, over 272 million people were migrants living outside of their home countries, with two-thirds being labor migrants.[17] This transition to "free trade" was certainly not the result of Mexicans freely exercising their democratic rights.

This method of capitalist accumulation, which I will refer to as the North American model (NAM), enforces inalienable rights for capital mobility while criminalizing the movement of labor. For example, border enforcement policies are enabling the maximum exploitation of the working classes on a regional scale, even as workers in the US and Mexico are being fused together through different forms of integrated supply chain production, where manufactured products are built in stages across national borders.

The North American model includes the hyperpolicing and repression of undocumented workers within the US and the maintenance of segmented labor markets across nations. In practice, labor markets like these serve to create and maintain a superexploitative low-wage threshold within the regionalized economy. That is, employers can leverage undocumented workers' vulnerability in order to suppress wages and working conditions to below the actual social sustainability and reproduction of the workers themselves, thereby forcing the workers to live and work under precarious, dangerous, and impoverished conditions.

Through a seemingly endless raft of immigration policy at all levels of government, the state has battened down the lowest possible socioeconomic threshold for the benefit of capital accumulation. Furthermore, it has been working incessantly in this trajectory to restructure labor markets across the economy in this manner through expanding immigration enforcement, restrictions, and other punitive measures from the macro to the micro level.

Restricting citizenship and national origin within the US economy allows for different labor status conditions, which undergird wage differentiation within the nation. Policed borders then serve as a bulwark to maintain wage differentials between nations, even as workers increasingly perform the same labor, work for the same firms, and contribute to the fabrication of the same products.

While the NAM has seen the careful construction of new labor regimes predicated on depressed and differentiated labor markets, it also yields unintended contradictions. Supply-chain production, common transnational employment, and other production linkages within this model are concurrently interconnecting and integrating workers in unprecedented ways. The potential for transnational solidarity, class struggle, and union organization is pointing a way forward for labor in this era and showing a road map for how we can build a movement to open the borders.

## Open Borders for Capital, Controlled Borders for Workers

In the current stage of US-led neoliberal capitalist globalization, the capitalist class in its different capacities and strata have all aligned to benefit from the arrangements of free trade and its consequential displacement of people who are compelled to migrate across borders in search of work. International capital has exponentially extended its capacity to exploit workers across national borders. Other sections have profited enormously by equipping the *migra-state,* while still others have made voluminous gain through the exploitation of workers whose labor value has been artificially degraded and depressed through state mechanisms of criminalization.

At the top of this arrangement sits finance capital, which creates the rules, regulations, and policies of international capitalist political economy (the NAM). Through its "investments" it profits from all stages and processes of labor exploitation within the maintained dichotomy of an open border for capital and restrictive border for labor. This has been accomplished in rapid succession in the short history of US-Mexico free-trade integration: a flood of capital export in the form of new speculative investments, market buyouts, takeovers, and other methods that have accelerated the concentration of ownership and control. The result is a new architecture of dominance that reroutes the bulk of financial transaction and exchange through the circuitry of US-based capitalist firms and investments. Furthermore, the NAM has been coupled with the wiring of state and private financial entities to facilitate fluid and unrestricted transnational capital and profit flows. As one study of this phenomenon observed, neoliberal capitalism, which is dominated by finance capital, brings "all aspects of economy and society under its thumb."[18]

The capitalist class also benefit from displacement migration, which is a logical outcome of the free-trade model of wealth transfer from labor to capital both within and between nations. Small and large sectors of the productive economy utilize migrant labor as a means to extract more labor value to keep their businesses in operation, make more profit, and accumulate more capital. Within capital's own national territory, finance capital needs the productive process of migrant labor exploitation in order to profit from migration itself.[19] Through everything from ownership of the largest productive firms that use migrant labor to selling weapons or prison beds to the state or charging migrants exorbitant prices for sending remittances, finance capital has become arterial throughout all aspects of the migration-related sectors of the economy—and has subsequently increased its wealth astronomically.

The triumphal ascendancy of US-led capitalist globalization, in practical terms, means that national borders have been eliminated for capital. The model created from the opening of Mexico continues to be replicated across the world. Money in the form of investment moves seamlessly across the globe searching for profit, settling across boundaries without checkpoints, without being apprehended by armed agents or being detained and subjected to cruel and discriminatory treatment.

Through investment in ownership and control over whole transnational industries, capitalist firms leverage their operations into an international economy of scale. Nevertheless, they can only profit through the exploitation of labor and therefore rely on borders to differentiate, divide, and further subdivide workers along national and international lines. Once profits are accrued, they freely return and overflow bank accounts without need for passports or papers. There is no regulatory or repressive state for capital—only *agreements*.

While the most powerful states have enabled the rise of a system where capital has internationalized, they have also simultaneously constrained the movement of large swathes of the international working class. This has become reality through the growth and ossification of militarized border zones and the building up of various legal and political regimes to repress migrant people.

Along the US-Mexico border, migrating people die crossing deserts attempting to circumvent border walls and guards. They are killed by bullets, extreme temperatures, drowning, or preventable infections born of squalid conditions intentionally gestated in concentration camps as part of a program of intentional cruelty. Life is squeezed from men, women, and children as they desperately try to cross a border merely to survive and work.

Without papers, they live in fear of arrest and detention while they work. They look in all directions and keep their heads low in public spaces, to account not only for police presence but also for those whose racial and xenophobic hatred for migrants leads them to orchestrate violence. Life passes by, and these migrants live without basic opportunities or rights, and with diminished hope for a progressive future.

Within the boundaries of the United States, the criminalization of migrants' mobility and labor engender poverty and social-political isolation. This precarious condition adds value for capitalism, which breaks down and undermines working-class economic and political organization—and with it the confidence and ability to resist or beat back state violence through collective mass protest action. This situation creates optimal conditions for the superexploitation of their labor.

Racialized violence and inequalities intrinsic to border militarization and labor control through the manipulation of citizenship have been ongoing features of modern US capital accumulation, and have become more essential to its everyday functioning. They are the hardening joints of a sclerotic system, increasingly dependent on the force of institutional violence to extract surplus value from a growing and subjugated population. Migrant labor is interconnected to the population by class position but disarticulated from the nation-state through "illegalization," which creates segregated and unfree labor within the working class based on racial and national discrimination.

Criminalization of cross-border labor and the deployment of state violence and repression are intentional efforts to prevent migrant workers from forming or joining unions, participating in social, political, or civic class-based activities to improve and uplift their condition, and to otherwise prevent their integration and consolidation into the US working class in a way that allows for cohesion, solidarity, and coordinated action. As long as borders are nonexistent for capital—yet remain present and closed for labor—wages and working and living conditions for all workers will continue to stagnate or decline.

## The Case for Opening the US-Mexico Border

The slogan "The border crossed us" has resonated from the migrant rights movement in the last few decades. It captures the reality and popular conception that physical borders only exist to repress people and enforce inequality. It also embeds a historical understanding: that the US-Mexico border crossed the people in multiple ways.

The border was first imposed through Anglo colonization and theft of the land from Indigenous and Mexican people after the invasion and occupation of 1846–1848. At the turn of the twentieth century, the border continued to shift farther south for US capital, in order to allow for dominance over the Mexican economy into the years leading up to the Mexican Revolution. The border changed again in the 1940s to allow for the US state to bring millions of contract laborers (braceros) into the US to carry out low-wage labor within different industries.

After a fifty-year experience with state-managed, protectionist capitalism following the revolutionary period of 1910–1940, the border was again extended southward to allow US-based investors and speculators to recapture the Mexican economy. Most recently, the border as enforcement regime has spread throughout the interior of the United States to police and repress migrant laborers and hold millions of people in legal suspension and without rights.

Over the course of this book I lay out the case for opening the US-Mexico border to allow for the free movement and settlement of migrating people seeking employment or refuge. In Part 1 I chart the origins of US capitalism and how it developed as the preeminent global economic power through stages of military colonization, imperialism, and racialized systems of labor exploitation that laid the foundation for the original stages of capital accumulation. I focus on the most recent period of neoliberal capitalism and how finance capital leveraged state power to reopen post-revolutionary Mexico to capital export through the doctrine of free trade.

This process combined the projection of military power, disproportionate US economic size and scale within global capitalist markets, the fostering of transborder capitalist class relationships, and the crisis of the global capitalist system itself. This text explains the transition from state capitalism to the primacy of US capital ownership, and control of the commanding heights of the Mexican economy is explained and described as the return of *semicolonization.*

Further, this semicolonization describes the condition of foreign control through primarily economic means—while in concert and partnership with the dominant sections of the Mexican ruling class, whose cohesion and subsequent rise to power occurred in tandem with the procession of US imperial policy. While the condition of semicolonization affords some autonomy for the Mexican state and capitalist class, it is confined within the parameters of compatibility with US policy.

The imposition of free trade and free-market capitalism was a transition point for the reorganization of a US-centric global model. The semicolonization of the Mexican economy enriched the US capitalist class as well as its ascendant partners in Mexico and served as a staging ground for exporting the Mexican model internationally.

Opening the border for capital led to massive internal displacement in that country. As authentic labor unionism declined, jobs disappeared and the state downsized its social welfare provisions. This drove migration to the United States, even as the implementation of international free-market capitalism coincided with the restriction of movement of workers across borders—the paradox is the heart of the NAM.

Contrary to current practice, it is clear that if the US-Mexico border allows for the free movement of capital, the rich, and the general population of people from the US to cross into or settle into Mexico without restriction, then so too should workers from south of the border be allowed free movement and settlement into the US if they need or choose to do so. The contradiction of the half-closed border has become even more apparent as workers in Mexico and the United States are now linked transnationally, working for the same capitalist firms, and integrated into the same industries across the border.

Part 2 of this book builds on the conception of transnationalization, showing how the North American model of capitalism has established manufacturing linkages, interconnected distribution and transportation nodes, and created conditions where workers perform the same or interdependent types of labor across borders. This transnationalization of the working class through direct and indirect forms of integration makes the case for opening the border so that workers receive "equal pay for equal work." Therefore, the border needs to be opened for labor to make any advance. This includes the imperative to create cross-border unions and collective bargaining agreements and labor rights and other democratic practices that are now blocked by the racial, national, and legal differentiations imposed by the border and immigration enforcement. The transnationalization of working-class struggle also shows a tremendous potential power for workers to open the border through their own actions.

The emergence of cross-border strikes and solidarity movements shows the early manifestations of international class-consciousness and the immense power the working classes have when they unite and collaborate across borders. This potential suggests their ability to match and surpass the preponderance of power otherwise vested in state-backed international capital that is bulwarked by enforced borders. Building support for transnational workers' movements and strikes will allow for the necessary organization and capacity-building of cross-border unionization and coordinated action to fully equalize and increase wages, expand social and democratic rights, and undermine the current conditions that displace people and force them to migrate.

Part 3 focuses on the role of Mexican migrants in the US economy. As a growing segment of the US-based workforce in the 1980s and '90s, migrant workers became a significant factor in efforts to build and expand unions. The Immigration Reform and Control Act of 1986 (IRCA) resulted in an amnesty, or legalization of undocumented workers. Imbued with rights, they filed into organized labor. The IRCA also contained the first comprehensive measures of labor criminalization, opening the door to the draconian, cruel, and punitive enforcement methods and armed agencies of immigrant repression now ubiquitous in society.

The fact that immigrant workers joined unions en masse—and would likely do it again if another legalization were to occur—has led both the Democratic and Republican capitalist parties to firmly oppose another amnesty. Meanwhile, they have collaborated in building up Immigration and Customs Enforcement (ICE), the detention complex, and other components the migra-state—the inflating and expanding state apparatus devoted wholly to repressing migrants. The case for opening the border lies in the empirical evidence that when workers attain civil and legal rights, they unite and join with other workers to build unions and the labor movement. Unionization is the key to uplifting the wages and working conditions and expanding political rights for all workers. This historic phenomenon has been witnessed before and is urgently needed to negate the racial and national segregation that underpins social inequality, poverty and privation, and the reactionary political movements that spawn from these conditions.

Part 4 makes the case for building the movement to open the border. There is evidence to show that growing parts of the US working class are being drawn into open opposition with the functioning of bordered capitalism. This includes campaigns to abolish ICE, close the detention camps, and defund the border wall. There is a growing list of actions taken by workers to oppose the migra-state at the point of production, converging with wider social movements led by a new generation of socialists and class-conscious workers who understand how migrant repression is a permanent function of capitalism—and that it weakens, divides, and debilitates the whole working class. For this reason, a new anticapitalist movement is developing against bordered capitalism and will need to continue to grow and deepen its roots in the class struggles within and across borders in the years ahead.

# PART I

# Opening Borders in Response to Capitalist Crisis

*A major effort of US policy toward Latin America should be to point up the merits of and assist these countries to develop a reliance on private enterprise and the process of private investment decision-making.*

—*Congressional Report on Inter-American Economic Relationships of the Joint Economic Committee of the Congress of the United States, 1962*

# ONE

# The Colonial Origins of Free Trade

The construction of the capitalist economy of the United States occurred through colonialist methods. These include the pilfering and exploitation of Indigenous lands and violent removal of the people, racialized slavery and regimented labor migration, and the repopulation of stolen lands through exclusive citizenship policies and settler colonialism.

Indigenous nations were denied inclusion and forcibly displaced, eliminated, or concentrated into territorial prison camps. Their brutal and systematic dispossession from the land over the course of nearly two hundred and fifty years opened the path to privatization, commoditization, and, ultimately, capitalism. The consolidating ruling classes were sure to disqualify them from citizenship and any form of basic right or legal recognition, and with that, they precluded any means to resist the process of genocidal displacement through the colonizer's legislative or judicial systems.[1] The long process of physical elimination and forced removal and relocation has since passed to one of systematic under-development through the reservation system and cultural genocide through aggressive assimilation and historical erasure from the national imagination.[2]

Enslaved Africans were denied access to citizenship—and humanity—so that the value of their labor could be savagely extracted. For more than one hundred and fifty years, enslaved labor was multiplied throughout an expanding agricultural sector and factored into the supply chains of capitalist industrialization.[3] Along with the stolen land of the original inhabitants, their stolen labor brought together the key elements of what Karl

Marx described as the original accumulation of wealth that lay the basis for the rise of US capitalism. As he explained in *Capital,*

> The discovery of gold and silver in America, the extirpation, enslavement and entombment in mines of the aboriginal population, the beginning of the conquest and looting of the East Indies, the turning of Africa into a warren for the commercial hunting of black-skins, signalized the rosy dawn of the era of capitalist production. These idyllic proceedings are the chief moments of [original] accumulation. On their heels treads the commercial war of the European nations, with the globe for a theatre.[4]

The march of capitalism included the conquest and colonization of the northern territories of Mexico in 1848, after an invasion and occupation by US slaveholding settlers beginning in 1835.[5] Colonial expansion continued into the Caribbean and Asia, with the occupation and forcible acquisition of Puerto Rico, Cuba, Philippines, Hawai'i, Samoa, Guam, and Wake Island between 1890 and 1903.[6]

By the end of the nineteenth century, following a period of rapid industrialization, unprecedented capital accumulation and concentration, and the legal foundation of the rights of capital to perpetually expand through incorporation and national mobility, a qualitatively different character emerged within the capitalist class. This marked the arrival of monopoly capitalism—the process that eclipsed competitive capitalism through the aggregation and consolidation of large capital and firms that came to dominate and control national and colonial markets. Monopoly capitalism also coincides with the growing preponderance of capital and its impact on political structures, through which various representative agents of the rising class learned to exercise greater influence over the state and military and utilize them as instruments for further advances internationally.

Expansion was initially driven by the need for capitalist producers to export their excess agricultural and manufactured goods. Eventually, the scale of accumulated surplus capital outgrew the potentiality for profit from within national boundaries. This compelled them to look beyond their own borders to export their capital investments in order to find new and ever more sources of profit.[7]

The rise of the United States as a regional and then international power through the buildup and deployment of unrivaled military capacity, capital export, and market dominance facilitated the unprecedented transfer of wealth from a growing list of formerly colonized nations into the US and the hands of private, state-connected banks and other incipient multinational firms. This process positioned sections of monopoly capital to acquire such unprecedented infusions of wealth through the nodes of military imperialism that a further transfiguration in class organization was catalyzed in the articulation of finance capitalism.

*Finance capitalism* refers to the orientation of a distinct class of superwealthy investors (now explicitly international in outlook), who sought to open markets on a global scale to freely move and invest their amassed stores of capital. Alongside military imperialism, "free trade" emerged as the mantra of finance capitalism—the fundamental notion that the rights of capital supersede all others. It is against this historical backdrop that concurrently expanding capitalist nations began to come into direct competition and conflict over whose capital gets to enjoy the fullest extent of free trade.

Military invasion, interventionism, and occupation paved the way for the imposition of free-trade policy and the subsequent freedom of movement across borders to freely engage in different economic activities to extract surplus value from the labor processes of conquered or subjugated nations. In this trajectory, capital mobility necessarily creates conflict among international rivals, domestic capitalists in the receiving nations, and the working classes whose labor and natural resources it seeks to exploit. Within the imperialist system, the dominant capitalist classes sought to *open* foreign markets only to then dominate them for themselves. As Rudolph Hilferding described in 1910,

> It is the largest banks and the largest branches of industry which succeed in obtaining for themselves the best conditions for the valorization of their capital in foreign markets, and acquire the rich extra profits in which lesser capitals cannot even dream of participating.
>
> The policy of finance capital has three objectives: (1) to establish the largest possible economic territory; (2) to close this territory to foreign competition by a wall of protective tariffs; and consequently (3) to reserve it as an area of exploitation [for itself].[8]

In the early twentieth century, Vladimir Lenin observed and described the emergence of imperialism as a stage of capitalism transcending traditional colonialism as a means for capital accumulation on an international scale. The emergence of finance capital and the advent of modern capitalist imperialism marked an evolutionary step in the operational behavior of the capitalist state. The dominant capitalist classes reduced the ranks of their competitors and formed into financial oligarchies, monopolized national markets, forced open markets on a regional level through military intervention and disproportionate economic leverage, and then set out to project this model of control and dominance internationally. By the second decade of the twentieth century, rival and competing centers of world capitalism had gone to war to contest and redivide control over conquered global markets.

## The Making of Free Markets

By seeking out new markets for capital export, these dominant capitalist classes ran up against a closed colonial system in which subject nations were already seized by rival capitalist powers to facilitate their own capital export. Gaining access to new markets already enclosed within the existing division of colonies and spheres of influence, specifically to invest in the exploitation of labor, land, and natural resources, necessitated a military buildup. Conflict, war, revolutions, and counterrevolutions became characteristic of the process of redividing the globe and reordering the hierarchy of international capitalism.

The conception, pursuit, and sanctification of US-directed free-trade began under the moniker of the "Open-Door Policy," by forcing open national economies (as existing colonies, semicolonies, or independent nations) so that US capital could be exported, invested, and expanded.

Despite its original colonialist trajectory, by the turn of the twentieth century the US capitalist class had changed course. It opted for an aggressive form of imperialism, leveraging military power to open foreign national markets to facilitate capital export. Instead of increasing direct colonial holdings, the US Marines were sent in to forcibly impose "free-market" arrangements at gunpoint. Oppositional governments, social and political movements, and any other form of barrier were toppled; compliant regimes were installed and subsequently backed by US political and military power.

In the first three decades of the twentieth century, for example, US military forces invaded Puerto Rico, Cuba, Honduras, Nicaragua, Guatemala, Costa Rica, Mexico, Colombia, Panama, Haiti, and the Dominican Republic. Beyond Latin America, forces were also deployed to Russia, China, and Turkey. The threat of war was used against its imperialist rivals to compel them to share the spoils by giving its capitalists access to the markets within their own spheres of influence.[9]

Marine Corps major general Smedley Butler, the highest ranked and most decorated marine of his time, participated in the invasions to open Latin American economies. He later lamented his role and criticized the use of the military as an instrument to advance the interests of capitalists. In a speech he gave in 1933, he described his service in the following terms:

> I spent thirty-three years and four months in active military service as a member of this country's most agile military force, the Marine Corps. I served in all commissioned ranks from Second Lieutenant to Major-General. And during that period, I spent most of my time being a high-class muscle-man for Big Business, for Wall Street and for the Bankers. In short, I was a racketeer, a gangster for capitalism.[10]

Successive US governments built the empire and supplanted European states and rival capitalist classes across Latin America and into Asia. This model of imperial free-trade policy became based on the US maintaining its economic primacy through imposed free-trade regimes backed by disproportionate and asymmetric military might. This imperial model enabled the US state to reorder the global economy by the end of World War II and work to gradually undermine existing systems of national development outside its control. The exploitation of labor was central to the process of capitalist expansion.

## Imperialism and Reserve Armies of Labor

The exploitation of captive and enslaved labor was a primary factor in original capitalist accumulation and the building of the economy. Further expansion necessitated subsequent infusion of new groups of workers from beyond existing national boundaries, so the state enticed migration. Building on the colonial framework, racial and ethnic exclusions were built into the first definition of citizenship in the Naturalization Act of 1790. The state prohibited colonized and enslaved Indigenous and African peoples from accessing citizenship, initiating a system of state labor regulation that determined citizenship rights within the constructs of racialized capitalism and colonialism.

Building on the construction of disempowered systems of slave and captive labor, English colonial and then United States immigration policy was invented and implemented within this framework. As a result, immigration policy was crafted at each phase of capitalist development based on legal frameworks that excluded, subdivided, and hierarchized migrant workers along racial and national lines. This was reflective of original colonial policy, excluding basic rights and citizenship to African and Indigenous peoples, and its integral effect in creating permanent patterns of segregation and social marginalization. Immigration has policy formed within this mold and has further progressed in tandem with cycles of capitalist development.

Furthermore, evolving immigration policies have been developed in conjunction with the specific episodes and characteristics of global colonial and imperial expansion that have fueled waves of displacement and out-migration into the present. The colonization of Puerto Rico and the Philippines and the opening of China (US Open-Door Policy), for example, further added racialized subjects to this colonial framework. This colonial immigration model has been fine-tuned to undergird all of the phases of capitalist expansion, providing a lever for capitalists to increase the exploitation of a stratified workforce. Racism and xenophobia are therefore normalized as an ideological means to undermine class unity and to socially legitimize and reproduce class divisions. Within labor markets, bosses and contractors quickly learned that they could pay migrant workers of color less, make them work harder, and fire or replace them more easily. This became a widely employed method for increasing the rate of capital accumulation throughout US history.[11] Workers from the colonies, from Puerto Rico to the Philippines, began to move into the US through the circuits of capitalism and within the framework of regulated colonial citizenship.[12] This was followed by further elaboration and formalization with succeeding waves of labor immigration from other parts of the world.

The practice continued throughout the imperialist phase of expansion, where the state systematized racially and nationally regulated labor importation projects in dialectical rhythm with economic growth and the internationalization of capital export. As imperialist expansion facilitated the transfer of wealth from colonized and semicolonized countries back to the rich nations, so too did economically displaced people move in the directions of these economic links and capital and profit flows. For instance, Mexicans were already incorporated into the US as racially restricted laborers after colonial occupation in 1848, but a much larger population of migrants began to cross the border in the first three decades of the twentieth century. Between 1900 and 1930, over one and half million Mexicans migrated as US capitalists began their first phase of imperialist expansion into Mexico, creating the conditions of imperialist semicolonialism in the lead-up to the Mexican Revolution of 1910.[13]

Citizenship rights bestow some basic legal protections and guarantees. The racialization and restriction of access to citizenship concentrated more power over their workers in the hands of capitalists. Capitalists learned that the more that they denied rights, divided, and socially isolated workers, the more they could increase the rate of exploitation—the more they could work them and the less they had to pay them. Capitalists wielded a set of tools, backed by the power of the state, to police the activities of their workers, in effect significantly shifting the existing balance of power between labor and capital in favor of the latter.

This allowed them to utilize and deploy other forms of class oppression, i.e., racism and xenophobia embedded in citizenship restrictions, to extract more surplus value. This refers to the rate of unpaid value produced by workers that capitalists appropriate for themselves. This is the core process of capitalism, and through the state the owners of capital in the US developed immigration policies into elaborate schematics for optimal effect. Workers from different parts of the world were drawn into the gravitational pull of US capitalist imperialism as migrants and incorporated into the US as what Marx described as "reserve armies of labor." The owners of the means of production maintain a percentage of the working classes in perpetual under- or unemployment, a reserve army of labor. The size of this army will fluctuate with the expansive and recessive phases of the capitalist cycle, with more drawn into employment during periods of growth and again pushed out during downturns or when no longer needed.

The existence of the reserve army not only economically depresses some sections of the working class at all times, but also is leveraged by owners against the employed sections in ways that lower wages in order to increase capital accumulation. The existence of an unemployed workforce in every industry can be wielded as a threat of replacement by owners when needed, especially to cross picket lines during strikes or replace militant workers during union drives or other workplace actions. This strategy can also be used to blunt and deflect class anger toward those competing for jobs.

While the US working class has always been expanded and replenished by infusions of immigrant and international workers, the restricted access to citizenship for Black, Latin American, and Asian workers has structured their entrance into labor markets through the strictures of a reserve army of labor and used by capitalists in a similar manner. Since the 1980s especially, this has been coupled with the additional state-imposed vulnerability of these workers also facing arrest, detention, and deportation if they are undocumented and try to change or resist their conditions. The net effect is that the maintenance of a reserve army of transnational and undocumented workers has become the optimal arrangement for suppressing wages and conditions for all workers. As Marx summarized in *Capital*,

> The overwork of the employed part of the working class swells the ranks of the reserve, whilst conversely the greater pressure that the latter by its competition exerts on the former, forces these to submit to overwork and to subjugation under the dictates of capital. The condemnation of one part of the working class to enforced idleness by the overwork of the other part, and the converse, becomes a means of enriching the individual capitalists.[14]

Furthermore, racialized citizenship controls restrict how the undocumented reserve army is incorporated into the economy by depriving migrants of the rights afforded to citizen labor, such as the right to organize unions and collectively bargain, vote and engage in civic activities, petition for grievances, enjoy freedom of movement, etc. Furthermore, the state created special agencies and armed forces to police the presence and activities of noncitizens starting in the late nineteenth century.[15] These mechanisms became more elaborate and entrenched in relation to migration from south of the US-Mexico border from the second half of the twentieth and into the twenty-first century.

This arrangement frames the methods through which capitalists could reap exceptional benefits via bypassing the costs of social reproduction, while simultaneously enabling the superexploitation of migrant labor. As Ana Alicia Peña López explains, "Migration diminishes the costs to employ workers, since the country receiving the immigration does not have to pay to produce and reproduce them (in terms of health, housing, education, training, etc.)"[16] Furthermore, through the criminalization of labor, the conditions for superexploitation thrive when workers have virtually no means to resist conditions of exploitation under capitalist relations of production. Under these circumstances, capitalists will increase the rate of exploitation (i.e., push wages lower, increase working hours, pay less into workplace protections) to below the point where workers can actually sustain themselves economically or even physically. "Paying workers below the level [of self-sustenance] not only implies the degradation and pauperization of the reproduction of Mexican labor that works in the United States, but it is the key to migration dynamics between Mexico and the United States."[17]

While the US state maintained open borders for international migration as part of working-class formation in the early stages of nation building, colonialist citizenship restrictions were codified and expanded into law in synchrony with each succeeding wave of migration. A kaleidoscopic array of racialized and nation-based restrictions was packaged into "immigration law" to govern the multitudes of different workers who entered into the country and those already present.

Restrictions or limitations were placed on people from Africa, Asia, Eastern and Southern Europe, and Latin America. Eventually, the state regulated all racial and national categories with the passage of the Immigration Acts of 1921 and 1924. Since then, immigration and citizenship policy have been intentionally engineered on the basis of (Northern European) white supremacy and nationalism to legally stratify and subdivide a multiracial, multiethnic, and multinational working class in terms of access to and quality of citizenship.

Therefore, the trajectory of US immigration policy springs from an exclusionary framework that recapitulates the anti-Black and anti-Indigenous components of the original colonial model. The different components of the colonialist and imperialist model of immigration culminate in what we see today: racialized citizenship disqualifications and an appetite for disenfranchised labor as fuel for capitalist growth, alongside secondary forms of racial criminalization and the demonization of migrants fleeing countries directly impacted by imperialism. In the dominant capitalist states, the political administrators are predisposed to develop their immigration laws and policies in ways that primarily serve and advance the interests of the capitalist class—or replicate the actions of their main competitors if they provide an advantage.

Since its inception, a common trait that has run through immigration policy is the social and political marginalization of migrating workers already in the country. Different groups of working-class migrants have been deprived of access to citizenship (or full citizenship), which has allowed for the creation of socioeconomic subdivisions that facilitate increased exploitation of their labor. In the same way as the dubious construct of "race" has been used to craft policy to serve economic interests, so too have citizenship policies been invented and repurposed in different ways to be compatible with the needs of the bourgeoisie in each period.[18]

## The Colonial Origins of Free-Trade Policy: The Case of Puerto Rico

Contemporary free-trade policy gestated in the womb of colonialism, as can be learned from the experience of Puerto Rico. The acquisition of Puerto Rico in 1898 as a colony after the United States defeated Spain in the Spanish-American War opened the door to a flood of US capital export into the country, which was initially administered under a military-colonial dictatorship. The relations of subjugation imposed by the United States on Puerto Rico allowed for the island nation to be rendered into an economic laboratory for capitalist accumulation.

The construction of free-trade policy was done through a sweeping set of legislative policies carried out in Washington, DC, with no consultation from the people on the island. These included the wide-scale privatization of land and state-owned industry, the fixing of US and Puerto Rican exchange rates, extending of US tariff protections to production on the island, and restrictions placed on foreign trade and shipping.[19] Furthermore, the Foraker Act of 1900 consolidated all administrative power over the country's political and economic affairs into the hands of the US government.

US investors swiftly established control over all aspects of the economy, including taking effective control over transport, communications, finance, agriculture, and manufacturing. Large swathes of the most productive land were bought up by speculators and converted to export production for US markets. This, along with increased capitalization of agricultural production, led to the intensification of dispossession of rural peasants and farming families, who swelled into a larger population of poor and landless workers already underdeveloped by centuries of Spanish colonization. Furthermore, the effects of transition to the US dollar as the main currency led to a 40 percent wage reduction after 1899, even as the cost of basic staples remained constant or even doubled.[20] The expanding ranks of the impoverished rural working class were drawn into US-based export production.

Through this export model, cheap Puerto Rican labor was reconstituted in export industries to service US consumption and produce enormous profits for the new class of landowners. By 1930, 92 percent of Puerto Rican exports, mainly sugar, went to US markets.[21] The traditional Puerto Rican landowning oligarchy proved unable and unwilling to present a challenge to the new order, and the largest and most successful were able to adjust and profit from the labor-export model.

The exploitation of colonized Puerto Rican labor was maximized due to the low level of union density and militancy in agricultural production until the 1930s.[22] The Puerto Rican colonial government itself promoted migration to the US and partnered with US-based firms that wanted to hire cheap workers for their operations. After World War II, US capitalists saw the potential to expand this method of capital accumulation to other markets and forms of segmented production on the island, especially as the federal government exempted Puerto Rico from minimum wage requirements and the colonial government repressed efforts to expand unions into the export zones. The level of unionization in the United States had reached its highest point right after the war, with wages increasing across the manufacturing sector.[23] In response, the US government engineered Puerto Rico as a low-wage and union-free alternative for capital investment in export-based manufacturing.

In 1947 the US Congress and the Truman administration passed the Industrial Incentives Act, dubbed "Operation Bootstrap." This law developed the prototype of "maquiladora" production, a scheme designed for the maximum exploitation of colonized labor as a primary motivating factor in the transnationalization of US capitalism. It granted capitalist investors a ten-year full exemption from income, property, excise, municipal, and corporate taxes if they invested in manufacturing operations in Puerto Rico. Furthermore, all costs associated with industrial licenses were waived for investors; they were provided government funding, building space, work-training programs, low-interest loans, and other forms of aid.[24]

This paved the way for multinational corporations and investment companies to pour into the island and take advantage, simultaneously fueling substantial migrations of displaced populations from inland regions to the cities where factories were sprouting up in and around port towns. Between 1950 and 1960, manufacturing wages on the island remained between 29 percent and 41 percent of average US wages, leading a wide number of industries to outsource production to join in the low-wage bonanza.[25]

By 1967, 2,367 manufacturing establishments employed 121,537 Puerto Ricans on the island. According to the Department of Commerce, total investment in manufacturing in Puerto Rico increased from $93 million in 1949 to $621 million by 1967.[26] According to another source, total externally held investment increased from $1.7 billion in 1960 to $18.6 billion in 1977; while 91 percent of the profits generated by industrial investment and 90 percent of industrial production in 1974 were tied to foreign capital.[27] The "success" of the Puerto Rican free-trade model led the US government to then attempt to export it to other countries in the region. The 1983 Caribbean Basin Initiative formalized the US government's intention to pursue similar free-trade style agreements with Caribbean, Central American, and North American nations.

Despite the growth of an urban industrial working class in Puerto

Rico, the maintenance of low wages and enforced, nonunion production led a growing number to choose migration to the US. In 1950, for example, the total population of Puerto Rico was 2.2 million, while twenty years later it was only 2.6 million. Most of the population growth of the working class was siphoned off into the US. For example, total employment in Puerto Rico decreased from 603,000 in 1950 to 543,000 in 1960.

A total of 684,000 Puerto Ricans migrated to the United States between 1950 and 1970, comprising the new ranks of a low-wage migrant working class especially in Miami, New York City, and Chicago.[28] As one historical study concluded,

> The US military invasion and the subsequent large-scale investment in Puerto Rican agriculture inserted the Puerto Rican worker into the larger network of colonial and semicolonial populations who were to serve as the reserve workforce for the imperialist chain emanating from the United States.[29]

Into the third decade of the twenty-first century, wage differentials between Puerto Rico and the United States have persisted, as have wage differentials between Puerto Ricans in the United States and other citizens. On the island, average per capita income amounts to a little more than one-third ($13,000 in 2019) of per capita income on the US mainland ($34,000 in 2019), while 43 percent of the Puerto Rican population lived in poverty in 2019 compared to 11 percent of the rest of the US population that same year.[30] More than a third of the Puerto Rican working population earns the minimum wage. The unemployment rate for working-age youth has reached double and triple the US rate over the last decade, while only about 40 percent of the total working-age population is consistently employed.[31]

In the US, Puerto Rican male workers earned 11 percent less than their white male counterparts for the same work, while Puerto Rican female workers made 25 percent less.[32] They have higher rates of poverty, unemployment, and housing scarcity, and lower rates of education then the rest of the citizenry.[33] With deepening economic crises, perpetual underdevelopment and disinvestment, and the effects of natural disaster and imperial neglect, Puerto Rican workers continue to migrate from the island to the United States in droves.[34]

By 1970, US capitalists were eager to replicate and export the lucrative

Puerto Rican colonial model, especially in Mexico, with a working class over twenty times the size of Puerto Rico's. US capitalist penetration into Mexico's economy was partially curtailed in the period of 1940–1982 as the postrevolutionary government set out along a path of managed capitalist development under Mexican control. Nevertheless, the limitations of state-managed capitalism as a strategy for development and independence from imperialism revealed themselves throughout the period.

Despite the historic Mexican Revolution, US capitalism reasserted its access and eventual control. The first significant reopening of the Mexican economy to US capital occurred during World War II and accelerated throughout the subsequent US-directed Cold War. By the 1970s, US-aligned sections of the Mexican bourgeoisie were positioned to dismantle the postrevolutionary protectionist constitution, with the support, guidance, and direct participation of the United States.

# TWO

# The Contradictions of Capitalist Development in Postrevolutionary Mexico

Since its independence in 1821, Mexico has been subjected to ongoing foreign intervention and a perpetual theater of inter-imperialist rivalry.[1] By the late nineteenth century, Mexico had been integrated into the global capitalist economy as a semicolony. Foreign capital had become predominant within the economy, and competing imperialist powers vied for control over political affairs.

In 1910, there was a popular uprising and revolutionary overthrow of the nearly forty-year dictatorship of Porfirio Díaz, which represented an alliance of interests between foreign capitalists, the large landowning oligarchy, the commercial bourgeoisie, the military hierarchy, and the Catholic Church. While these elements were defeated on the battlefield and politically subordinated to the emergent revolutionary regime, they were not fully dismantled or wholly appropriated.

While industrial and agricultural workers were the detonators of revolutionary movement from below, and provided the bulk of battleground forces, their attempts to lead toward socialist revolution were repressed and defeated.[2] Given the small size and battered condition of these forces, alongside the underdeveloped state of the domestic capitalist class, power passed into the hands of a cohering middle-class layer of revolutionary generals, intellectuals, bureaucrats, and landowners whose leadership emerged most intact.[3]

The conclusion of the military phases of the revolution and the foundation of the 1917 constitution gave way to the second phase: consolidation of a postrevolutionary state. For over two decades, the ruling factions jockeyed for power amid periodic explosions of class struggle and counterrevolutionary violence. Eventually, they consolidated as a ruling class and exercised their power through internal brokering processes and power-sharing agreements. This was formalized through the creation of a one-party state, administered through their self-styled Institutional Revolutionary Party, or PRI.[4]

Every six years, a leader that reflected the confluence of social and political factors and the corresponding type of leadership needed for the given period was negotiated and appointed from within the party apparatus. This allowed for flexibility to move further left or right, depending on shifting balances of class forces in society. This was especially the case in their need to co-opt and demobilize revolutionary workers and peasants. The new ruling groups created their own state-controlled "popular" organizations in an attempt to co-opt and peel them away from the radical organizations and further revolutionary aspirations. Over this period, the state was willing to negotiate with and make concessions to state-aligned unions and peasant groups in order to co-opt and eventually control them, and deployed force and violence to repress radicalized worker movements.

Concession and co-optation became a primary strategy, especially as the embers of revolution continued to reignite episodes of class struggle into the 1930s. After succeeding in crushing radical movements and taming the working classes, the emphasis shifted toward capital accumulation—which depended on the subjugation of industrial and agricultural workers.

In order to consolidate its power, the new ruling factions of the PRI established a mechanism of class rule referred to as *corporatism*.[5] Through this method, class organizations of the incipient bourgeoisie, the urban working class, campesinos, and the popular sectors (middle-class professionals and students) were either co-opted or contrived and affixed into the PRI-controlled state.

Atop this governing structure, the PRI maintained control for seventy years through a variety of mechanisms, including: strengthening the state's bureaucratic apparatus vis-à-vis the social classes; pitting classes against one another; establishing state-controlled organizations and clientele networks; making periodic concessions; providing privilege and establishing relations of patronage in exchange for loyalty; enforcing state mediation and arbitration over all substantive conflicts and matters; and meting out brutal repression, primarily against workers, students, and peasants to crush periodic outbreaks of struggle and resistance where the previous methods failed.

Despite the façade of the state being above the class struggle and a neutral mediator, the state as a whole became a vehicle for increasing capital accumulation. Mexico's vast rural population was the fulcrum of national capitalist development, and the exploitation of their labor and extraction of surplus value was the motor of state economic growth. Freed from the land, the rural population merged into the labor armies for capitalist agriculture and state industry. Along the path to further development, according to this model, Mexico could export its agricultural products to world markets and generate first domestic and then international markets for manufactured goods. Ultimately, this aspirational model saw Mexico emerge as an industrialized and advanced capitalist nation that could transcend its colonial past and take its rightful place as an independent world power.

Alongside methods of state accumulation, there were domestic sources of capital investment. While the Porfirian-era bourgeoisie had lost political power, they were not expropriated, and they had a mutual interest in rebuilding the economy. Even the defeated landowning oligarchy, including the most feudal and backward *hacendados*, retained vestiges of their land, wealth, and power.[6]

## Rehabilitating Porfirian Bankers

As part of the new state-building calculus of the PRI, and because of the urgent need for sources of investment, the new regime sought out rapprochement with their defeated enemies. Members of the former

Porfirian ruling class were officially rehabilitated as patriotic investors and partners as a new convergence of interests superseded old rivalries.

For instance, bankers who worked as part of or in collaboration with the Finance Ministry during the Díaz regime were rehabilitated and recruited to help design and develop the postrevolutionary financial system. Many of these *porfiristas* were educated north of the border and made their fortunes in partnerships with US investors before the revolution. They lost power but still emerged as the richest and most powerful people in Mexico, who largely retained their wealth and privileges. In exchange for loyalty and service to the new government, they were reintegrated into the new ruling class.

This cohort made their participation in the reconstruction of Mexico's financial system conditional on the establishment of a set of guarantees for their class. These included: that the new Finance Ministry be independent of the state, that the existing banking sector (that they controlled) remain private, and that they have a say in all financial governance matters.

In 1928, this group was inaugurated as the Mexican Bankers Association. Its leadership was given a semiofficial position and virtual control over financial affairs. The membership moved between the private sector and leading positions in the Finance Ministry, and typically appointed their own successors as well as the board members of the Bank of Mexico.[7] Within the new state, they were assigned direct channels by which to advise the Mexican government on all financial matters.

They were able to enshrine and expand their class privileges while under the formal jurisdiction of the state. For instance, they retained control over private financial markets, made it customary to maintain free exchange convertibility (free movement of money across the border), established a tight monetary policy, and maintained little or no taxation on profits and luxury goods.[8] Furthermore, private banks were fused with the Bank of Mexico, Mexico's central bank, which financed and underwrote their operations.

By opposing exchange controls and allowing for the transnational mobility of money, capitalists gained a potent tool and weapon. For the following four decades, they were able to move their money out of Mexico and into US and international banks at will. This allowed them, for instance, to carry out recurring cycles of "capital flight" and leverage the movement of their growing fortunes out of banks and national circulation to discourage or punish the state when policies that they opposed were passed. This culture of coordinated class action against the state began in earnest during the government of Lázaro Cárdenas and later played an instrumental role in dismantling state capitalism altogether.

Once in charge of the banking sector, the Mexican Bankers Association went about expanding the speculative infrastructure of the finance system. In 1953, private investment banks (*financieras*) were legislated into existence and capitalized (and largely unregulated) through the Ley de Sociedades de Inversión. One year later, the state created the stock exchange with the Ley de la Comisión de Valores, which opened the door for domestic capitalists to invest and hold ownership shares (stocks) in the largest private and public firms in the country. These two institutions grew exponentially faster and quickly surpassed public and commercial banks in capitalization.[9] They enabled the gradual rise and ascendancy of a class fraction of Mexican finance capitalists and, when later deregulated and privatized, served as the point of entry for foreign capitalists to buy up large swaths of the economy.

The state also encouraged foreign investment to accelerate development but faced a lockout of international credit and market access as punishment for daring to wage revolution. Therefore, it was paramount for the state to promote partners with international connections, standing, and experience to rebuild credibility for the new regime.

Rapprochement and reconfiguration of the ruling class was also pushed by US and international creditors, who aimed to tame and control the postrevolutionary regime and steer it back into the fold of subordination within the imperialist world-system. In the drive to rebuild national capitalism, the PRI gradually fused with the Porfirian-era bourgeoisie and recapitulated its methods of class rule and international connections. This included the assurances of a bilateralization of formal and informal power sharing between the state and private capitalist sector.

Fragile and vacillating between nationalist posturing and conciliation with *porfirismo* and international capital, different ruling-class fractions with varying ideological and class orientations gradually aligned behind the general goal of national development—albeit with widely varying definitions. Their collaboration was mediated through state capitalist development that would ostensibly break free of foreign domination and underdevelopment, even if still operating within and dependent on international capitalist markets.

The Great Depression, outbreak of World War II, and the emergence of a bipolar Cold War further complicated the process of nation building, especially in the shadows of expanding US capitalism and empire. In this context, Mexican state planners concluded that national capitalist development would not be possible without negotiated realignment and subordination to US international objectives. Furthermore, there was also a convergence of interests in the 1930s and '40s: US capitalism was expanding internationally, and the PRI desired foreign investment; the US state was engaged in repressing Communists and other radical movements, and the Mexican government did the same; when the US entered into World War II and needed to increase agricultural imports, Mexico was eager to access US markets for its exports.

By 1940, the new ruling class consolidated and learned to share power in accordance with capitalist development, now formally shrouded in revolutionary rhetoric and with motifs of popular national development.[10] Its overarching goal, from this point on, was capital accumulation through the development of the productive forces and natural resources under state control. Achieving this goal was predicated on three major factors: the concentration and capitalization of agriculture for export, the transformation of the large rural population into armies of labor, and the rise of the postrevolutionary Mexican bourgeoisie through state-managed capitalist development. This historical process fits into the category of what Karl Marx referred to as a *bourgeois revolution*.[11] The Mexican model embedded numerous contradictions that limited its extent and scope. It occurred at a late phase of the bourgeois revolutionary cycle, in a historically colonized and underdeveloped country, and under the conditions of domination by US imperialism and overt opposition to the project of Mexican economic development, lost access to cheap labor and natural resources, and the rise of a potential competitor along its southern border.

## Proletarianization and Reserve Armies of Labor

In theory, the PRI corporatist arrangement gave all Mexicans a voice in governance, a populist notion designed to assign legitimacy to the new state as the embodiment and conclusion of the revolutionary process. In practice, it gave the state a toolbox to attempt a managed process of capitalist development, while suppressing class antagonisms and repressing class struggle from below.

An initial step of this process was the displacement and proletarianization of the immense rural population to make way for capital-intensive investment in agricultural development and export. This began with the dual model of state-administered production for national consumption, referred to as the ejido system, and a private ownership model based on capital-intensive investment, mass production, and export to foreign markets.

Article 27 of the Constitution of 1917 stipulated that the state become the steward of agricultural development, and that land, resources, and supports be distributed accordingly in order to stimulate capitalist production. In practice, the process was slow, especially as the first postrevolutionary governments sought rapprochement with domestic and international capital. As an extension of US policy, US creditors made lending to the postrevolutionary government conditional on ending expropriations.

Land redistribution stalled, and concentration continued. The circumstances changed during episodes of peasant rebellion, land occupations, and other forms of protest to push the governments to fulfill their revolutionary promise.

Ten years after the end of the military phase of the revolution, the agrarian landscape was fragmented. The semifeudal hacienda system was partially broken up, with about ten million hectares of land distributed. But most land was still concentrated in the hands of large landlords. The agricultural census of 1930 showed that 13,500 people controlled 83 percent of the land in the private sector.[12] The situation changed significantly thereafter, as increased class struggle in the countryside spurred government action. The most significant episodes of redistribution to landless and small farmers were carried out by the state in two periods, in the 1930s and 1970s, when strikes, land occupations, and other forms of class struggle by peasants and landless workers reached its height—and when nationalist-oriented reformist presidents came to power.

For instance, campesino radicalism reached a high point during the *sexenio* of Lázaro Cárdenas (1934–40). By the mid-1930s, landless peasant strikes were erupting across the country. In the Laguna cotton-producing zone of northern Mexico, for instance, over one hundred strikes occurred in 1935 alone.[13] Strikes and landless peasant occupations extended from Baja California to the Yucatán Peninsula in rapid succession.

The Cárdenas administration was compelled to intervene and administered land expropriations and ejido formation in response.[14] To contain the outbreak of rural radicalism (and prevent worker-peasant radical convergence[15]), the Cárdenas government created the Confederación Nacional Campesina (National Confederation of Peasants) in 1938 and incorporated it as an auxiliary of the PRI state. Between 1934 and 1940 nearly eighteen million hectares were distributed to 772,000 *ejiditarios,* nearly double the number of hectares distributed by all previous postrevolutionary governments combined.[16]

Some redistributed lands were assigned as small, private plots (*minifundias*), but the majority were restructured into the ejido system. The ejido was a state-administered land tenure system that became an important mechanism of agricultural capitalist development. The state retained ownership of the parcels and bureaucratically administered operations down to the local level. Recipient communities were allowed to collectively farm the land, sustain themselves, and produce for national markets. As a developmental project, ejidos were seen as a means to increase production for national consumption and decrease rural unemployment.

The state subsidized the ejido economy as an arm of national capitalist development, and in return benefitted from the labor value embedded in the productive processes while also meeting the consumptive needs of the growing urban population. This ejido system provided a state-guaranteed base of employment, sustenance for rural families, and steady production for domestic markets. It was also the driving force of population growth between 1940 and 1970.

Nationalists in the ruling party came to favor the ejido system. The class fractions preferring land privatization, economies of scale, and export as a means to increase private profit saw it as a fetter to capitalist growth. The two competing models came into conflict in the post–World War II period and eventually into existential struggle. Push-pull battles over the ejido sector played out in the ruling party, especially in relation to the level of class conflict over the period. Nevertheless, the compulsive pressures to accumulate in order to build up an industrial economy won out, tilting policy toward land concentration and industrialization and the proletarianization and out-migration of the rural population.[17]

Between 1940 and 1960, state and private banking capital investment in agriculture increased ten times per hectare and per active laborer. Capitalist bankers favored direct lending to the private landowners, while the state financed the development of infrastructure such as roads, irrigation systems, and energy production to incentivize industrialization and growth.[18]

The greatest beneficiaries were large private landowners with properties of up to 5,000 hectares (*latifundistas*), who increased holdings to control 63 percent of the arable and productive land in the country, while ejidos covered 32 percent.[19] Private and state investment in large-scale capitalist production increased by twenty-five times between 1940 and 1960, with the highest concentration going to technologically intensive production using farm machinery, irrigation systems, etc. This scale of investment for this type of agriculture increased from 40 million pesos in 1940 to nearly 3 billion pesos by 1960. Ejido investment also increased nineteen times. The ejido system was expanded again by another 12.8 million hectares during the presidency of Luis Echeverría (1970–76) during another period that saw intense peasant and landless worker unrest.[20] Lands under ejido cultivation came to cover nearly half the country's land mass, but the allotments were drawn from more marginal and less arable lands.

Despite its resilience, the functioning of the ejido sector became wrought with contradiction and conflict. Class differentiation emerged within the system as the size of distributed allotments and state resource inputs (credit, technology, water, and irrigation, etc.) favored larger farms.

Individuals came to dominate within the largest farms, market competition favored the better-equipped, and a host of other factors fueled displacement, concentration, and exclusion. Corruption was rife within bureaucratic governing structures, with payoffs and kickbacks becoming normalized in exchange for officials permitting privatization and turning a blind eye to profiteering through leasing and renting. Furthermore, those in the governing party who favored "free-market" agriculture actively opposed increased support for the system at the federal level.[21] State support for the ejido began to decline in relation to the private sector by the late 1970s. Support for privatization crystallized after the creation of free-trade zones in agriculture with the implementation of the Border Industrialization Program (discussed in next chapter).

Small, private landowners (*minifundistas*) also saw a decline. The number of smallholdings nearly doubled between 1930 and 1950 to over one million tracts of land, but they were gradually reduced in number and size, with a substantial proportion absorbed into larger holdings after this period. By 1960 they operated on less than 4 percent of the land.[22] Ancestral and communal lands used by Indigenous farming communities were also reduced through privatization and dispossession. As Roger Bartra explained,

> This is why when capitalism is introduced into agriculture by the revolutionary path. . . it destroys the communal and seignorial forms of property and opens the way for peasant private small property. Subsequently, capitalist development's own laws will take charge of dissolving the peasantry in a process of polarization. But the important thing is that peasant property can be sold and rented, in a way that the land can be concentrated again . . . thus permitting the concentration of capital.[23]

Displaced small farmers, Indigenous farmers, and "excess" generational workers who had been squeezed out of ejidal economies were absorbed into an expanding agricultural proletariat.

By 1950, there were 1.5 million landless workers, who made up 30 percent of the rural population. By 1960, this number increased to 3 million and 55 percent of the population.[24] One study in 1960 showed that a population of 960,000 workers remained in the countryside as a wage-earning workforce on the large capitalist farms, while another 600,000 worked on ejidos (split between bureaucratic administrative positions, collective and individual farmers, and additional hired wage workers).

A third segment of 298,000 workers were drawn into the United States as braceros. The Bracero Program was a state-negotiated labor contract system that transferred Mexican workers into US capitalist agricultural production (and railroad construction) between 1942 and 1965.[25] Not all bracero applicants were enlisted, leading thousands of unenlisted workers to move into the United States anyway, forming the first waves of migrant "undocumented" labor. A last group of the "excess" rural population was compelled to migrate into Mexican cities and into the urban proletariat employed in the expanding state sector or into the social margins as informal labor. The rural population declined significantly over the period, from 65 percent of the economically active population in 1940 to 39 percent in 1970.[26]

In all cases, the process of proletarianization and exploitation of the Mexican rural population served as fundamental mechanisms of state and private capital accumulation—including the first transnational manifestation of this phenomenon in the postrevolutionary period. This role contributed to the state-managed effort to industrialize the economy through a method of capitalist development referred to as Import Substitution Industrialization (ISI).

## Labor Suppression

The nationalist vision of capitalist modernization relied on the subordination of labor to the prerogatives of capital accumulation under state management. During the final phases of the revolution, the Mexican left was repressed and independent and radical unionism was smashed. Labor unions were incorporated into the one-party state apparatus, and class struggle was mitigated and contained through a combination of complex patronage systems and brutal state repression. An independent, anticapitalist or militant workers' movement would have been the very antithesis of state capital accumulation, which itself depended on the subjugation and control of labor for maximum exploitation within the shifting balance of class forces at the time.

In 1916, for example, the bourgeois revolutionary government of Venustiano Carranza used loyal sections of the military to crush a general strike led by the anarcho-syndicalist labor federation Casa del Obrero Mundial. With the direct support of his lieutenant and soon to be successor Álvaro Obregón, Carranza backed the formation of the Confederación Regional Obrera Mexicana (Regional Confederation of Mexican Workers, or CROM) as the government-aligned union alternative in 1918.[27]

During the second half of the 1930s, the urban and industrial working classes rose up again in the greatest strike wave in the country's history.[28] The new labor movement broke away from the decrepit CROM as strikes took on an explicitly radical and anticapitalist character, especially as the Mexican Communist Party increased its influence within different sectors. The fear that labor radicalism could produce a break with the state and threaten existing property relations led the government of Lázaro Cárdenas to launch a new union movement.

Cárdenas formed the Confederación de Trabajadores de México (Confederation of Mexican Workers, or CTM) with the support of the Communist Party. Through the CTM the government was compelled to nationalize the railroads in 1937 and the oil industry in 1938, after industry-wide strikes demanded expropriation and workers threatened to take over the industries themselves.[29] Other sectors of the economy were later nationalized under similar circumstances, such as the US-owned American and Foreign Power Company in 1960.

Labor militancy and radicalism in the period pushed the state under Cárdenas to implement the guarantees of Article 123 of the Mexican Constitution, which established a comprehensive framework of labor law within the framework of capitalist development. Reforms included: state recognition of collective bargaining rights and the right to strike (for labor and capital), rules determining maximum work hours, minimum wages, overtime limits and pay requirements, regulations regarding job rights with stipulations for legitimate and wrongful termination, and a range of others. The overarching goal of the new state was to establish and codify the "harmonization of class relations" into law, in the interest of maintaining labor stability and increasing productivity.[30]

Federal and state labor boards were established to determine the legal parameters governing industrial conflict and to administer and arbitrate over strikes, lockouts, and other activities from a theoretically neutral standpoint. Despite the progressive appearance of these infrastructures, they were top-down and bureaucratic in nature and vested all power in the state to be the final authority governing class relations as determined by "national interests." Through its power to authorize unions and determine the legality of a strike, the state cultivated a loyal and compliant leadership. Labor law enabled union leaders to negotiate and sign contracts without approval by the membership, the entrenched leadership held public-vote elections to ensure loyalty, and in many unions it became customary for them to select which workers received jobs at any given site.[31]

These practices eroded traditions of militancy, independence, and self-organization and were inevitably used as a cudgel against the discontent of rank-and-file workers and dissident movements. Nevertheless, amid the rising wave of class struggle in the 1930s, it seemed possible that the state could be pushed left and made to fulfill its revolutionary obligations to the working class under *cardenismo,* especially according to the calculations of the shifting formulations of the Mexican Communist Party that led them to align with Cárdenas.[32]

Bolstered by legality, the influence and leadership of the Mexican Communist Party, and worker-led militancy across the established industrial sectors of the economy, the CTM grew quickly. Membership more than doubled in its first year of existence, from 200,000 to 480,000 between 1936 and 1937; and then nearly doubled again to 949,000 members in 1939.[33]

Despite the gains, the sweeping reforms contained a fatal flaw for the future of labor. Cárdenas leveraged his government's support for worker militancy to the point of nationalization but conditioned it on loyalty to the ruling party and formal incorporation of the CTM into the state apparatus. In effect, Cárdenas increased the legitimacy of the federal government, and thus the party and state, in the eyes of the working classes precisely at the time that it was building its own organizational and political capacity to confront and expropriate capital.

By implementing labor reform, tilting state support for class struggle at its most exacting point, and finally by insinuating the machinery of the party-state as permanent arbiter between capital and labor, the functional role of cardenismo succeeded in steering and dissipating the remaining reverberations of revolutionary momentum into the ruling party. Along with the direct legwork of the Communist Party, the process saw the construction and formalization of a labor bureaucracy now dependent on the state for legitimacy.[34] While cardenismo as a ruling ideology was short-lived, its legacy was not easily wiped away. It would take decades of inner ruling-class conflict and capitalist class consolidation and political organization, as well as episodes of violent state repression, for organized labor in Mexico to be fully subdued and denuded of its once-radical orientation.

After Cárdenas, the CTM maintained its position within the state as the official representative of all organized labor, and its leadership continued to be integrated into the party hierarchy, creating the illusion that workers now had a permanent seat at the governing table.

In reality, this arrangement codified state control over labor, and made future organizing and strike action dependent on government consent. The danger of this dependence became clear after the departure of Cárdenas and the rightward shift of the PRI as it embarked on an intensive project of state-led industrialization. State capital accumulation was contingent on establishing the control of owners and managers over labor at the point of production, suppressing authentic labor activism in all forms, and maintaining the highest rate of exploitation of labor possible.[35]

The rise of the post-Cárdenas right expressed itself in the formation of various groups inside and outside of the state explicitly opposed to further labor reformism and land redistribution. In 1948, the head of the Mexican central bank (Banco de México) linked arms with the Mexican Bankers Association to repudiate the Cárdenas-era state-building strategies, claiming that "public spending, salary increases, agricultural reform, and oil and railroad nationalizations had all been misguided policies."[36]

As a semiofficial institution of the state, the CTM was gradually allowed to expand its presence across the growing state-controlled sector until the 1980s, when it reached 1.5 million members.

The largest and most independent and militant unions either remained outside of the CTM and the corporatist structure or split off at some later point. These include: the railroad workers (Sindicato de Trabajadores Ferrocarrileros de la Republica Mexicana; STFRM), the electrical workers (Sindicato Mexicano de Electricistas, SME), the miners and metalworkers (Sindicato Nacional de Trabajadores Mineros Metalúrgicos Siderúrgicos y Similares de la República Mexicana, SNTMMSSRM), and others. Unions formed after 1940, such as the Mexican Teachers Union, remained outside of the CTM but were also incorporated into the PRI, producing a split by 1979 and the formation of a radical dissident teacher's movement called the Coordinadora Nacional de Trabajadores de la Educación (CNTE). Together they added another 3.5 million workers to organized labor's ranks, with over 5 million workers, or 22 percent of the formal workforce in unions by 1980.[37]

Collective contracts were extended to cover much of the state-owned economy by 1960, guaranteeing wages and other benefits. The state-linked unions became internally structured to serve as vehicles for the distribution of welfare benefits and services. The co-optation of the symbols and rituals of the revolution led the state to use the concept of the Mexican nationalist worker as a prop in public ceremonies and holidays.

The institutionalization of the CTM and other unions linked into the PRI state allowed for them to be internally restructured and qualitatively changed over time. In a paternalistic way, the state became the guarantor of union stability and continuity through its management of the economy, but it needed workers to be submissive.

Subsequent state leaders maneuvered to replace union leadership with functionaries and loyalists who further constrained class struggle in exchange for personal privileges, patronage, and ambitions for power. This next generation of dutiful and self-serving appointees became known as *charros*, who became lifelong fixtures in the unions in exchange for their service. The CTM and other state-controlled unions gradually became the state's primary means to stifle and disorganize working-class independence and action.

Nevertheless, this system of labor management could not fully prevent workers from engaging in militant action. The state occasionally offered workers higher pay and incentives when there was economic growth but could also take back or constrain wages in different ways depending on the capitalist economy and state imperatives. When economic crises increased in frequency after 1960, the state pushed the costs onto the working classes in the form of increased inflation, wage cuts, layoffs, currency devaluation, privatization, and a variety of other ways.

When workers fought back and took militant action, or pushed beyond the control of their own PRI-aligned leaders, the state deployed raw force to crush the movements—often with support of other state-aligned unions.

## 1958–1959 Railroad Strikes

In late 1957, railroad workers in Mexico City began to organize to push for their leadership to take action to raise wages, which had stagnated amid rising inflation, as well as to provide medical and housing benefits to workers' families.[38] Through the locals the workers forced the issue to be addressed by the national general executive, which for nearly a decade had been dominated by a PRI-backed charro named Samuel Ortega Hernández. Ortega Hernández and his appointees had consolidated power at the national leadership but had to contend with some locals that had retained traditions of militancy and democracy.

When the national leadership balked and obfuscated, workers took action. They held their assemblies and formed committees in the railroad locals led by militants, often Communist Party members or followers. Beginning in Mexico City and Oaxaca, a dissident movement took shape and converged into the Gran Comisión Pro Aumento General de Salarios (Grand Commission for a General Wage Increase).

Over the first few months of the 1958, the Comisión sent delegations to the different locals across the country to appeal directly to the membership to join the movement. By June of 1958, the majority of the railroad locals were won over to affiliation with the commission and elected their own representatives. This organizing from below surged despite open and active opposition from the national leadership, which deployed a variety of methods to oppose and derail the movement at every step.[39]

The wave of upsurge culminated on June 26, 1958, when railroad workers began several hour-long strikes in Oaxaca and Mexico City, demanding that the railroad companies double their monthly pay of 175 pesos to 350. The following day, the strikes spread to include sixty thousand railroad workers representing twenty-six of the twenty-nine union locals across the country—effectively shutting down the national rail system.[40] Additionally, groups of strikers' wives began their own campaign of blocking trains in different states where the locals were situated. Their protest campaign even spread to include the wives of railroad workers in the United States, who blocked Mexico-linked train routes from Chicago and Detroit in an act of solidarity with their Mexican counterparts.[41] Another round of strikes halted the trains again on June 28, this time also bringing out oil workers, electrical workers, teachers, and students on strike in solidarity.[42]

It was at this time of growing support that the Mexican president Adolfo Ruiz Cortines personally intervened in an attempt to placate the workers with support for a compromise raise of 250 pesos. Following in the footsteps of Lázaro Cárdenas, Ruiz Cortines positioned himself in support of the workers as a means to contain and diffuse the movement. He even met directly with the Gran Comisión, sidelining Samuel Ortega Hernández as an observer during the negotiations. The workers agreed to the 250 peso raise and emerged from the struggle triumphant, handing the state and railroad companies a defeat while creating a model for how to defeat charrismo.

The struggle then carried back into the union, where the commission-affiliated groups fought to depose and remove entrenched charro leadership at all levels and replace them with their own elected leaders. The insurgent workers convoked an "extraordinary General Union Convention" on July 12 to consolidate their movement, elect a new executive leadership, and proceed with their demands. The workers ousted Samuel Ortega Hernández and his underlings and elected Demetrio Vallejo, a militant rank-and-file leader and Communist as general secretary.

The overthrow of one of the most prominent charro leaders was not acceptable to the state and the companies that ran the railroads. In the days that followed, labor minister Salomón González Blanco declared the convention vote nullified and unilaterally announced the reinstatement of Ortega Hernández. Furious at the state's action, the workers declared another strike for July 31, 1958, to rally around Vallejo and their reclaimed union. Rather than placate the workers, the state shifted to the iron fist, sending in police to seize the locals and arrest the dissident leaders. Workers were offered raises and bonuses to return to work but refused to budge. They compelled the government to hold new elections, which

Vallejo won in a landslide with 59,749 votes to Ortega Hernández's 9.[43]

The struggle between the new leadership and the state came to a head when Vallejo pushed to restructure the corrupted rail fee system in order to increase wages. One point of contention was a practice that gave lower rates and subsidies to US mining and metal corporations, a concession the state refused to address. On March 25, 1959, workers went out on an unauthorized strike to force the government's hand. In response, the new government of Adolfo López Mateos dropped all pretense at negotiation. The state unleashed an torrent of repression against the striking workers, declaring a state of emergency, seizing the national railroad system and placing it under military control.

Over the course of several days, railroad worker pickets and protests were forcefully broken up by groups of police and military. In the melees, several workers were killed and untold numbers wounded personnel. Over ten thousand workers were fired, and over three thousand were arrested, with one hundred fifty leaders targeted and charged as Communist conspirators. To set an example and discourage further challenges to state control of the union movement, newly elected Demetrio Vallejo was sentenced to eleven years in prison for sedition and conspiring with the Soviet embassy to foment strikes.[44] While the state repressed the leadership and most militant workers and declared the strike illegal, it still conceded to most of the demands to prevent continuation of the movement. As Vallejo concluded, "We didn't [win all our demands] . . . but this wasn't because of betrayal to the railroad workers . . . but the [united opposition] of the railroad company and their agents, the old charros, the government and its repressive machinery, the soldiers and police, and the cowardly and servile merchant press. . . . We fought almost by ourselves, and still triumphed."[45]

The brutal repression of independent and militant unionism confirmed that the model of state capital accumulation through labor exploitation could not allow for any deviation. Subsequent leaders conformed to work hand in glove with state imperatives while draping its conservatizing role in the rhetoric of nationalism and shared social development.

Gradually, the state became less concessionary and more repressive. The consolidation of control, especially over the rural and urban working classes, was a major turning point. It underwrote the new state's vision for managed capitalist modernization, a project that became known as Import Substitution Industrialization.

## State-Led Capitalist Industrialization

The outlook for independent national economic development in 1940 was not ideal for Mexico's new ruling class. The conclusion of World War II saw a fundamental reordering of global political economy, with US empire and capitalism in a phase of historic expansion and Cold War conflict rearing its head. The Mexican economy was in shambles, already underdeveloped, and still partially in ruins from the revolutionary period.

Within this context, the consolidated postrevolutionary state embarked on a project of rapid industrialization and state-capitalist class formation between 1940 and 1982, repackaging traditional liberal thought in revolutionary language. As Julio Moreno notes,

> Ironically, political leaders selectively recast processes and ideologies embedded within Mexican liberalism. . . as they pushed for reconstruction, industrial development, and commercial growth under the banner of the Mexican Revolution.[46]

Import Substitution Industrialization was premised on the idea that a strong state could substitute for a weak capitalist class and lead the historic process toward industrialization through protectionism and the mobilization and intensive investment of state resources. This strategy required restrictions on foreign capital investment, the exclusion of industrial imports through high tariff walls, direct financing through organic capital accumulation and access to credits, state ownership and management of industry and natural resources as a means to further accumulate, and the elaboration of policies designed to stimulate population growth and increase consumption through the fostering of domestic markets.[47]

This model relied on partnerships with international capital and firms willing to do business in Mexico under these circumstances. Through partnerships, Mexicans would gain technology transfer and professional training, rely on steady state funding for research and development, and have access to a large and docile workforce. A Mexican industrial base would emerge and replace foreign firms within domestic markets and then eventually compete with them internationally. This process would nurture a progressive and nationalist capitalist class geared toward aggressive development and increase national income and social growth, and Mexico would eventually find its place among advanced industrial capitalist or "first-world" nations.

The strategy was deployed alongside private-sector capitalism and seen as working in conjunction toward national development. As part of the negotiated bifurcation of the capitalist economy, the operations of the Finance Ministry were autonomous, and financial markets were deregulated. After all, both fractions viewed access to foreign capital and collaboration with multinational entities as essential to their respective visions for national economic growth.

With this mission, the Finance Ministry blocked all efforts to limit or restrict its power and function. Attempts to impose exchange controls were thwarted, for instance, which allowed for recurring bursts of capital flight as a means to evade unfavorable state policy. Private financial markets remained open and largely unregulated, fed by an increase in US and other international-origin loans, credits, and investment partnerships. Eventually, open borders for finance capital nurtured the meteoric rise of the Mexican capitalist class into direct conflict with the state.

After the US entered World War II, Mexico became a major exporter to the US war economy. Amid this wartime commodities boom, the administration of Manuel Ávila Camacho (1940–46) announced the Industry Transformation Law in 1941 and the 51 percent law in 1942. These laws declared the Mexican state's intention to foster industrial development in Mexico through state investment and by limiting foreign ownership to 49 percent within private firms. Later followed the Emergency Decree of 1944, which regulated the influx of foreign capital within the economy—primarily from the US—to preserve Mexican ownership of key industries. The new law gave the Mexican federal government direct oversight over all foreign investment activities in the country to enforce an eventual complex economic overlay of nearly two hundred ownership laws and restrictions.

The postrevolutionary Mexican state also incorporated the Calvo Clause into its laws governing international investment as a means to limit the influence and leverage of foreign capitalists. This prohibited the intervention of foreign courts and diplomatic privileges to adjudicate on behalf of their capitalist investors on economic matters in the Mexican economy, a historic practice that was seen as instrumental to imposing semicolonial economic control.[48]

The state also incorporated the nation's natural resources as a factor of production by implementing Article 27 of the Mexican Constitution, which nationalized Mexico's mineral, water, and land resources and created a restricted zone which forbade foreigners from owning land within one hundred kilometers of the Mexican borders and fifty kilometers of its seacoasts.

Successive governments took further action to "Mexicanize" capitalist development through state management that guided foreign and domestic policy in this direction.

> It was under these conditions that the state established the principle characteristics of its role in the economy: invest in infrastructure and the production of energy, foment the growth of industry through the extension of credits, tax exemptions, the provision of subsidized goods and services through the public sector, and a set of protections and guarantees to shield domestic industry from foreign competition.[49]

After 1940, the state's drive for accumulation to finance rapid industrialization, especially in the context of partnership with US capital and foreign policy initiatives, led to a shift in the balance of power within the state in favor of utilizing the countryside more aggressively as an instrument for original accumulation. Subsequent generations of rural workers (one million people in population growth per year between 1940 and 1970) not incorporable into the ejido structure were proletarianized as landless workers, migrated into urban industry, or contracted to work to the United States as braceros.

Between 1946 and 1952, during the administration of Miguel Alemán Valdés, tariff regimes and other forms of restriction were established for all major industries covering over 97 percent of the economy. The state also financed the development of state credit banks and a private banking system capitalized with public money. Between 1970 and 1982, the Mexican state under Luis Echeverría invested substantial amounts of oil-generated revenue and borrowed money into the establishment of a broad complex of 1,155 state-managed industries that employed over a million workers and generated 18.5 percent of the national economy.[50]

As part of building an industrial capitalist economy, state planners understood the need to improve the material condition of the population and to increase the sustainable social reproduction of workers. Substantial state investments were made in public education, health services, and employment with wage guarantees. A welfare system was also created and managed by the state, increasing access to subsidized food, utilities, and housing. These measures increased the standard of living for most Mexicans. Mortality rates dropped and fertility rates increased, with the population more than doubling between 1940 and 1970 from 20.2 million to 50.7 million people.[51]

The first four decades of the Mexican Revolution were a partial success in the direction of state capitalist development, representing the final phase and denouement of the Mexican bourgeois revolution. The capitalist class created by ISI and linkages with foreign capital grew to the point where it no longer accepted subordination to the postrevolutionary state. This outcome was bolstered by the trajectory of US imperialism.

The United States emerged from World War II as the main global power and began to exercise its power to reopen markets for capital export on an international scale, starting in Mexico. The gravitational push and pull of US capitalism and postwar preeminence persisted and regained its currency and influence amid Mexican economic affairs. Whether through dependency on investment, the threat of sanction, common cause against communism and worker radicalism, or the promise of mutual benefit—the Mexican state continued to keep the partnership with international capital and incrementally reined in the scope of its own anti-imperialist rhetoric.

By the 1960s a new majority of Mexican capitalists emerged and expressed itself through self-conscious class organizations with links to US capitalists. Concurrently, the actively pursued the opening of Mexico's economy as a zone for capital export, and by the 1970s was working to undermine the ISI regime in league with its aligned counterparts in the Mexican state and Mexican capitalist class.

The postwar reorganization of global political economy, with the US state and capitalist class at its center, provides the international context for the reordering of power and priorities in Mexico. Cross-border linkages between the US and Mexican ruling classes never ceased but, in fact, deepened into the Cold War. US banks and investors increased their active involvement in the Mexican economy despite formal restrictions. As memories of the revolution faded, so too did the border as it related to capital.

Eventually, the growth, evolution, and maturation of the Mexican capitalist class led it to dump the model of the PRI state and cut the cords of managed capitalism after 1982. In tandem with the trajectory of US-centered capitalist expansion and global financialization—and driven by their own appetites and aspirations—the rising free-market fractions of the Mexican bourgeoisie took the reins of power directly.

# THREE

# Mexico within the US Imperialist Orbit

In addition to internal factors, the demise of state capitalism in Mexico was shaped by external factors as well; the foremost factor was opposition from the United States. The attempt to chart an independent economic path, industrialize, and advance as a potential competitor to dominant capitalist nations—all within an expanding US-centric imperialist system—did not proceed without conflict.

Prior to the Mexican Revolution, access to Mexican labor, land, markets, and other natural resources was essential for the original accumulation of capital that allowed the United States to scale up to the level of a Pacific empire.[1] Following World War II, between the years 1945 and 1973, the US economy entered its longest sustained phase of capitalist expansion. This expansion coincided with unmatched military spending, leading the US to become the preeminent global economic and military power.[2] Mexico was factored as a strategically important theater of capitalist accumulation by US policy makers, and entered into the cross hairs of imperial stratagem.

The US state initially worked with the PRI to advance its regional interests within the constraints of Import Substitution Industrialization. This was especially the case in the context of the emerging Cold War, as the US and Mexican governments had a shared interest in seeing the suppression of labor and agrarian radicalism. After state consolidation and the end of the war, the dynamics changed.

International banking institutions led and crafted by the US feared the disproportionate growth and preponderant weight of US capital. The rise of

US finance capital and its circulation internationally (as credits and loans) allowed for indirect reentry into protected economies like that of Mexico.

Other points of entry developed as the Mexican state came to rely on US export markets for its products, as a shock absorber of surplus agricultural workers, and an erstwhile ally in the Cold War. By the 1960s, the Mexican government had become more receptive to opening the border for US capital.

Eventually these linkages created fraternal bonds, lucrative partnerships, and financial fusion between sections of US and Mexican capital. Transnational economic relations among the capitalist classes fostered a sense of solidarity, shared interests, and mutual support. By the 1970s, these relationships informed the desire for unlimited accumulation through the complete opening of the Mexican border and markets to international investment, and in turn opposition to ISI and all other limitations on the supremacy of finance capital.

Internationally, the main centers of global capitalism have worked against the rise of new competitors in the so-called developing world. By the twentieth century, the most advanced capitalist nations had accumulated vast quantities of capital and built up their own economies through various forms of conquest and wealth transfer from other nations and populations. These occurred in different forms, including: enslaved labor, territorial acquisition and colonization, the pilfering of natural resources, the removal and separation of Indigenous peoples from their lands, the establishment of systems of labor superexploitation of oppressed populations, and the export of capital.

These dominant powers used protectionist measures to foster their own capitalist growth and industrialization, while actively seeking to export their capital to other countries and contributing to deindustrialization as part of the colonial relationship. This refers to the role of preponderant foreign capital being invested into the domestic economy of a subject nation through the forced freeing of those markets, and subsequently subsuming and eventually eliminating forms of autonomous industrial production. Due to the disproportionately larger scale of foreign capital—backed by immense military power, greater global market scale and access, technology and infrastructure, and resulting political inequities—foreign ownership gradually displaces and replaces domestic production. Through this transposition of capital, higher rates of wealth can be accumulated than in the home country, where markets are more saturated and competitive.

The dispossession of domestic capital and existing land tenure systems in the subject country ensure that existing productive capacity, land, and natural resources are more readily available and can be acquired more cheaply under conditions of colonization. Furthermore, the largest transnational capitalist firms can extend monopoly control over newly acquired markets and leverage accumulated capital gains against competitors internationally.

The contemporary global capitalist system reflects this legacy in the form of an international division of labor between the so-called developed and developing nations, which is the balance sheet of the first stage of original capitalist accumulation through colonization. Unequal relationships of power have been codified, perpetuated, and widened through the unilateral formation of international financial organizations, pacts, policies, and practices, that underwrite new forms of wealth transfer and reconfigure economic predominance.

The United States emerged from World War II as the dominant economic and military power, rivaled only by the Soviet Union. The shift to this bipolar model led to a reordering of the collapsed global imperialist system. The Cold War was the manifestation of this scramble for global repositioning, as the US and Soviet Union competed to carve new empires out of the smoldering ruins of the old.

## US Imperialism and Capitalist Globalization

US capital accumulation in Mexico began with the occupation and forced military cession of the northern half of the country in 1848. Between 1865 and 1910, US capital export to Mexico surpassed all Mexican domestic capital investment combined, creating the conditions of semicolonialism.[3]

During the Mexican Revolution, the US state played an active role in toppling unfavorable regimes, arming preferred factions, moving troops across the Mexican border in 1911, and invading Mexican national territory in 1914, 1916, and 1917. The armed forces were used to protect US investments from revolutionary expropriation, or to tip the balance in favor of preferable factions in the decade-long military phase of the revolution.[4] The Mexican revolutionaries toppled the regime of Porfirio Díaz but not the US empire that backed it up. In the ensuing decades, between 1920 and 1940, the United States sought out ways to goad the postrevolutionary regime toward compliance, exploiting its underdevelopment and the desperate need for capital.

In 1944, the US-initiated United Nations Monetary and Financial Conference held an international gathering to prepare the ground for a new postwar economic and political order known as the Bretton Woods Conference. The conference brought together the representatives of forty-four nations allied to the US to construct a postwar framework for commercial and financial relations.[5] The US also created the Washington-based Organization of American States in 1948 as a political transmission belt to coordinate and advance aligned efforts toward regional integration.

The 1944 conference outlined the basic architecture of the free-market order envisioned by the triumphant US capitalist class and their closest allies a system that has persisted through various stages to the present. Signatories pledged to raise funds to support rebuilding the national economies devastated by war and to integrate them into a new international system of free trade. The strategy included measures to stabilize currencies and create fixed exchange rates, establish global trade rules and regulations, and administrate through international oversight and enforcement bodies.

Over a three-year process, the conference produced the General Agreement on Tariffs and Trade (GATT, later renamed World Trade Organization), the International Monetary Fund (IMF), and the International Bank for Reconstruction and Development (IBRD, later renamed the World Bank) were created. A leadership structure commensurate to economic size and funding contribution was formalized, giving the US and Great Britain alone over 50 percent of the vote. This ensured effective control and veto power over all decision making. Mexico, on the other hand, held less than 1 percent of assigned votes. Combined with the other eighteen Latin American and Caribbean nations in attendance, they held a mere 8.38 percent of votes.

The IMF began accumulating an annual chest of funds, in accordance with the size of each member's economy. In the first phase, this allowed the United States to become the predominant creditor nation in the first phase of redevelopment. In subsequent phases, reconstructed European and Japanese capitalism partnered with the United States, especially when redeveloping the economies of colonized and historically underdeveloped nations. The veneer of legitimacy was added through the performance of a representative vote, even as the hierarchical design of these organizations ensured the representatives of the US capitalist class steered the ship. With the architecture of capitalist globalization in their hands—swelling stocks of accumulated capital at their disposal and the backing of the world's most powerful military to enforce the new order against rivals and outliers—the US ruling class initiated a new global capital-export regime under the mantra of development through free trade. As US Secretary of State Dean Rusk expressed the aspirations of US capitalism in 1965:

> But we know we can no longer find security and well-being in defenses and policies that are confined to North America, the Western Hemisphere, or the North Atlantic community. This has become a very small planet. We have to be concerned with all of it—with all of its land, waters, atmosphere, and with surrounding space.

By 1960, for instance, US-based capitalists had displaced their European counterparts as the dominant global investors, accounting for 59 percent of total volume of capital-export that year. What's more, the combined sales (in all major industries) from US-owned foreign enterprises abroad surpassed US-based manufactured exports by 1965.[6] Mexico became a major contributing source of growth during this period.

The US economy, remained intact and revitalized amid the generalized ruin of war. There was little to stop the United States in its advance toward imperialist hegemony except the Soviet Union—which had global designs of its own to extend its political and economic influence.[7] Seeing the accords as "predominantly of American authorship," the delegation from the Soviet Union withdrew from the meetings, characterizing the new organizations as "branches of Wall Street."[8] The ensuing Cold War seeped into every aspect of global politics and became a recurring justification for US military and economic intervention in Latin America.

Through the Bretton Woods system, US capitalism became the dominant global economic force outside of the Soviet Bloc countries. US-based banks, investment groups, and corporations became international in scope as the financiers, investors, and suppliers of global redevelopment. The Washington-based agencies compelled compliance through the strategic control and circulation of capital, loans, and credits; and by codifying these arrangements into legally sanctioned agreements that traded access to this system in exchange for opening of markets for export US capital and products.

Increased opportunity to shift investments in production to other countries where labor costs were cheaper led to a spike in capital export. Between 1950 and 1971, for instance, US corporations increased the rate of foreign direct investment at an average of 50 percent higher than the rate of investment in domestic production.[9] The US economy tripled in size over this period, and US corporations and international investment bankers dominated global trade and finance, comprising about 40 percent of total global GDP by 1960.[10] This period of capitalist expansion is referred to as the Postwar Boom in national lore but more accurately signifies the globalization and financialization of capitalism within the postwar, US-centric model.

New opportunities to profit through the internationalization of capital soothed the rivalries of the previous era and facilitated opportunities for new partnerships between capitalist classes within aligned nations. The dominant nations continued to fiercely compete but could also find common cause in expanding this system into new markets for mutual benefit.

The hegemony of the US-centric imperialist system was complicated by the emergence of a rival nuclear power in the Soviet Union (and its alignment of satellite states), as well as the revival of nationalist movements that charted a separate path toward capitalist development. This was especially the case in Latin America, where a long history and bitter memory of colonialism and US imperialist dominance inspired models of national capitalist development after World War II.

Over the course of five decades, the Cold War framework fueled a costly international arms race, wars in Asia, military interventions, and coups, with a major focus on Latin America.[11] The period also saw a prodigious expansion of US military placement on a global scale, with the number of bases and installations in other countries increasing from two in the 1920s to sixty-four by 1969 and positioned in sites and regions that reflected the geostrategic interests of US capitalism.[12] This coincided with an increasing appetite to expand capitalist globalization south of the US border.

The postwar model of capitalism in the United States experienced its first significant downturn during the global recession of 1973. In the period between 1973 and 1982 the US capitalist class saw its control over global economy diminish. Revived capitalist economies in West Germany and Japan made inroads into international trade and finance, followed by the consolidation of twenty-seven European states into a rival economic bloc known as the European Union.[13]

Beginning in the late 1970s, the dominant currents of the US ruling class began to reimagine and retool methods for capital accumulation amid global decline.[14] Both political parties coordinated a fundamental shift in governing philosophy and policy toward a more aggressive form of capital accumulation through the intensification of labor exploitation. The core of this strategy revolved around the systematic decimation of wage gains, labor rights and protections, and redistributive measures of the previous generations. Led through the state, unions were ground down into fragments, welfare provisions were whittled down or dismantled, and a general transition toward redistributing social wealth from poor and working-class people to the rich began.[15]

Concurrently, US investors and multinational corporations looked to the state to execute similar measures to increase capital accumulation and bolster sagging rates of profitability internationally. This started with a strategy to force open protected markets to the south, starting with Mexico.[16]

## Reopening the Mexican Border to US Capital

US imperialism in Mexico has a long and largely unbroken history, maintaining continuity through and beyond the revolution. Despite losing its hold over the commanding heights of the Mexican economy after the toppling of the Porfirian state, US capital still retained its most precious assets within the country, including major oil, mining, and railroad concessions.

Within the turbulent postrevolutionary period, the US government compelled its fragile Mexican counterpart to make significant concessions using a number of tactics. These included: withholding official recognition of the presidents, cutting off international credit, and threatening blockade and military invasion. Between 1923 and 1928, the Mexican state under Álvaro Obregón and Plutarco Elías Calles had agreed to limit land expropriations and compensate for accrued losses, pay back all outstanding prerevolutionary debt, and affirm and protect private US investments.[17]

After the rail and oil nationalizations the next decade, the US government demanded compensation and again cut off access to international credit but refrained from further action. Given the volatility of rising class struggle and the vulnerability of the new ruling group in Mexico, which policy makers used to contain the social movements, the US government scaled back threats of direct intervention lest they provoke a further radicalization.

## Wartime Investments

With the coming of war, the US government initiated the Good Neighbor Policy to restore favorable relations with Mexico, especially as it sought military alliance and new sources for raw materials. Wartime economic mobilization and the vast need for a variety of inputs opened up possibilities for production linkages between the two countries, coalescing with the new government's aspirations for foreign capital supports for industrial development.

In 1942, the two governments signed the Suárez-Bateman binational agreement, which established mechanisms for economic coordination between the two countries amid the outbreak of war. The US Federal Reserve and the Mexican central bank formalized an agreement to peg the currencies to facilitate cross-border exchange of capital and raw materials. The US offered Mexico above-market rates to direct its exports to the US alone. This arrangement stimulated possibilities for increased output and exchange.

The plan was to initially allow for US-owned enterprises in Mexico to ship materials across the border such as lead, copper, and zinc from the

Guggenheim-owned ASARCO mining company, the largest in Mexico. The US government shifted state resources toward resource development in Mexico. For instance, the Mexican government agreed to increase the land under cultivation by 3.3 million acres with direct subsidies from the United States in financing of $25 million for dam construction, irrigation projects, technology, and other inputs.[18] To facilitate financing, US bankers were sent in. According to one historical account,

> Warren Lee Pierson, president of the US Export-Import Bank, accepted an invitation to visit Mexico in August 1943 to study various project proposals that would absorb that country's growing dollar reserves.[19]

The bank loaned money to the Mexican government to develop cross-border transportation infrastructure, electricity production, railroad modernization, and technology for agricultural economies of scale. By 1947, the IBRD, the Export-Import Bank, and private US banks had loaned the Mexican government over $10 million as part of these development schemes.[20]

Despite the Mexican state's hope for wartime collaboration becoming a vehicle for substantial investment and technology transfer to facilitate the industrialization of Mexico, the effort fell far short. US investments were concentrated in sectors of the economy that aided US capital in Mexico and cross-border transfer of natural resources, but these did little for domestic industrial production. When the war ended, the US ambassador to Mexico abruptly announced the termination of further state investments in Mexico.[21]

Nevertheless, capitalists within the US government or connected to politicians involved in the wartime effort continued to pursue their own interests in Mexico through the economic channels that were established. The scramble for Mexico's opening economy and the promise of rich reward—even with state restrictions—drew in a of growing horde of investors, corporations, and speculators of all stripes. Between 1955 and 1958, for instance, over $100 million in US investments poured into Mexico each year.[22]

The first phase of state-managed industrialization between 1940 and 1970 relied on opening up partnerships with US capital. The first generation of multinational corporations were allowed to invest in the Mexican economy in two key ways: by taking minority shares in Mexican-owned industry or by setting up subsidiary companies within the national territory to supply domestic markets that weren't in direct competition with Mexican firms.

For instance, firms like Owens-Corning Fiberglass, Allied Chemical, B. F. Goodrich, Bayer, Morton Salt, DuPont, and International Nickel, transnationalized by entering into partnership with Mexican industrialists.[23] Multinational producers of consumer goods established subsidiary companies that operated wholly in Mexico. Kimberly-Clark established Kimberly-Clark de México in 1931, for instance, becoming the country's primary supplier of paper products. Sears, Roebuck, the US-based department store chain, opened seventeen stores in Mexico between 1940 and 1956, becoming the largest retailer in the country.

The events of World War II and the ensuing Cold War changed the course of regional politics, opening a pathway for the US state to reinsert its influence in Mexico and for capitalists to regain a foothold in the economy.

In the case of Mexico, lending was tied to the reopening of protected markets, the suppression of radicalism, and the formation of a capitalist class in its own image. As previously mentioned, the aftermath of World War II saw the United States enter into a period of sustained capitalist expansion. State policy makers began a multilayered project of increasing capital export on an international scale, while channeling resources through the architecture of its foreign policy objectives.

Different US-controlled banking institutions packaged and circulated private and state capital as credit. These included the newly created Export-Import Bank (1934), the International Bank for Reconstruction and Development/World Bank (first known as IBRD; 1944), and the Inter-American Development Bank (1959). The credit was distributed to make a profit for investors and was also tied to the state's political objectives. For instance, a US-based multinational cotton-trading firm called Anderson Clayton became the dominant supplier of credit to the ejido sector, surpassing the state-managed National Ejidal Bank by the early 1970s.[24]

As the Cold War proceeded, the US shifted direction once again. In the war of position with the Soviet Union, especially after the victorious Cuban Revolution in 1959, the US saw Mexico as both a large untapped resource and a potential hot spot for spreading agrarian insurgency. Capitalist investment and development became a strategy to combat the spread of rural radicalism in that period, as well as a means to procure new markets for capital export.

Despite its nationalist posturing, the Mexican government's desire for investment opened these portals for US capitalist reinsertion into the economy. These included US-Mexican business partnerships, an agricultural modernization project, and the creation and expansion of free-trade zones.

## Imperial Agriculture and Migration

When the right wing of the Mexican ruling party took the reins of government after 1940, they transitioned toward the utilization of agricultural export as an engine for capital accumulation to fund industrialization. As previously mentioned, this project necessitated a radical reorganization of the countryside, including accelerated land privatization and concentration linked to expanding US markets and a channeling of state investment into agricultural export economies of scale. These rapid shifts uprooted large swathes of the rural farming population, inducing proletarianization and out-migration.

Conciliation with the US government and foreign capital opened other doors for state accumulation. Alongside growing export outflow of raw materials and natural resources was the export of surplus workers. The transformation of the Mexican countryside systematically dislodged and impoverished rural Mexican workers in the decades following the war. Many were drawn north as transnational laborers known as braceros, whose disenfranchised labor provided vast quantities of capital to both US agricultural capitalists and the Mexican state for over two decades.

Between 1941 and 1945 the onset of World War II saw about sixteen million US workers drafted into the military, and millions more joined the exodus from agricultural regions to urban centers in search of better job prospects in war industries.[25] Most never returned, creating a checkerboard of vacancies in the lowest-paying echelons of farm work.

The need for cheap labor converged with the Mexican state's concern with a swelling population of landless workers in Mexico. This led to the mutually beneficial bilateral agreement to export surplus Mexican labor into the US economy. The Bracero Agreement outlined an innovative plan for the transnational exploitation of Mexican workers. According to the agreement braceros were contract labor, which in practice prohibited them forming unions or collectively bargaining to increase pay. Furthermore, the braceros were formally excluded from citizenship and had to return after the harvest season.[26]

US growers were able to continue paying substandard wages. They were empowered to deport unruly workers at will. Even though they were required to provide transportation, housing, and food to the braceros, they could circumvent those obligations as there was little or no enforcement of these provisions.

The novel form of labor exploitation proved so beneficial in its first few years that agricultural capitalists leveraged their power through the state to extend it beyond the war's end. For over two decades, agricultural wages remained stagnant, unions virtually disappeared, and the value generated by superexploitation transferred immense wealth into the hands of the grower class. Between 1942 and 1959, for instance, the average farm wage dropped by 13 percent nationally.[27]

The elaboration and institutionalization of the Bracero Agreement signified a new method in labor procurement and exploitation. The US state induced Mexican labor migration, while simultaneously denying these workers access to citizenship rights, creating the conditions for structured and systematic superexploitation. It was the prototype for what has since evolved into "undocumented" migration. Along with the Cold War–origin elements of border enforcement, armed agents, and state violence, this trajectory of state policy explains the overlapping of migrant labor exploitation with so-called national defense. This has led to the militarized institutionalization of migrant repression.

## Braceros: Restructuring Capitalist Agriculture

Between 1942 and 1964, 4.6 million braceros formed the ranks of a mass labor-export scheme. They moved into US fields and railroads, while thousands of others who were disqualified from the program concentrated in the northern border regions and eventually constituted the first ranks of "undocumented" labor, enticed by a wide range of capitalist industries to cross without state authorization.[28] The outflow of migrants also became a political expedient for the Mexican ruling class. By exporting displaced farmers and impoverished workers, they diffused the conditions for rural unrest. More significantly, the superexploited labor of braceros became an important source of capital accumulation for employers and foreign cash for the Mexican government. By 1950, remittances had become the country's third-largest source of hard currency and a crucial funding mechanism for the Mexican state's industrialization projects.[29]

Millions of rural workers not absorbable into the restructured Mexican economy were encouraged to journey to US-directed bracero recruitment centers stationed in different parts of the country. The most fit and able bodies were selected by US agents, while those deemed unfit were denied. Workers were shipped to the border for six-month intervals. They could not apply for citizenship, and part of their wages were deducted and transferred to the Mexican government; the money was only accessible to them after their return.[30]

For twenty-three years, this migratory population entered and labored in the United States without labor rights, guarantees, or recourse. They were brought in by the state and incorporated into the agricultural workforce by capitalist growers as a reserve army of labor. Over two decades, their vulnerable position was exploited as a bulwark against unions in US fields, to leverage wages downward to create a substandard wage floor, and to eventually restructure agricultural work into the least organized, lowest-paying, and least protected sector of the economy.[31]

For the Mexican state, cross-border labor migration also served as a social pressure valve for impoverished workers who were denied the promises of the revolution for social development and could become a detonator for renewed rebellion in the countryside. They also became a lucrative source of investment through the repatriation of their wages to Mexico.[32]

## Cold War Containment

After World War II, there was a weakening and reordering of the imperialist system. This created the openings for insurgencies and revolutionary movements developing in parts of Asia, Latin America, and Africa.

The United States and its European allies transitioned into the Cold War, opening up a new phase of imperialist reorganization. US policy makers focused on the potential for radicalization of disgruntled rural populations south of its borders becoming the backbone of a Communist insurgency across Latin America and other parts of the world.

As a national security doctrine elaborated by then secretary of state George F. Kennan in 1947, containment entailed the "long-term, patient but firm and vigilant containment of Russian expansive tendencies."[33] Containment strategy sought to arrest the spread of Soviet power in two dimensions. "Strongpoint defense" called for the concentration of military force and power at strategic geopolitical locations abroad where US interests were threatened, and "perimeter defense" called for securing of the "rim of the heartland" from enemy penetration.[34] This latter component of the doctrine was institutionalized throughout the Cold War and colored national policies in all forms, including border policy.

Cold War ideology carried over into US funding and support for anticommunist movements in Central America, which became a strategic region during the Cold War. In 1954 a US-supported military coup toppled the reformist government of Jacobo Árbenz in Guatemala. This was due to its alleged socialist ambitions in pursuing land nationalization at the expense of the US-based United Fruit Company, a multinational corporation that controlled much of that country's arable land.[35] Central American Cold War flashpoints, in the eyes of then president Dwight D. Eisenhower, placed the threat of a "possible Communist outpost on this continent" within striking distance of America's southern border.[36]

This framed the financial dimension of US-led Cold War containment strategy in the region, especially after the successful Cuban Revolution of 1959. Furthermore, the growth of US capitalist firms during the war situated them to prosper immensely on an international scale after the war with the help of the imperial state. Therefore, the policy directives of the US state combined capitalist expansion and Cold War strategy and positioning. This meant forging a new political anticommunism and state-building in its own image, with newly imposed trade relations that facilitated capital export and increased profits for its emerging multinational firms and investors.

The US government created the Inter-American Development Bank in 1959 to facilitate the financial side of this strategy. The IADB was set up to distribute loans to Latin American and Caribbean nations, with funds raised through the sale of bonds to international private investors. Like the other global financial institutions created by the US government, it was constructed to guarantee that its own delegations retained veto power. Alongside the IMF and World Bank, the IADB weaponized lending to contain radicalism and nationalism, open up new markets to international capital, and encourage privatization of agriculture.[37]

In exchange for continued economic cooperation, the Mexican government worked through the IADB to allow US investments into Mexican agriculture as part of its project to expand agricultural industrialization for export to increase state income. This converged with US interests, which saw it as a means to develop poor agrarian regions, export US capital, and restructure regional production and distribution systems in ways that linked them to US capital and consumption markets.

The US government had been subsidizing grain producers since the Great Depression by purchasing their surplus grain and distributing it in conjunction with the plan to develop a new global agricultural distribution system. In 1965, the US tied grain distribution to countries facing famine to structural adjustments in their agricultural economy. "Future deliveries were made dependent on the satisfaction of a number of conditions by the receiving countries—primarily a shift of emphasis from industrialization to agricultural development, expansion of population control, and an open door to US investors."[38]

This model of capitalist production requires more technological inputs, machinery, and land concentration—to the benefit of US exporters and a newly reconstituted landowning capitalist class in Mexico. Economies of scale produced higher profits, which in turn drove an increase in the value of land. This further contributed to land concentration into fewer hands, greater economies of scale, and more cheaply produced exports for US markets. Agricultural exports rose from $40 million in 1964 to $100 million in 1969; and doubled to $200 million by 1977.[39]

US economic and foreign policy objectives increasingly converged and overlapped, gearing up more explicit designs for the opening up of Mexico. In 1978, for instance, the US National Security Council identified Mexico as an "economic power of strategic value to the US," especially after the discovery of huge oil deposits in the preceding years.[40] Further economic penetration into Latin America in the 1970s was inhibited by "developmentalist" economic policies of the postwar period. Mexico, the second largest economy in Latin America at the time—and closest to the US border—was the beachhead for the US empire's designs to restructure the capitalist system first in Mexico and then across the hemisphere.[41]

The next opening for US capital came in 1964 and 1965 when the US and Mexican governments negotiated the Border Industrialization Program (BIP). The Bracero Program was ended in 1965 as a result of two factors: a successful campaign of US labor unions against contract labor (led by the United Farm Workers) and the gradual preference by growers for cheaper and more accessible undocumented labor.[42] With the structures of undocumented labor migration in place (without the need for state management), US capitalists could shift the locus of labor exploitation *into* Mexico with the establishment of free-trade zones to US manufacturers and investors within fifteen miles of the border region. The opening of Mexican border economies to US capital for investment in maquiladora assembly and agricultural export-oriented production was a first phase in the eventual dismantling of Import Substitution Industrialization.

This stage of capitalist reorganization was designed to open the border and allow investors to have access to labor *inside* Mexico as an even more effective method of accumulation. Whereas immigration provided the ranks of a reserve army of labor within US labor markets, the BIP began the process in earnest of transnational working-class formation—still maintained as unequal by the developing mechanisms of border enforcement and subdivision.

The BIP served as an entry point that eventually reordered the northern border region of Mexico as an extension of US-based production. Through these openings, US companies and investors implanted within the Mexican economy. They formed business relationships that served as the initial conduits for transborder capitalist-class formation and as vehicles for aligned political action.

# FOUR

# The Maquiladorization of Mexico

Even though the Mexican economy required that private industries be "majority Mexican-owned," the state turned a blind eye toward violations. Factional disputes within the state and between different groups of capitalists produced negotiated power-sharing agreements that allowed for economic regionalization and degrees of autonomy. Consequently, economic differentiation outside of the state capitalist model paved the way for increased foreign investment, growth, and expansion of new models of production and labor exploitation and capital accumulation that existed outside of the corporatist structure.[1] This transition laid the foundation for the increased fragmentation and ultimate irreconcilability between the growing free-market class fractions and the declining ranks of the defenders of ISI.

Furthermore, some US multinational corporations were allowed to operate subsidiaries inside Mexico early in the postwar period and not be hampered by tariffs, creating virtual monopolies in some sectors of the economy. These Mexicanized subsidiaries cultivated important transnational linkages and entry points for US capitalists to influence policy decisions in Mexico.[2] Pervasive corruption also played a role in allowing more powerful sectors to of the capitalist class to carve out forms of local control and autonomy, especially in the northern border states where the bourgeoisie has had longer and deeper connections with US capitalism.[3] For example:

> From 1940–65 . . . industrialists in Mexico and in the United States transformed borderland economies, making the region the fastest-

> growing area of both countries. Mexican and US investment in agriculture, ranching, and manufacturing industries; infrastructural developments including highway, railroad, and monorail construction; the building of new customs gateways, factories, and oil pipelines; and tourism and free-trade initiatives implemented by local, state, and national governments all demonstrated the increasingly dense economic connections promoted by businesspeople and politicians on both sides of the border.[4]

In fact, US investment increased at an average of 10 percent annually during the period of the most comprehensive state protectionism after 1940, and increased exponentially by the 1970s.[5] The managed partnership with US capitalism was in theory a necessary evil. The increase in foreign capital was to be controlled and leveraged to serve the development of industrial infrastructure, to facilitate technology transfer, and ultimately to engineer the modernization of Mexico and its gradual entrance into the developed world. In practice, the quantitative openings for US capital created qualitative changes that led to Mexican deindustrialization in favor of US capital import, while retaining and further strengthening authoritarian and patriarchal forms of working-class exploitation.

Access to *more* Mexican labor and other fruits of the Mexican economy enticed more investment. By the 1970s, the US state had factored the complete opening of Mexico as part of its *plan* for increased national development—a process which necessitated a structural transformation away from state control of the economy. Partnership with Mexican capital gave it new leverage.

After 1965 new methods to exploit Mexican labor as a form of capital accumulation replaced the Bracero Program. Among these was the preference for undocumented labor north of the border, and for Mexican labor *inside* Mexico.

> As labor-intensive production became increasingly uneconomic, US firms turned offshore, breaking up production into stages and carrying out the labor-intensive processes in countries where wages were low.... The border is fairly accessible, and transportation from almost any point in the United States to the border is cheap when compared to overseas trade.[6]

Initially, the maquiladora system was conceived of as a mutually beneficial island of production that would absorb Mexico's displaced agricultural workers and not undermine Mexico's domestic manufacturing economy. The system was supposed to absorb the populations of displaced and unemployed workers in the north of the country so Mexico could benefit from workers' reinvestment of wages back into local economies. Once functioning, the maquiladora economy took on a life of its own, becoming a major source of capital accumulation for transnational capital and foreign exchange for the Mexican state.

According to the BIP, US investors were allowed to import raw materials duty-free into their assembly facilities in Mexico; the materials were then finished and exported back to US markets duty-free so as to not compete with Mexican manufactured goods. This policy was structured to allow US capital to begin the process of outsourcing what became known as supply chain production across the US-Mexico border in order to take advantage of lower Mexican labor costs. Aside from procuring new sources of capital and profit, the system was designed to leverage lower Mexican wages to allow for US manufactured exports to be more competitive in international markets against those of other industrialized nations.[7]

By design, the implementation and maintenance of the program was predicated on continued access to large pools of cheap labor. At the inception of the program in 1968, manufacturing wages on the Mexican side of the border were on average six times lower than their counterparts in the United States.[8] The industry was initially located in the young and densely population Mexican border cities, which contained large working-age populations, especially young women, many of whom were migrant workers already displaced from other parts of the Mexican interior, who did not have established roots in the border cities. Due to the precarity of employment and the devaluation of female-gendered labor, the architects of the maquiladora model structured production around the superexploitation of primarily women workers.

Young women of working age were typically un- or underemployed in the formal sectors of the economy. They were excluded from male-gendered work where collective union contracts were more commonplace, they had fewer protections under existing labor law and custom, and were less likely to relocate or migrate across the border than their male counterparts. The latter occurred as result of the fact that young, single women tended to live in their parents' households, while older women workers were commonly single mothers who were the main providers for their children after their husbands or partners migrated north.[9] Transnational capital built upon and exacerbated the existing gendered division of labor in order to maximize exploitation of the already devalued labor of women. By 1980, for instance, about 85 percent of all maquiladora workers were women, and women have continued to comprise the majority of workers as the maquiladora model spread across the country.[10]

The growth of the sector has also been underwritten by the maintenance of suppressed wages. The threshold of maquila wages has been kept artificially low by the concerted effort and collusion of private capital and local and state governments to keep unions out, coupled with the implementation of an enforcement regime to criminalize migration into the United States—and, in effect, to build a bulwark against cross-border unionism and labor integration.

A further draw for US investment in maquiladora production came for US suppliers. On average, no more than 5 percent of the maquiladoras' intermediate inputs and raw materials have been locally supplied over the fifty-year period of the open border capitalist project. Instead, they typically come from subsidiaries of the same companies or other suppliers based in the United States.[11]

The total value of US investments jumped from about $1.1 billion in 1960 to $2.3 billion by 1968, especially concentrated in manufacturing. Over the decade of 1960 to 1970, total US foreign investment totaled $2.6 billion, while the repatriation of profits topped $3 billion—a gain of $400 million.[12] After the introduction and initial profitability of the BIP, more US investment poured in. By 1975, US investment in manufacturing flowed in from over 187 different US corporations, with 162 operating as transnational extensions and 412 operating as subsidiary companies, primarily concentrated in chemical-pharmaceuticals, cosmetics, processed food production, automotive, rubber, and electronics and appliances.[13] By the end of the first year of the BIP in 1965, there were twelve maquiladoras employing 3,087 workers. By the summer of 1971, the number multiplied to 293 plants employing 31,000 workers; these again nearly doubled to 531 plants in 1982 with over 156,000 workers. By the latter year, maquiladoras were also in operation deeper into the interior of the country.[14]

This concentration of investment into maquiladora production occurred through (mostly) US investors taking "control of the most dynamic sectors of local industry through the direct purchase of already existing productive operations."[15] In other words, US investors typically bought out highly productive Mexican enterprises instead of adding additional productive capacity. US investment increased from 7 percent of total investment in Mexican manufacturing in 1940 to 74 percent by 1970.[16] For example, the opening up of foreign capital through the BIP led to the demise of Mexico's young automotive sector.

An attempt to generate a domestic auto manufacturing industry in the 1960s through ISI was frustrated by open-market competition with larger US and multinational firms. Lacking comparative levels of capital, credit, technology, and transportation infrastructure, six Mexican-owned auto assembly and auto parts firms (both private and state-owned) eventually sold off their holdings to the multinationals.[17]

This capital concentration signaled the beginning of US dominance over Mexico's export sector. The "success" of the BIP in manufacturing, led other groupings of transnational investors to clamor for its expansion. Already by the early 1970s, US multinational firms such as John Deere, International Harvester, Monsanto, Dupont, United Brands, and Ralston-Purina had become the primary suppliers of machinery, fertilizers, and insecticides, and controlled processing and merchandising of agricultural products.[18]

The free-trade zone model was initially confined to the border zone and to assembly processes in order to placate nationalist concerns. In 1983 it was extended into the interior of the country. Like in the United States, where manufacturing moved to the southern states where unionization was historically weaker and wages substantially lower, a similar process happened in Mexico. Lower wages in southern Mexico and other parts of the country became even more alluring than the benefits of proximity to the border. Maquiladora operations eventually extended into every state of the country. By 1985, maquila production was the second largest source of foreign exchange after oil.[19]

In 1986, the BIP model was expanded to allow for the unfettered export of US agricultural capital.

> Beginning in 1983, Mexico began the process of reforming its agricultural policies as part of its overall effort to direct the economy toward international markets, eliminate excessive regulation and state intervention in the economy, and establish an environment to stimulate investment and private sector participation. The Mexican government reduced guaranteed prices on most commodities, reduced the role of and budgets for agricultural parastatals . . . and called for privatization of others.[20]

At the time, there were approximately twenty-eight thousand ejidos (after the final round of land distribution during the administration of Echeverría), with the economic participation of more than 20 percent of Mexico's rural population and covering half of Mexico's total land mass.[21] The opening up of the border region to US capital in agriculture began the process of dismantling the state-supported ejido system and its eventual absorption into the private sector.

Mexican farms were converted into partnerships with US grower-shipper operations, converting agricultural production of fruits and vegetables in the north into highly capitalized agro-industrial export zones for international markets—with substantial profits transmitted back to the US tax-free. These zones were initially developed in Baja California, Sonora, and Sinaloa but later expanded through the interior of the country with the transition to free trade.

> Concordant with NAFTA, the Mexican government agreed to drop all protective tariffs and taxes on agrarian goods, supports to farmers ultimately disappearing by 2008. However, the goal of making ejidos more productive through these changes has proved elusive. . . . The fundamental controversy over the reforms was that the ejido system allowed ejidatarios to sell off their communal property, or their share of communal interests, to private interests.[22]

The abolition of the ejido system was complete, opening the door to full privatization of the land.

The BIP was so successful an endeavor for US investors and a growing free-market wing of the PRI that its expansion became urgent. According to a 1987 US General Accounting Office report to Congress,

> As of February 1986, about 68 percent of maquiladora plants reportedly were entirely or majority U.S.-owned. Value-added in maquiladora plants increased approximately 53 percent, from about $828.2 million in 1983 to about $1.265 billion in 1985.[23]

The rapid expansion of the sector was further facilitated through the Mexican state with the passage of the Foreign Investment Law of 1973. This sectioned out three categories: state-owned, Mexican-only private ownership, and foreign-Mexican "partnership" industries. The national commission of foreign investment (CNIE, or Comisión Nacional de Inversiones Extranjeras) was created to regulate foreign investment, and was gradually given leeway to open up whole sectors to 100 percent foreign ownership. This created the first phase of parallelization of the economy between the Mexican-only sectors and those opened up to foreign ownership for export. A few years later, when state oil revenues plummeted, the Mexican government expanded the purview of FIC to take on a larger role in opening more arenas in the economy to foreign investment.[24] The US International Trade Commission reported,

> During 1984–87, U.S. imports under items 806.30 and 807.00 increased by 140 percent to $68.5 billion, at a faster pace than total U.S. imports which rose by 24 percent to $402 billion.[25]

Decreased public and private investment was commensurate with increasing foreign investment in manufacturing, resulting in deindustrialization. For instance, Mexican private investment as a percentage of total capital investment in manufacturing fell from 46.4 percent in 1977 to 36 percent in 1980.[26] Instead of investment into productive capacity, Mexican investors moved more of their money into speculation and services, especially in those sectors where foreign capital was dominant. This signified the retreat and gradual abdication of the terrain of manufacturing investment to international capital.

In 1993 the Mexican government modified the Foreign Investment Law to allow for 100 percent foreign ownership within all maquiladora operations. In a final pivot toward Mexican deindustrialization, the government fully opened up all Mexican markets to maquiladora products in 2001. This led to another wave of foreign investment and local buyouts and supply inputs to break into and corner previously closed Mexican markets.

Furthermore, GATT membership opened up Mexican markets to more than one hundred nations, dropping import duties from 120 percent to about 20 percent, leading to a flood of international capital and products.[27] This led to a persistent surge in imports of manufactured goods, increasing annually after 1982. As a share of GDP, they climbed from 10 percent in 1982 to more than 30 percent by 2007. From 1988 to 2006, imports of manufactured products expanded at an average annual rate that more than doubled that of exports. Over that same period, the import of manufactured goods rose to account for 95 percent of total imports.[28]

The combination of various factors drove Mexican deindustrialization, the changing composition of the Mexican capitalist class, and subsequent emigration of Mexican workers. These include: the free movement of US capital into Mexico and concentration in maquiladora export-oriented production, the removal of restrictions on maquiladora production and its expansion into local markets, and the lowering of tariffs for goods produced internationally. These drove a substantive shift in the trajectory of industrialization and a transfer of ownership of the means of production from Mexican to international entities.

Whole Mexican industries evaporated as markets became flooded with cheaper-made goods, displacing workers across the economy.[29] Some were absorbed into the "new" economy, working in maquiladoras or other foreign-owned industries and enterprises. Many more were pushed out of labor markets altogether, forced to look for work north of the border.

While neoliberal economists hold up increased industrialization rates in Mexico and point to a substantial growth of exports after the passage of NAFTA, they tend to ignore the underlying realities that prop up these trends. The post-NAFTA Mexican economy has undergone a change of ownership, as US and international capital now control the commanding heights of the economy with Mexican capital as a junior partner. Production for export, from automobiles to ventilators, is contingent on the suppression of wages and superexploitation of workers integrated into the economy at lower wages and higher productivity rates. Lastly, this new economy has not been able to absorb millions of workers, who have been compelled to migrate or move into the informal economy.

# FIVE

# The Burial of the Mexican Revolution

The bourgeois revolution in Mexico succeeded in some of its underlying objectives. State capitalism created an industrial base and a banking system and curated into existence a self-conscious capitalist class and enormous urban working class. As a component part of the corporatist framework, the bourgeois sector increased disproportionately in power and influence in relation to the other social classes, eventually rendering the postrevolutionary state arrangement defunct.

Nevertheless, the postrevolutionary state ultimately failed in its objective to navigate Mexico into the community of advanced capitalist nations. After losing its hegemony in Mexico during the most radical phases of the Mexican Revolution, when millions of workers and peasants entered the stage of history and waged existential struggle *against* imperialism, US capital restored semicolonial control of Mexico's economy by the conclusion of the twentieth century.

The postrevolutionary Mexican government's strategy of state-led capitalist development ran into the retaining walls of a fiercely guarded imperialist system dominated by yanqui capitalism. US economic expansion after World War II began the process of reintegration along conciliatory lines, but further growth after the end of the postwar boom was contingent on the virtual economic reconquest of Mexico. A tilting balance of power between the state and national capitalists in favor of those class fractions linked to international capital produced a qualitative shift in governance. This was escalated by several factors: Cold

War ruling-class alliances and US military aggression in the region, US-induced economic crisis and capitalist restructuring in Mexico, and a transnational capitalist class convergence toward overturning ISI in favor of free markets.

US capital exporters (i.e., investors) gradually reestablished majority ownership and control over major sectors of the Mexican economy through the aegis of their rising counterparts in Mexico. US-linked and allied capitalists in Mexico enthusiastically took power for themselves, privatized the state sectors, and reopened the economy to US capital in exchange for a cut of the spoils. This transnational alliance restored Mexico's functional subordinacy to the imperatives of US capital accumulation—effectively exhausting the inertia and burying the populist and nationalist aspirations of the Mexican Revolution once and for all.

## Neoliberalism: Capitalism Restructures Internationally amid Crisis of Accumulation

Capital accumulation in developed nations ran into significant limits in the early 1970s, culminating in the global crisis of 1973. A decline in the rate of profit as a result of increased international competition brought about jarring recession and the conclusion of the postwar boom in the United States. Military Keynesianism, the postwar model of US capitalist accumulation, had reached its limits.[1] This set of arrangements had depended on rebuilding and linking capitalist economies globally through the US-centric Bretton Woods system and expanding trade, consumer markets, and capital export, especially between the United States and other developed capitalist countries.

Postwar decolonization and international capitalist reorganization brought more newly independent nations into the fold of this system but did little to address the long-term effects of underdevelopment, deindustrialization, and the persistence of colonial-era dependencies and inequalities. While the new international order discouraged direct recolonization, it maintained and reinforced colonial-era disparities, and perpetuated an exploitative international division of labor through methods of financial dominance.

Existing international divisions of labor were reinforced and widened through increased capital export, asymmetrical economic integration, the "freeing" of protected national markets, and eventually foreign implantation and the reestablishment of semicolonization through economic hegemony. This began the process of interlinking capitalist classes internationally and across borders, as the new system allowed for a widening circle of participants and partnerships.

In the context of Soviet containment and inter-imperialist rivalry, this was backed up by a perpetual buildup and international deployment of military power to enforce compliance. The United States deployed quick and heavy-handed repression of nationalist, radical, and revolutionary movements that rose in resistance to this system, especially in the postcolonial nations.[2] US interventions to topple noncompliant regimes or to support aligned regimes in repressing popular movements took place in multiple countries in the postwar period. A partial list includes: Guatemala (1954); Cuba (1961); Guyana (1963); South Vietnam, Laos, and Cambodia (1963); the Dominican Republic (1965); Indonesia (1967); Iraq (1972–75); and many others.

These direct invasions to force regime change and to open support and aid for sanguinary repression made clear the costs of noncompliance. Postcolonial nationalist and nonaligned governments, ruling fractions, or oppositional popular movements that thwarted US hegemony were not going to be tolerated. After the end of the Cold War in 1991 and the dissolution of the USSR and Soviet satellite states, these oppositional currents were further isolated, diminished, or smashed.

The crisis of accumulation that developed gave rise to radical ideological shifts in the power centers of the ruling parties, who embraced anti-statist positions and turned aggressively against economic protectionism in the postcolonial and developing countries.[3]

As part of this political repositioning, the capitalist class spearheaded an offensive to reorganize the state to serve as a vehicle to directly restore lost profitability. The scale of this turn led to a seismic transition in the capitalist governance model, with both Republican and Democratic Party centers coming into renewed alignment. Since the 1970s, bipartisan administrations have carried out a fundamental social reordering to transfer socialized wealth back into private hands: tax cuts, social budget cuts and elimination, deregulation, privatization, the diminishing of worker's guarantees, and the expansion of a regime of legal rights for capital.[4]

The state was used to expand access and mobility for US capital internationally. The US Federal Reserve, which determines the interest rates for all dollar-denominated loans, unilaterally increased interest rates under the rubric of fighting inflation—knowing full well that the Mexican state (and other Latin American governments) did not have the reserves to pay higher rates on existing debts. In other words, the Fed intentionally pushed the Mexican economy into financial meltdown.

This political ambush, called the Volcker Shock after the Fed chair Paul Volcker, was the final blow against the teetering ISI model.[5] With the economy on the ropes, the US state went to work coordinating bailouts and loans from US banks, the IMF, World Bank, and other aligned creditors. The state then acted through these institutions to compel the dismantling of the forty-year-old ISI regime and its replacement with "free-trade" agreements.

## The End of Import Substitution Industrialization

US capitalists operating within Mexico impeded and deterred technology transfer and limited or avoided investment in the production of capital goods as an official position, "based on the premises that to do so would save US jobs, preserve US competitive advantage in advanced technology, and reduce competition from low-cost imports produced with US technology transferred abroad."[6] The imperialist logic ensured that investors could continue to transfer wealth out of Mexico in the form of accumulated capital and profits in perpetuity without simultaneously cultivating rival producers.[7] As one high-ranking official commented, "We are not in the business . . . of technical assistance in Mexico."[8]

Despite the substantial growth of an industrial base, Mexico's economic penetration into global markets and supply chains was blunted by the dominant capitalist countries. The model reached its growth limits and stagnated by the early 1970s, coinciding with the onset and impact of global economic recession. Foreign investment dried up: private and state-owned industries were compelled to lay off workers. As the working-class standard of living dwindled, so too did their purchasing power, decreasing domestic consumption.

The state became increasingly dependent on its oil exports, which spiked in price after 1973 due to international shortages caused by the OPEC oil embargo. To compensate for lost income in other industries, the administration of Luis Echeverría borrowed heavily from international banks to continue to fund the state-managed economy. When oil prices crashed again in 1976 with the end of the embargo and onset of a recession-driven glut, the state was left exposed to mounting debt and the balance of payment shortages. This confluence of factors touched off ten years of recession, capital flight, rising inflation, and collapsing investment in state industry.

The IMF intervened, offering the Echeverría government a $1.2 billion bailout, with the first installment financed through the US government, in exchange for a series of economic reforms that amounted to the first blow in a series of many to come. The Mexican state de-pegged the peso from the dollar, accepted a 38 percent devaluation of the peso, and opened the door to further dependence on these oppositional neoliberal institutions to introduce Trojan-horse policies, especially as access to international credit through traditional channels dried up. Meanwhile, corruption remained rampant and intensified as state income declined in the 1970s amid global recession.

In 1979, the US government formed a public-private partnership with the largest banks and companies to strategize for the opening of Mexico to a new era of capital export. According to the federal plan:

> The over 120 companies and firms . . . represent a cross section of US businesses with extensive international operations. The participating companies, which are some of the largest enterprises in the US, represent four sectors: Agribusiness (9%), Extractive (16%), Manufacturing (45%), and Services (30%). Of the 81 industrial corporations participating, 80% are on the Fortune list of the 500 Largest Industrials; 77% of the participating banks are on the Fortune list of the 50 Largest Commercial Banks.[9]

Instead of partnership and "technology transfer," the intention of the neoliberal, free-market reopening of Mexico was for US capital to supplant state-managed ISI. In the context of a deepening economic crisis in Mexico, reimplantation of capital was positively spun as a way to bypass traditional state-mandated technology transfer through direct investment that could also resolve the brewing crisis. As the report asserted, US reentry would increase consumption and prevent mass out-migration: "Without [US] enterprise in Mexico, we can't cope with the labor problem, we can't cope with the demand problem, and we can't cope with the dependency problem."[10]

The period of 1976–82 was definitive for the death and burial of the legacy of the Mexican Revolution. The 1976 crisis created the opening for a confluence of factors to converge in making Mexico the test case for neoliberal restructuring. As one study observed:

> The 1976 Mexican crisis and US and Mexican officials' responses to it exposed the tensions created by the growing global financial interdependence of the 1960s and 1970s. That interdependence reflected five interrelated phenomena: the rapid expansion and global integration of private financial markets; the US Treasury's increasing reliance upon those markets to finance rising US budget deficits; the growing competition among international commercial bankers to extend loans to increasingly insolvent borrowers in the developing world; developing country officials' growing reliance on foreign bank loans to finance their development projects and balance of payments deficits; and the rising level of systemic risk in the global financial system.[11]

Taken together, the United States and the global capitalist powers saw and seized the means and entry point for ending the cycle of nationalist and developmentalist movements in their former colonies and traditional spheres of influence and control. Rather than take direct military control to reestablish hegemony over the subject economy, the elaboration of mechanisms to facilitate capital export served as the means to displace national capital. In other words, Mexican state capitalism had to be demolished and replaced with free markets to allow for a restoration of the supremacy of US capital. Those in the US found allies in fractions of the Mexican capitalist class who began to push the same line—calling for cuts in public spending, diminished state regulation, free trade, and the encouragement of foreign investment. Proponents of this view within the government were the central bank head Romero Kolbeck and minister of finance Moctezuma Cid. This was also the viewpoint of most large-scale businessmen in industry, commerce, and finance.[12]

The reassertion of US imperialist dominance in the hemisphere also coincided with the revived Cold War offensives of the 1970s and '80s. The US state and its various agencies underwrote multiple efforts to crush radical and socialist movements challenging this framework. These included the ongoing dirty war to overturn the Cuban government, support for the overthrow of Salvador Allende in Chile in 1973, direct support for the Contras against the Sandinista Revolution in Nicaragua after 1979, and support for the bloody repression of guerrilla and popular movements in El Salvador, 1979, and Grenada in 1983. US troops were also used against one-time allies who fell from favor, such as Manuel Noriega with the invasion of Panama in 1989.

The counterrevolutionary offensives of the United States primed relations with the domestic bourgeoisies of these respective nations, who shifted back into alignment with US strategy to suppress dissident movements in their own nations.[13] The confluence of these factors gave rise to a newly configured and politicized capitalist class in Mexico. This movement was led by those *grandes* of capitalism who were both created by the postrevolutionary state and also orchestrated its demise.

## Rise of the "Men of Business" in Mexico

The postrevolutionary state incorporated the inchoate bourgeoisie as a subordinate yet essential partner in the nation-building process. State-led industrialization through public-private partnership, the direct financing of a banking sector with availability of easy credit and other inputs, the capitalization and concentration of the best land into a new landowning class, the subjugation and social production of labor, and the channeling of foreign investment into Mexican-owned enterprise were all designed to enable the growth of the capitalist economy. Out of this cocooned process emerged a reconstituted capitalist class, one that discreetly agreed to avoid direct intervention in national politics in exchange for retaining their privileged position.

Between 1940 and 1970 the number of industrial establishments grew from 13,000 to over 130,000, accounting for 34 percent of gross national product.[14] Despite the growth, capitalization was concentrated in a small number of enterprises. The 1,117 largest of these accounted for 64.3 percent of total production and 66 percent of total invested capital in 1965. Foreign capital was most concentrated in 938 of the largest of these firms in "partnership" with Mexican capital, accounting for nearly 27 percent ownership of the total assets.[15]

Over this period the Mexican bourgeoisie tied to foreign capital grew in size, wealth, and confidence. Through various stages, the group enlarged and redefined its role in relation to the government. By 1962, a subgrouping of the twelve largest bankers and industrialists organized a new group that assumed nationwide representation for their class, called the Consejo Mexicano de Hombres de Negocios (CMHN, or the Mexican Council of Men of Business).

The Mexican bourgeoisie was reconstituted over the course of the 1970s with the dominant fraction, led by the CMHN, gravitating toward neoliberalism. Through layers of class organization, these figures insinuated themselves more aggressively into national politics and eventually toward direct conflict with the tenets of state capitalism.

Through their control of banking and continued influence over the Finance Ministry policy purview, they integrated Mexico's economy into US-centric international finance markets. They legalized the internationalization and consolidation of the banking system into fewer megabanks, allowed for the dollarization of banking, and expanded their control over the stock market. As Sylvia Maxfield points out:

> The number of representative offices of foreign banks increased dramatically, Mexican banks were encouraged to operate internationally, and foreign borrowing ballooned. . . . [T]he promotion of private financial markets with relatively little success regulating credit allocation, free exchange convertibility, and little or no taxation on luxury goods shaped the way international integration affected Mexico's industrialization effort.[16]

International credit became cheaper and more readily available than in domestic markets through state financing. This allowed Mexican capitalists to finance their own investing, buy out smaller firms and concentrate control over whole sectors of the economy, engage in foreign exchange speculation, and profit by recycling cheap credit and lending it at higher interest rates within domestic markets through their banks.[17]

The rise of Mexican finance capital was engendered through several overlapping factors, including the global economic crisis in the 1970s; the reorganization of US capitalism and renewed projection of power through the interventions of the IMF, World Bank, and the GATT/WTO and other auxiliary organizations; the collapse of the Soviet Union; and the right-wing shift of Socialist International (of which the PRI was a member) toward accommodation with neoliberalism and global financialization.[18]

From the 1970s to the 1990s these underlying shifts induced a corresponding ideological realignment. Through the circulation of international capital in the form of debts, credits, and different forms of investments—and backed by unmatched US global military power and reach—the revamped US-centered imperialist system accelerated the financialization of global capitalism, especially now in the postcolonial and "developing" world.

This international reconfiguration shifted toward class linkages between capitalist classes in the richest and poorer nations. This convergence took place around three specific indicators that were imposed or achieved through consensus: support for external exchange (free trade), opening once-protected economies for foreign capital investment, and unencumbered international flows of profit.[19]

The transition in the US (and other rich and imperialist nations) was mirrored within capitalist classes internationally, as new fractions consolidated through partnerships, trade pacts, political alliances, and the application of other forms of pressure applied during periods of economic turbulence. This historic process saw the rise of new sectors of Mexican capital, with links to US and other nodes of international capital, and with an appetite to develop in their image. From their vantage point, in order to accomplish this, Mexico's economy needed a reset.

State capitalism was dismantled in several stages, beginning in the 1960s, as international economic forces exerted pressure and sharpened the internal divisions within the Mexican ruling class. This played out as a tug-of-war between aspirational internationalizing capital and the decrepit and weakening forces of national capitalism. The crystallization of those fractions of the Mexican capitalist class tied to US capital outgrew and ripped away the hull of economic nationalism in favor of open markets. They then enthusiastically inserted themselves into the global financial system as a pathway toward unfettered accumulation.

This process rolled back the most radical and progressive gains of the revolutionary period and led the Mexican economy to become one of the most open to foreign capital in the world by the turn of the twenty-first century. Each stage of opening has produced spasms of economic displacement, closely corresponding with episodes of migration to the United States, which has played a consistent role in Mexico's development.

## Cold War Alliances

As a representation of the first stage of self-consciousness vis-à-vis the state, the CMHN began to articulate its own ideas, concerns, and vision for the direction of government. The success and potential spread of the 1959 Cuban revolutionary model to other parts of Latin America—including Mexico—was of great concern for them. They began to assert greater influence, initiating direct consultations with sitting presidents to suppress all manifestations of radicalism.

The CMHN pushed for closer collaboration with the United States through the 1961 Alliance for Progress. This anticommunist policy initiative spearheaded by the administration of John F. Kennedy provided direct military assistance to Latin American nations in order to suppress left-wing movements. It remilitarized the region, facilitated a wave of military coups in the 1960s, and set up two decades of brutal and systematic intervention, fascist terror, violence and torture, and civil war across the hemisphere.[20]

In Mexico, the state moved into alignment with the United States to suppress radical agrarian and student movements. The governments of Gustavo Díaz Ordaz, Luis Echeverría, and José López Portillo utilized US military assistance and direct CIA support to wage a decades-long dirty war against rural populations in the south of the country. Thousands of peasants and students were detained, tortured, killed, or disappeared during this period.[21]

In 1982, Mexican businessmen organized a hemispheric gathering of Latin American capitalists called the Foro Empresarial Iberoamerica in Monterrey. This was a movement toward unifying the transnational interests of capitalists opposing communism and socialism in favor of creating open markets. The fear of revolt and revolution pushed the once nationalist Mexican bourgeoisie further into reactionary alliance with US imperialism, afraid of radical movements that were increasing in relation to widening inequality in Mexico. Vijay Prashad explains this phenomenon:

> What such developments show is that among sections of the bourgeoisie, there is a slow erosion of national loyalty and the growth of cosmopolitan extra-national sentiments that are more in tune with a global bourgeois calculation of economic interest... and therefore a political realignment among certain states whose bourgeoisie is eager for a pro-United States engagement, even as this might be counterproductive for the vast mass of its population.[22]

## Capitalist Class Organizes

The period of the oil boom opened up a massive speculative frenzy in public and private borrowing and from international banks, mainly based in the United States. For instance, lending to the Mexican government alone increased from $2 billion in 1972 to $17 billion in 1981.[23] Billions of dollars were cycled through the Mexican state and invested in the economy, with much of it used to build personal fortunes.[24]

After 1975, these capitalists concentrated wealth, forming the nuclei of groups that began to expand and consolidate into their own independent associations. Under the leadership of the biggest players of the economy, the Mexican capitalist class began to achieve levels of capital accumulation at a rate that eclipsed that of the state. They flexed their muscle and tempered decisions of the state by moving their money in and out of the country through different forms of flight.

The Mexican capitalist class expanded in horizontal and vertical dimensions, with hundreds of regional and sectional associations consolidating into interconnected blocs. In 1975, the “Great Men” took the initiative to organize these groups into one national, centralized structure known as the Consejo Coordinador Empresarial (CCE, or Business Coordinating Council).

Through the CCE, these groups began to insert themselves more directly into politics and entered into municipal and state government, as well as the federal Chamber of Deputies. The organization moved to unite all echelons of the capitalist class behind its leadership. By 1994, for instance, the ranks of affiliates to the CCE had grown to over five hundred thousand “businessmen” from every sector and region.[25]

Emerging from the chrysalis of the 1976 economic crisis was a transformed capitalist class. The ’70s generation was no longer a direct by-product of the postrevolutionary epoch. Imbued with newfound class confidence and international aspirations, they scuttled the old agreements and discretions with the state.

One leading CCE member at the time expressed the capitalist class’s reimagining of the state in the following terms:

> Perhaps the new state should be promoter and not actor, coordinator and not governor, one that provides stimulus and finance, but doesn’t manage; a state that supports private initiative to grow and innovate, to fill gaps and identify opportunities, that doesn’t operate directly in the economy and also prevents the formation of state or private monopolies. It’s a state that continues building infrastructure, social protection, and other activities that the private sector is not able to provide, and also, collaborate with the private sector on these when possible.[26]

Candidates with ties to the CCE began to directly vie for power in the northern border states, where the bourgeoisie has a history of assertive independence and where transnational linkages to US capital fused new alliances and an appetite for growth.[27] The CCE operated chiefly through the reinvigorated Partido Acción Nacional (PAN, or National Action Party), a traditional conservative Catholic and pro-business party that was allowed to operate as a nonthreatening loyal opposition since the 1930s. The PAN opposition became a vehicle to expand the model of the BIP free-trade regimes into all sectors of the economy, especially to allow for increased financial investment into supply chains to produce for export markets. Eventually, the PRI also began to fissure.

The crisis of 1976 was followed by a near-total collapse in 1982, which was accelerated by the decision of the US Federal Reserve to nearly double interest rates on the dollar from 11 percent to 20 percent, driving Mexico into an interminable second-balance-of-payments-crisis.[28] This pushed Mexico and other Latin American nations with mounting debt even further past the brink of insolvency and into more IMF-brokered negotiations. With international credit cut off to these nations amid the various crises of the 1980s, they were forced to enter into more Faustian pacts.

Over the course of the crises of 1976 and 1982, the Mexican capitalist class began to move their wealth out of the Mexican economy, engaging in capital flight as a means to abandon the flagging economy. It was also a direct political act to express their discontent and to undermine the state, deepening the crisis.[29] They abandoned investments in Mexico and purchases through the peso. Unprecedented capital flight, combined with the increase in purchase of dollar-denominated imports contributed to a substantial rise in inflation.

The wealthiest Mexicans held their wealth in dollars, and typically in the over one thousand foreign banks in operation in the country, which allowed them to move an estimated $50 billion out of the country and into US banks and real estate investments between 1978 and 1982 alone.[30] In the last months of 1982, outgoing president López Portillo nationalized the private banks through emergency decree in a futile attempt to stanch capital flight. In advance of its implementation, Mexican capitalists and bankers carried out the largest wave of capital flight in Mexico's history, moving another $100 billion out of the country.

Between 1976 and 1985 the total value of capital flight from the country was the equivalent of 71 percent of total national debt growth that occurred over the same period.[31] In other words, the state had to borrow money to make up for the disparity, causing the slide toward bankruptcy that led to IMF-directed structural adjustments.

This episode of massive capital flight was carried out to preserve and later repatriate fortunes when the economic situation improved, but also to destabilize the existing government. Sectors of the capitalist class even called for a general strike, taking up the banner of war against the government.[32] Despite the threats, the whole banking system was nationalized by the end of 1982. Nevertheless, the character of the nationalization and the outcomes had the opposite effect of taming the business sectors—they now came out in full opposition to the state.

Like in 1976, the 1982 crisis IMF bailout was negotiated by the United States on Mexico's behalf, illustrating how the US state and finance capital provided the guide to opening of Mexico's markets. The terms of the IMF were again favorable to business in that they required significant downsizing of public health services, education, and other social provisions. These coincided with the interests of the rising men of business, who wanted to see an end to the interventionist state.

Furthermore, the PRI sought to appease the disgruntled capitalist class, who treated any act of nationalization as a "step toward communism" (i.e., a threat to their interests). In response to the public repudiation and overt threat, party leaders offered conciliatory and generous terms and a path to accumulate more power during the next president's tenure.

The selection of Miguel de la Madrid to succeed López Portillo and the bank nationalization in 1983 represented a shift in the ruling PRI toward quick conciliation. It also reflected the consolidation of power and placement of a faction within the PRI with closer ties to capital and toward political alignment with the aspirations of the bourgeoisie.[33] The former bank owners were compensated with a payout of 93 billion pesos, which was 36 percent higher than the actual valuation, and were allowed to reinvest in the banks (owning up to 34 percent in shares), positioning them for repurchase when the banks were reprivatized in 1992.[34]

Another benefit of the nationalization was that the state assumed their private and foreign debts, totaling over $21 billion.[35] The state then financed debt restructuring of the banking system with public money, while allowing public enterprises also hit by the economic crisis to fall into bankruptcy.

Furthermore, following the nationalization, the state began to deregulate the nonbanking financial sector and to sell off state holdings in 1984. This began with privatization of state-owned or regulated stock brokerages, insurance companies, mortgage companies, and other securities. Mexican investors, especially those operating through the largest *grupos* and large national firms, were able to buy these up on the cheap.

The expropriated bankers were also allowed to split off, retain, and augment these branches of their banking systems. Taken together, this legal regime of devolution created a wholly private financial sector that became quickly integrated into global financial markets. This act "converted banks from simple intermediaries that channel state credit into a parallel private banking system that was able to accumulate and circulate significant volumes of capital."[36] By 1987, this new financial sector controlled 64.4 percent of total banking activity, superseding in capitalization the state-controlled commercial banking sector.[37] Ultimately, control of this sector allowed capitalist investors to grow wealthier and eventually tower over the state.

As part of the same raft of privatizations, the state also sold off mining operations, chemical, cement, and food production facilities, and construction holdings. Within a period four months, over 341 enterprises were transferred to private investors.[38] Starting in 1984, the rate of private investment surpassed public investment for the first time, and within the five succeeding years, the imbalance widened. Whereas the total share of private investment in the Mexican economy increased from 55 percent to 80 percent between 1981 and 1989, the level of public investment dropped from 45 percent to 20 percent over the same period.[39]

The restructuring allowed for the reorganization and concentration of capital in Mexico on an unprecedented scale. Capitalists that weathered the transition consolidated into mega-investment groups with slick single-word names akin to sports teams: Monterrey, Alfa, Vitro, Visa, Chihuahua, and Cydsa. These groups bought up privatized holdings across the economy, taking ownership control or substantial holdings in different enterprises, financial firms, and infrastructures. These large conglomerates are owned and run by a single owner or family. Investment and planning decisions are centralized among top partners, or a ruling family head, who wield complete power over the group and the internal structures, and operations supersede outside scrutiny and legal authority. By 1980, there were over one hundred of these grupos controlling hundreds of businesses and private banks, operating a larger share of the economy than the state, and politically linked through the CCE.[40] By the end of the decade they were in control of the state.

De la Madrid also issued the Plan Nacional Desarollo (National Development Plan), showcasing his intentions to prioritize the growth of the private sector. According to the Plan:

> Development requires a private sector capable of launching large economic projects under conditions of competency and efficiency, and is able to incorporate new technologies as well as assume the financial risks of its activity. This is a private sector with the entrepreneurial spirit that knows how to recognize and adapt itself to new market conditions, and is able expand development and integration into new areas.[41]

In 1986, in accordance with IMF-prescribed structural adjustments designed to open the economy, de la Madrid also signed on to the GATT. This "agreement" was constructed and controlled by the richest capitalist nations, primarily the United States, countries in Western Europe, and Japan. The goal was to create a community of nations that accept the conception of free markets and can therefore formalize international trade and trade rules. Within the imperialist system, the richest nations leveraged their disproportional weight to compel other nations to join as a condition for access to their larger markets, capital flows, and other benefits of participation.

In Mexico, this began the process of extending the BIP export model through the rest of the country and economy. This positioned a consortium of 317 of the largest export-oriented firms, formed into their own groupings under the umbrella of various *grupos* and the CCE, for substantial growth and expansion as a component of transnational supply chain production.[42]

The quantitative shifts away from ISI measures, framed by the imposition of austerity measures, the growth of the export sector, and the concentrating power of the men of business and their international aspirations, gave way to a qualitative shift in the governance structure that amounted the overthrow of the once-dominant state-capitalist factions of the party. The national sections of the bourgeoisie that had gestated under ISI and remained dependent on the state for their survival also saw their power and influence wane.

The internationally linked capitalist class began to publicly assert its demands on the weakened Mexican state, using its new leverage in the economy to wrest more concessions. Key demands included the defunding and dismantling of the remains of the revolutionary state, an end to one-party PRI rule and *presidencialismo* (centralized authority in the president), and downsizing and restructuring the state bureaucracy to serve rather than regulate capital.

The marching men of business compelled the state to sign several national pacts between 1987 and 1989, as a form of public parading of the state into submission and as a condition for supporting the continuation of the PRI in power.[43] Concession to these pacts, and unity behind the selection of Carlos Salinas de Gortari in 1989, represented the full convergence between the capitalist class and the triumphal free-market wing of the PRI.

# SIX

# A New Generation of Mexican Businessmen

In conjunction with a further succession of demands for privatization by the IMF as contingent for loans between 1986 and 1988, the state abided to the pacts and carried out the prescribed diktats. These included the privatization of state-owned firms, the reprivatization of the banks, the downsizing of the welfare state, and the full integration of Mexico into the global financial system through the deregulation of investment and the aggressive pursuit of free-trade agreements.

For example, between the years 1970 and 1982 the number of state-owned enterprises rose from 391 to 1,155 and grew to account for 18.5 percent of the economy and to employ over a million workers.[1] The number dropped from 1,155 to 412 during the administration of de la Madrid between 1983 and 1989, and then again down to 216 in 1994 during the administration of his Carlos Salinas de Gortari.[2]

Not just inefficient but even profitable sectors such as the telecom and commercial banking sectors were privatized. Furthermore, public services and infrastructure were opened up to privatization, including highways, ports, and railroads. Public education at all levels was opened up to private investment. State financial regulations and controls were removed and state banks sold off. State-controlled land, water, and other preserves were privatized or opened up to private ownership and exploitation.[3]

The process of state liquidation occurred behind the scenes, where transfers of public wealth into private hands occurred quickly and opaquely. The upper echelons of the ruling PRI and the new mandarins of the capitalist class acquired the accumulated public wealth of the Mexican people practically overnight. While most of the privatized enterprises were maintained by Mexican capitalists, these were primarily the big grupos. In many cases, cheaply acquired industries were flipped to US and other international investors. As a result of the liquidation of public industry, the state became more dependent on private investment, shifting it into a position of increasing accommodation to the needs of investors. In the *sexenio* of Carlos Salinas de Gortari alone—through which NAFTA was implemented over the heads of the Mexican population—a new crop of billionaires was born. Prior to NAFTA, Mexico only had one billionaire. After its passage, twenty-three more billionaires were created.[4]

The project of privatization was not to shrink the state in Mexico but to reorganize it into an instrument for national and foreign capitalists to transnationalize the economic system through linkages of finance, production, and distribution subservient to US operations.[5]

State sell-offs were designed to help pay off the public debts now financed as part of debt restructuring through the IMF, and corrupt dealings in this process allowed for insiders to transfer accumulated private debt to the public as part of these opaque transactions.[6] As one observer noted: "Big business, accused of looting the national treasury, reemerged and presented themselves as the saviors of the nation."[7] While the social functions of the PRI-state were discarded, the capitalist class retained and utilized the top-down structure of the corporatist state to push through the radical changes. Big business organizations displaced the state bureaucracy as traditional arbiter with the ruling executive.

One of the most significant transitions occurred early in the Salinas de Gortari regime: the 1989 Foreign Investment Regulations. This opened up 80 percent of the 750 economic activities in the country to 100 percent foreign ownership. It also accelerated the denationalization of the economy in other ways. Between 1982 and 1991 Mexico's economy went from being 100 percent regulated by tariffs, exclusions, permissions, and other regulatory features to only 3 percent.[8]

Foreign investment in export production increased exponentially over this period, especially in relation to the growth of the maquiladora sector. Supply chain production for export soared to account for 60 percent of all manufacturing by 1991.[9] The benefits of oil production disproportionately benefitted the owners of industry. By the late 1970s, 20 percent of oil subsidies, development funds, and fiscal exemptions went to the ten largest grupos.[10]

Furthermore, in 1990, Salinas's government allowed the creation of dollar-denominated treasury bills to be issued on speculative markets to enable the government to raise funds. The financialization of the Mexican economy allowed for international capital to move more freely in and out of the country. Capitalists could again use the threat or insinuation of capital flight as a means to directly leverage their financial power against the state.

Between 1975 and 1990, the total value of foreign investment financing in Mexico, primarily from the US, increased from $75 billion to $465 billion—a 700 percent increase, which was most concentrated in the portfolio, or speculative, sector.[11] After the Mexican stock market (Bolsa) was opened up to foreign capital, the total value of foreign financial stock holdings nearly tripled from $1.5 trillion in 1983 to $4.4 trillion in 1990.[12] Investments flowed in, with the creation of 2,028 investment groups between 1989 and 1991 alone. These 1,280 were foreign capital majority, investing almost $18 billion, compared to 748 dominated by domestic capital and investing about $600 million.[13] The influx of dollar-denominated investment increased the trading in US dollars in the Mexican financial system by 558 percent between 1987 and 1992.[14]

The coordination with foreign capital also became directly linked at the top of the Mexican grupos, with foreign financing constituting 11 percent of total capital in the largest 104 groupings, with 45 of the groups ranging from below 50 percent to 100 percent.[15] By 1994, the 10 largest grupos were responsible for 55 percent of national sales, controlled 56 percent of natural resources, and 48 percent of employment.[16] By February 1994, there were over 1,500 co-investment projects initiated between Mexican capital and US multinationals, while 71 percent of all US foreign direct investment went toward buyouts of privatized firms in Mexico.[17] This established a new transnational and international capitalist class operating through corporations, banks, and investment vehicles. By the passage of NAFTA, US investors bought up 90 percent of Mexican government-issued, dollar-denominated treasury bonds and held 27 percent of total shares (valued at $56 billion) in the Mexican stock exchange.[18]

The denouement of the state capitalist fraction occurred through bank reprivatization. The state aided the process of concentration, consolidating the commercial banking sector from sixty in 1982 to twenty-nine in 1988 and to eighteen in 1994; with three megabanks controlling half of the national market. By 2019, the seven biggest banks controlled 85 percent of all banking capital.[19] Salinas de Gortari ordered the reprivatization in 1992, as the representational organs of the capitalist sector got impatient with the slow pace of the process and threatened to begin another round of capital flight.[20]

Nationalized banks were sold back to the wealthy grupos, passing the last vestiges of the financial sector back to the Mexican capitalist class. Much of the financial infrastructure was then sold off to international capital, especially investors from the US. By 1994, nine of the largest banks in the United States had the equivalent of 44 percent of their capital directly invested in Mexico.[21] Within the first year after the passage of NAFTA, ninety multinational financial corporations or their subsidiaries (two-thirds from the US alone) opened operations in Mexico to supply credit, sell financial products, or purchase Mexican institutions.[22] By the end of the decade, all foreign ownership restrictions had been removed from the private banking system. In fact, even oversight of these transfers was lifted. NAFTA rules guaranteed the automatic approval for foreign acquisition of Mexican-held assets valued up to $1 billion.[23] All other barriers to free movement and functioning of foreign capital were removed or gradually phased out.

So much US-based capital had penetrated into the Mexican financial system that the US Treasury Department treated it as an extension of the US economy. In 1994, the United States founded the North American Financial Group, a consultative body that included the Treasury Department, the IMF, and Canadian and Mexican representatives in order to "provide an intergovernmental structured method for the review of economic and fiscal policies concerning Mexico."[24]

The United States pushed specific policy recommendations via this body, including a plan to create a standing multibillion-dollar fund to inject into the Mexican economy to stabilize it during episodes of volatility amid the transition. Other configurations of diplomatic exchange followed, with hundreds of other high-level meetings concerning events in Mexico during the period of NAFTA's implementation. Through capitalization financed by the World Bank, the Mexican government created its own version of the Fondo Bancario de Proteccion al Ahorro (Federal Deposit Insurance Corporation) to use public money to underwrite the operations of the privatized Mexican banking system. US-led negotiators directed the Mexican government to de-peg the peso from the dollar and then compelled a 40 percent devaluation in December of 1994.[25] The devaluation of the peso enabled investors to buy Mexican assets more cheaply through dollar-denominated purchases. More significantly, it amounted to a massive wage cut for Mexican workers who are paid in pesos, thereby transferring the laborsaving costs back to owners.

The devaluation collapsed the peso. Financial speculators and those who held assets in pesos unloaded their holdings, causing the peso to plummet further. Working-class people watched as the value of their savings evaporated. As the panic spread, fear of another financial meltdown and social unrest led the Mexican capitalist class to engage in another episode of capital flight. Mexican and international capitalists with holdings and investments moved their wealth out of the country in a frenzy or dumped their pesos in favor of dollars. According to one study, capital was moved quickly into "offshore centers and tax havens [amounting to] $50 billion in 1993 and $55 billion in 1994, and additional 'capital flight' into the dollar is estimated at $40 billion in 1993 and $50 billion in 1994."[26] The Mexican Peso Crisis of 1994 became one of the first known economic crises in the era of financialization to be induced by capital flight.[27]

The US commandeering of Mexico's economy and attempts to radically overhaul the model of capitalism caused another system crash in 1995. Only one year into NAFTA, a deep recession wracked Mexico, pushing the government into another potential bankruptcy. Because of the extent of

US and international investment, this time the US—and, by extension, the global—financial system also faced a domino-effect collapse. In the type of bailout that has since become normalized, the US state rescued its speculative investor class by propping up the Mexican financial system with the largest bailout in history (at that time). The US government arranged a $50 billion bailout package, pooling funds from the US Treasury, the IMF, the Bank of International Settlements, and more than one thousand commercial banks that bought in hoping to gain handsome returns through the repayment schedule.[28] US-based international banking giant J.P. Morgan, for instance, administered the bailout and repayment transaction.

As part of the deal, Mexico had to surrender control of its state oil revenues. As John A. Adams describes in *Mexican Banking and Investment in Transition*,

> For the first time in Mexico's history, crude oil and oil products were tied to the repayment schedule. The Mexican Central Bank and government were also required to report to the US Treasury, on a weekly and monthly schedule, such items as all account balances, investment trends, inflation projections, money supply patterns, and how much money raised with US guarantees would be repaid. In all, over 100 economic and monetary indicators are filed on an ongoing basis by the Mexican government to allow the US Treasury and IMF to track the progress of the economic recovery.[29]

The US government could even deny Mexico access to its own oil revenues, if the purchase requests were deemed inappropriate or not in compliance with repayment schedules. Regular debt payments from Mexico to US banks occurred through this channel. In one reported case, the US Treasury sent two bailout installments of $5.2 billion *directly* to the Federal Reserve Bank of New York in order to pay off US-based creditors, completely bypassing the Mexican government in the process.[30]

Later, transborder finance transfer services between the Bank of Mexico and the US Federal Reserve banks were broadened with the creation of Directo a México in 2005. Through the aegis of the Federal Reserve, commercial and investment banks were able to move money in and out of Mexico on behalf of their clients. It also enabled and systematized the sending of migrant workers' remittances to banks in Mexico and other countries, which has continued to be a profitable aspect of financial integration.[31] According to the Federal Reserve Board,

> Directo a México helps US financial institutions capture a larger part of the rapidly growing US to Mexico remittance market. The program also supports customers by providing a secure, fast, low-cost, and convenient money transfer product for financial institutions to offer to their customers. The service that supports Directo a México, FedGlobal Mexico Service, is priced so that US financial institutions can offer it at extremely competitive rates.[32]

In sum, the US state through its Treasury and State Departments, the US embassy in the Mexican capital, the IMF and World Bank, the Federal Reserve, and other branches of influence and control became more transparent in direct orchestration of Mexico's economic policy. US-led foreign ownership of the Mexican financial system continued, growing from 16 percent in September 1997 to 54 percent by December 2000, and then again up to 76 percent by December 2002.[33] By 2006, 82 percent of all banking assets in Mexico were controlled by foreign—mostly US—banks.[34]

The end process of bank privatization and resale created a coterie of super-rich Mexican financiers who controlled whole sectors of the Mexican economy, in partnership with foreign capital. Carlos Salinas de Gortari heartily welcomed this group as a "new generation" of Mexican businessmen. This shift completed the process of recomposition of the bourgeoisie and the rise of financial capital in Mexico that works as junior partners with foreign investors in controlling banking, industry, agroindustry, commerce, and the service sector.

Mexico's super-rich reconstituted as a financial capitalist oligarchy comprised of the grupos, which shared in control of sectors of banking and big industry. These overlapped with the stock exchange houses operating through the Bolsa (Mexico's Wall Street), which manages the inflow and outflow of international investment.

The two richest men in Mexico to emerge from the period, Carlos Slim Helú (Grupo Carso) and Jorge Larrea Ortega (Grupo México), transitioned from multimillionaires to billionaires through cheap acquisition of state telecommunications infrastructure and mine holdings, respectively. Requirements for technology transfer, never really a successful component of Mexican economic development, were effectively abandoned as a requirement altogether under Salinas de Gortari.[35]

Following acquiescence into the GATT, this generation furthered its integration into the global financial system, joining into fifteen more international free-trade regimes between 1993 and 2019.[36] By 2020, Mexico was part of free-trade agreements that linked it to more than fifty countries and exposed it to 60 percent of the global capitalist market (as measured by GDP).[37] With the successful transition from state capitalism and ISI to free markets, US-led international capital has penetrated the Mexican economy to such an extent that Mexico has returned to its prerevolutionary status of being a semicolonized country.

## The Return of Semicolonization

The collapse of the Soviet Union and subsequent end of the Cold War were seismic political events that expedited a global capitalist reordering. Triumphal capitalist classes in the rich nations gained confidence to extend their range of influence within a reconfiguring imperialist order. The subsequent decline or dissolution of the largest and most powerful Communist-led parties and unions across the globe weakened working-class organization and resistance, enabled the further rightward shift of social democratic parties, and tilted the global political compass rightward toward consensual accommodation with free-market capitalism.

In the absence of an ideological adversary or military counter to its power, the US state moved swiftly onto the offensive to reassert its military power to remake the Middle East, Asia, Eastern Europe, Latin America, and the Caribbean.[38] The reassertion of US military power in strategic regions across the globe, the collapse of the left, and the vanquishing of ISI and forceful imposition of free-market capitalism combined to usher in the return of a state called semicolonialism. The Communist International developed this term to describe a nominally independent or sovereign nation that remains dominated and controlled by imperialist powers through various means—especially financial hegemony.[39]

The implementation of the free-market agreement was formalized through congressional action, but NAFTA was conceived of in corporate think tanks, board rooms, and other corridors of capitalist political power. Its eventual implementation required radical restructuring, political destabilization, and bypassing democratic norms. The North American model of free-market hegemony has reshaped the contours of the class struggle into one that is transnational. The impetus has been to restore and increase profitability, especially since the end of the postwar boom. Largely, impulses toward deepening regional integration, consolidation, and control arose as the United States and China engaged in the first steps of inter-imperialist rivalry and war of economic maneuver and positioning.[40]

In Mexico, the implementation of NAFTA required the overthrow of the ISI regime, electoral fraud on a national scale, uprisings, mass resistance and repression, as well as the weakening of state power and the rise of parastatal drug cartels, a political civil war, and convulsions and splits inside the ruling class. These have produced periodic implosions and left splits from the ruling PRI, beginning with the breakaway and foundation of the Partido de la Revolución Democrática in 1989 and the Movimiento Regeneración Nacional (MORENA, or National Regeneration Movement) in 2014—with both claiming to represent the continuity of the Mexican revolutionary legacy. Nevertheless, both of these parties quickly accommodated to free-market capitalism and ensured the Mexican capitalist class of their commitment to the preservation of neoliberal arrangements such as NAFTA and USMCA.[41]

In the United States the fallout was less severe, as support for NAFTA was consensual within the majority of the ruling class and the two pro-free-market parties that represent them. It is an extension of a coordinated state and capitalist class offensive conducted without quarter since the global economic crisis of 1974–75. Through all channels of governance, the trajectory of legislation, policy, enforcement, and court rulings have contributed to the significant weakening of unions, the atomization and stratification of different sections of the working class, the overall decline of wages across the board, and policies of austerity that have erased reforms and class gains from previous epochs. This has enabled a hemorrhaging of social wealth and its transfer from the working classes to the capitalist class.[42]

The attrition of unionization was followed by the return of the "runaway shop" and gradual relocation of industrial production further into the historically nonunion and lower-wage regions in the US South—which then continued unabated across the border with the concoction of free-trade agreements. NAFTA was fast-tracked over the widespread opposition of the US working class, with the effects of implementation predictably contributing to a scale of inequality not seen since the eve of the Great Depression.[43] According to one study,

> From 1982 to 2012 the share of total income that went to the top 10 percent increased from 35 percent to 51 percent, while that of the top 1 percent rose from 10 percent to 23 percent. Furthermore, the labor share of income in GDP has declined in relation to capital, whose piece of the pie climbed from 18.8 percent in 1979 to 26.2 percent in 2010.[44]

Furthermore, the behavior of capitalist states during pandemic of 2020 only widened the crevasse:

> The pandemic has reinforced this trend. As the virus spread, central banks injected $9tn into economies worldwide, aiming to keep the world economy afloat. Much of that stimulus has gone into financial markets, and from there into the net worth of the ultra-rich. The total wealth of billionaires worldwide rose by $5tn to $13tn in 12 months, the most dramatic surge ever registered on the annual billionaire list compiled by *Forbes* magazine.[45]

Over a hundred new billionaires emerged from the crisis to be added to the ranks in the US, amounting to 724, while the combined net worth of Mexico's 13 billionaires rose by nearly a third to $136.1 billion.[46] The passage of NAFTA was the culmination and codification of all the previously prescribed structural adjustments, and the launching point for further privatization, deregulation, and extension of capital mobility. The totality of the process was orchestrated and advanced by a changed guard of the Mexican ruling class who approached the transition to open-market capitalism with religious-like faith and zeal.

By the turn of the twentieth century, US-based capital controlled a majority share of most sectors of the Mexican economy—especially the financial and industrial sectors. US-led international capital dominated the Mexican stock exchange and owned the majority of Mexican Government Treasury Bonds (CETES). Most external and internal debt is held by US creditors and investors. US investors also dominate the Mexican Derivatives Exchange (MexDer), a speculative market exchange created in 1998 and modeled on the US version, to allow for international investors to bet on Mexican futures and options.

US-led capitalism operates independently of state control or regulation, and the state has become a more transparent lever for capital accumulation and wealth transfer. For instance, the Mexican economy has become dollarized, leading to the emergence of parallel and unequal financial systems. International investors and the richest Mexicans hold and exchange their money in dollars, and move it in and out of the domestic economy and across borders without restriction.

*Banxico* (the Bank of Mexico) holds substantial reserves in dollars and periodically injects money into the economy to stabilize the peso and to facilitate exchange transfers from dollars to pesos and vice versa depending on investor needs.[47] The complete dollarization of the financial system occurred in 2016, when Banxico established the Sistema de Pagos Interbancarios en Dólares (SPID). This is a central clearinghouse to allow for US dollar conversion wholly within Mexico, allowing Mexico-based companies to transfer all of their earnings to dollars on a same-day basis.

The successful reconquest of Mexico by US-led international capital was a test case and a transition point in an international offensive to restructure global capitalism into the twenty-first century. The use of the treasury, the Federal Reserve, and leveraging of dollar-denominated debt allowed the US state to overturn unfavorable regimes that obstructed capital accumulation without having to fire a shot. The international arm of US economic imperialism—the IMF, World Bank, and other lenders—were retooled to instrumentalize the Mexican model and to aggressively pursue replication in other nations. These institutions began what has become a permanent process of keeping subject nations underdeveloped, open to international capital, and in debt. Through bailouts and loans, coupled with other factors like open access, direct ownership, and exploitation of labor and natural resources in these countries, the wealth is transferred in debt-servicing payments to private banks and the value transfer of artificially suppressed wages passed on to investors.

The success in Mexico opened the door to spreading the model internationally. In the following decade, similar structural adjustment agreements were used to open up over a dozen other Latin American economies including: Venezuela, Uruguay, Dominican Republic, Costa Rica, Brazil, and Argentina. The model was also exported to Africa, Asia, and Eastern Europe.[48] This was then followed by further expansion of NAFTA-like trade agreements with the Central America-Dominican Republic Free Trade Agreement (CAFTA-DR) in 2005 and others incorporating various states across the hemisphere. The Mexican state has subsequently signed forty-four separate free-trade and bilateral agreements and twenty-seven "investment protection agreements" with other nations.[49]

The dismantling of state-led capitalism in Mexico provided a model and opened the field for the financial arms of US-centric imperialism—especially the International Monetary Fund and World Bank—to aggressively accelerate the deconstruction of ISI regimes globally.[50] This was especially borne out after another capitalist crisis in 1995, which saw another significant devaluation.

After this third economic crisis in Mexico since 1976, the IMF

> ushered in a new era of much larger lending, followed as it was by the East Asian financial crisis of 1997–98, the Russian meltdown of 1998, and the Brazilian exchange crisis of 1998–99 (point I). For the second half of the decade, the Fund had just 75 active borrowers, but it lent an annual average of $20.7 billion (SDR 14.7 billion).[51]

The majority of these loans had structural adjustment mechanisms attached to them, which ate away at all residual forms of protectionism, gave leverage to empower and entrench compliant regimes, and systematized wealth transfer from poor nations to international banks and investors through debt maintenance. The inflow of loans and outflow of debt servicing became a major factor in the transition to free-market capitalism and has become normalized as an important source of wealth transfer from the Mexican public treasury to US-based multinational banks.

As part of the transition from state-led capitalism to free-market capitalism and subsequent use of lending as a mechanism for structural change, Latin American and Caribbean debt increased from $57 billion in 1974 to $230 billion in 1980. According to IMF statistics, by 1988 these countries had paid out $110 billion to multinational banks to service their existing debts—while their total overall debt *increased* to approximately $410 billion over that same period. This massive transfer of public wealth to private investors through the mechanism of debt financing led to the period being referred to as Latin America's "lost decade."[52]

In Mexico, external debt to foreign banks (primarily from the US) increased from $13.5 billion in 1975 to $41 billion in 1980, while debt servicing payments as a percentage of total foreign exchange income increased from 7.1 percent to 18.3 percent between 1973 and 1980—even as the rate of total exports more than tripled over this period.[53] While Mexico exported more, including through the growth of the maquiladora sector and increased oil exports, it became more dependent on borrowing to service existing IMF debts and address other balance of payment deficits (including recurring episodes of capital flight).

In Mexico, external debt continues to grow. Between 2009 and 2020 it more than doubled from $165 billion to over $451 billion. The largest share of growth occurred in public government loans, which nearly tripled from $85 billion to $263 billion and became roughly equivalent to the total external foreign debt of all Latin American and Caribbean nations in 1980. By 2020, about three-quarters of this debt continued to be held in US dollars and issued from private US banks through the International Monetary Fund, World Bank, and the Inter-American Development Bank.[54] While the interest rates have changed over time, they continue to extract huge sums of wealth for investors. For instance, by 1989, the Mexican government made interest payments that alone amounted to 36 percent of the total foreign debt it held that year.[55] According to one IMF calculation, the projected debt-servicing payments Mexico will make in 2023 could reach up to 2.2 percent of total GDP, or about $24.5 billion.[56]

On a global scale, total external debt of developing nations increased from $334 billion in 1977 to $1.2 trillion by 1989, mostly in the form of public, government borrowing.[57] By 2018, total debt of developing nations increased six-fold to $7.8 trillion—a scale unprecedented in history.[58] The extension of predatory credit to poor and underdeveloped nations has expanded even further following the global economic crisis and pandemic of 2020, ushering in the makings of yet another "lost decade" on a global scale.[59]

While the indebted nations bleed out the wealth of the people, the ruling classes of these semicolonized countries like Mexico have partnered in the process. For example, from 1960 to 2017, Latin America's real income per capita (compared with that of the United States) remained unchanged over nearly five decades, rising from 20 percent of the US level to just 24 percent.[60]

By 2000, the richest tenth of the population of Latin America and the Caribbean captured 48 percent of total income in their respective states, while the poorest tenth earned only 1.6 percent, making it the most unequal region in the world.[61] By 2020, the richest 10 percent of Latin Americans were estimated to hold approximately 70 percent of the total wealth of the region.[62]

Since the turn of the twenty-first century, Mexico became the nation with the highest rate of inequality in the western hemisphere (equal to Chile and followed by the US).[63] The number of millionaires in Mexico grew by 32 percent between 2007 and 2012, and the richest four men in the country control 10 percent of total national GDP.[64] The widening chasm of social inequality mirrors similar developments in the United States and is the direct result of capitalist restructuring, with NAFTA as the spearhead of transposing this process onto Mexico.

One measure of the benefits of capital mobility has been US economic growth from the repatriation of profits. Between 1990 and 2000, US GDP grew at an average annual rate of 5.7 percent, with the overall corporate profits doubling from about $250 billion to $500 billion. The growing share of increase was commensurate with the implementation of NAFTA and a transfer of wealth from investments in Mexico. Profits then increased fourfold between 2000 and 2019, from about $500 billion to nearly $2 trillion.[65] Taxes on capital gains and earnings from the stock market were abolished creating an even sweeter reward.

After the recovery from the 1995 crash and bailout, the Mexican GDP grew by 9.1 percent—now heralded as a success story. Nevertheless, this growth was commensurate with the influx of US foreign direct investment in Mexico, which increased exponentially from $17.0 billion in 1994 to $109.7 billion in 2017.[66] Mexican FDI increased from only $2 billion to $18 billion over the same period, showing a much smaller profit flow from north to south.[67] Despite the rhetoric of success, economic growth did not equate to social development. The more money invested, the more profit was extracted; wealth concentrated in the accounts of international and Mexican capitalists.

Total US trade with Mexico grew fivefold, from $81 billion in pre-NAFTA 1993 to $600 billion in 2013 and $617 billion in 2018.[68] US investors account for about two-thirds of all FDI in the country and have come to account for nearly 30 percent of all Mexican export activity.[69] Illustrating the dominant role of transnational US capital in Mexico, the country sent 89 percent of its exports across the northern border and bought 73 percent of its imports from the United States by the turn of the twenty-first century.[70] US capital dominates the maquila export industry, bringing in inputs from the United States as imports and sending finished products back to the United States as exports. This arrangement shows how much the Mexican economy has been retooled to be dependent on US capital and markets for its well-being. For instance, Mexico's business cycle is closely tied to that of the United States, which is evinced by the fact that the recessions in the United States in 1994, 2001, and 2008 were followed quickly by recessions in Mexico, although deeper and longer.

US-Mexico integration has also transformed Mexico's financial sector. For instance, by December 2008, the share of foreign control of Mexico's banking system increased from 1.5 percent in 1993 to 74.5 percent after the Mexican government dismantled most investment restrictions during that decade. Foreign capital, led by the United States, Canada, and Spain, poured in. For example, US-based Citibank Corporation now forms the second largest commercial banking group in the country under the name Grupo Financiero Banamex-Accival (Banacci).

Even Walmart, which became the largest retailer in Mexico, moved into the banking industry, operating four hundred branches by late 2008. Citigroup and Merrill Lynch operate as the country's top two brokerage firms, while US-based MetLife is the largest insurance company in operation. US-based companies also control the largest market share in pension fund management and bond underwriting.[71] Mechanisms like Directo a México facilitate cross-border flows. For example, in 2005 the US Federal Reserve and the Bank of Mexico established formal linkages for easy money transfers—easing, for instance, the transfer of debt payments to US banks.

In addition to the legal ways wealth is extracted from Mexico, there are also parallel illicit methods. For instance, it is estimated that US and Mexican capitalists, bankers, and investors transfer about $50 billion annually from the people of Mexico into their own bank accounts across the border. In a comprehensive study of illicit cross-border wealth transfers conducted over four decades (1970–2010), it was found that the Mexican people have lost $872 billion through trade mispricing (multinationals transferring profits across borders without reporting them), capital flight, bribery and corruption, tax evasion, money laundering, and other forms of wealth transfer.[72]

# SEVEN

# Transnational Class Formation

In order for aspirational US capital to instrumentalize the state to undermine economic developmentalist regimes, laws, and policies in Mexico and Central America, allies were needed in those countries. The disruptive imposition of new rules and regulations that collapsed large sections of the economy in favor of the free movement and operations of multinational corporations was contingent upon sections of the domestic capitalist class in the subject nations who could steer their respective states through the process and hitch their economic fortunes to the new model.

US capital initiated the process and defined the terrain in which subordinate states would have to adjust themselves accordingly to have access within the new model, while also invoking the crystallization of like-minded counterparts internationally. This model for the globalization of capital movement was concurrently triangulated through international capitalist institutions, which sanctioned and codified the process into an international consensus. As Cypher and Delgado Wise explain in the context of Mexico,

> We are aware of the important exogenous forces unleashed in the era of World Bank "structural adjustment programs" that were cross-conditioned via a series of important IMF loans received in the 1980s and later. This massive and cumulative lending operation was, of course, fully supported by the United States, which urged upon the World Bank and the IMF the imposition of a neoliberal agenda

> for Mexico. In all of this, the meeting of the priorities of transnational corporations, above all those based in the United States, received uppermost consideration in the complex policy shifts that occurred—whether initiated directly by the Mexican state, the World Bank, or the IMF. In this sense, we find a *codetermination process* at work, involving both the power elites of Mexico and the United States.[1]

Class formation is thus a consequence of converging concentrations of capital in large corporations and the social overlap of these corporations and their executives in multiple institutional spheres. From a class perspective, an inner circle—whose collective outlook is generated from a unique structural level spanning numerous institutions, corporations, and state agencies—nests within the most interlocked sectors of the most influential corporations.[2]

The economy of Mexico (as well as most Central American and Caribbean states) is closely interconnected with that of the United States through transnational agreements, partnerships, and mutual class interests. The US state offers inducements, blandishments, legitimacy, authorizations, and a multitude of other forms of support and sanction to attain acquiescence and collaboration from its subordinate partners. Alliances also occur through shared class outlook. The capitalist classes in these nations form individual economic partnerships with US investors and corporations, send their children to the same US universities as their US counterparts, and share a similar disdain for working-class organization and opposition and any other obstacle to the full and unfettered functioning of neoliberal capitalism.

The Mexican political cohort that took the reins of state power from the late the 1980s on, whether from the PRI or PAN, shared a common background. All four Mexican presidents who presided over the full implementation of NAFTA, serving between 1989 and 2012, attended Harvard or Yale Universities for their formal education. In these Ivy League US schools, this generation of rich Mexican politicians were fully immersed in the neoliberal political and economic orthodoxy that guided their mandates. During their administrations, the practice became institutionalized with the state allocating resources to systematize US-educated elites for the foreseeable future. As one study reported about the trend,

> Mexico is increasing the number of students it sends to the US with paid tuition and a verbal commitment that they will return home. Yet because of Mexico's proximity to the US, the consequences will be felt more directly across the region, experts say, as students return to help Mexico update its economy.[3]

This practice of Mexico's dominant, ruling-class families sending their children to US universities to "train" has greatly expanded in recent years, approaching nearly 15,468 students by 2018.[4] During the Obama administration, there was even a proposal called "Project 100,000" to strive for the exchange of US and Mexican students to achieve higher educational integration, but this initiative was scrapped by the Trump administration.[5] Even the majority of graduate students who attend universities in Mexico list US companies as the most desirable companies to work for upon completion of their studies.[6] Besides grooming the next generation of a US-trained, business class, the corruption embedded in the implementation of NAFTA, USMCA, and CAFTA-DR helped produce new capitalist dynasties nearly overnight.

The NAFTA, USMCA, and CAFTA-DR projects have generated a new class of billionaires in the United States, Mexico, and Central America. A 2018 UBS billionaires report describes the process of how wealth accumulation and concentration has taken place relatively quickly over the neoliberal period,

> The past 30 years have seen a for greater wealth creation than the Gilded Age of the 19th century. That period bred generations of families in the US and Europe who went on to influence business, banking, politics, philanthropy and the arts for more than 100 years. With wealth set to pass from entrepreneurs to their heirs in the coming years, the 21st century multigenerational families are being created.[7]

In Mexico, the privatization of state industry was the catalyst for the accumulation of vast fortunes.

This class of nouveau riche cheaply acquired 390 privatized state-owned industries. Hundreds of billions of dollars of public money were invested for over a generation in economic infrastructure to build up a variety of industries including banking, manufacturing, construction, brewing, mining, telecommunications, media, and food production.

These were passed into the hands of well-placed capitalists and ruling-party elites through corrupt means, sprouting a new set of billionaires practically overnight. In some cases, they turned their original accumulation of public resources into multinational corporations, as did Carlos Slim Helú with his privatized telecommunications firm América Móvil. In others, they sold off their cheaply attained assets to US capital or formed partnerships to manage national subsidiaries of US-based multinational corporations such as Walmart and Pepsi.

In Honduras, a country of 8 million people with a total GDP of $21 billion, where 66 percent of the population lives in abject poverty, Camilo Atala Faraj has become the country's first billionaire. Atala has been linked by family and business relations to the murder and disappearance of human rights activists.[8] According to the BBC, Atala has been identified as a key player in the overthrow of the government of Manuel Zelaya in 2009.[9]

Guatemala has also produced its first billionaire. Mario López Estrada made the world's richest list in 2015.[10] As the scion of an old and rich Guatemalan ruling-class family, he rose through the ranks of government and leveraged his position to financial advantage. He was appointed as minister of communications to oversee state telecommunications operations during the administration of Marco Vinicio Cerezo (1986–1991).

While in office, López Estrada oversaw the privatization of the national telephone system in 1989, in which the government announced it would grant a monopoly to the newly formed Comunicaciones Celulares company (COMCEL). López Estrada then left the government to become a "private investor," buying up a 45 percent stake of the new COMCEL company in 1993. When the telecommunications system was fully privatized in 1999, COMCEL (now called Tigo) was positioned to emerge as the single dominant telecommunications company in the region.[11]

In El Salvador, Ricardo Poma and Roberto Kriete operate conglomerate grupos in the Mexican style. Grupo Kriete has amassed assets worth $6.5 billion, and Grupo Poma has accumulated assets valued at $1.4 billion. El Salvador is a country of 6.4 million people with a total GDP of $20.6 billion, a third of the population living in poverty, and nearly another quarter of the population living outside of the country as displaced migrants.[12]

## Profits for Capital, Degradation and Migration for Labor

After three decades of capitalist restructuring and the imposition of NAFTA, 53 percent of the population lives below the poverty line and an estimated 60 percent of the population works in the informal sector.[13] By the time of the pandemic shutdown and ensuing economic crisis of 2020, the absence of state support alongside the dependency of the economy on free-market-linked exports pushed millions more working-class Mexicans into economic distress. One study estimated that as many as 70 million Mexicans (about 60 percent of the population) experienced the conditions of poverty and privation by the end of the year.[14] This is the logical outcome of the free market for Mexican people, as four decades of publicly invested wealth was privatized and handed to international capitalists. Unionization rates and traditions of militancy, wage gains and improvements in living conditions that occurred in the period of ISI were wiped out after the 1970s. The land was privatized, and the ejidos were liquidated, leading to the dispossession of millions of people.

At the heart of free trade is the de-territorialization of capital in order to increase the rate of capitalist exploitation of labor—within and across borders. In the United States it has been an instrument to engineer a general weakening of the organizational capacity and negotiating power of the US working class. Simultaneously, destabilization increases the rate of migration and thereby access to migratory labor. Displaced workers experience the opposite effects. Through criminalization, they are doubly exploited: firstly, as a mechanism to restructure and introduce new forms of segregation based on citizenship in order to tier and subjugate the working class as a whole, and, secondly, to be superexploited for their labor.

Despite episodes of immense workers' struggle and persistent peasant uprisings in the countryside, the PRI deployed state repression commensurate with the demands of the domestic bourgeoisie to increase profitability. By the early 1980s, suppression of authentic unionization became a paramount function of the party as a means to increase domestic and foreign capital investment.

In 1994, the PRI sent in the military to repress an uprising of the Ejército Zapatista de Liberación Nacional (EZLN, or Zapatista Army of National Liberation). The Zapatistas, as they are called, began as an Indigenous-led peasant movement centered in the state of Chiapas that took up arms and seized several towns in the state in direct opposition to the imposition of NAFTA. While the uprising was brutally crushed after two weeks, it shook the pillars of the Mexican state. Zapatista resistance garnered international solidarity and exposed the deteriorating conditions and dispossession in the Mexican countryside. The uprising transformed into a political movement and inspired national opposition to the government, producing the historic first electoral defeat of the PRI in 2000.[15] Nevertheless, the succeeding ruling parties have all preserved NAFTA and deepened free-market policies once in power.

## Union Busting

The state set out to break the extant forms of independent labor unionism. In 2009, the government fired the forty-four thousand members of the Sindicato Mexicano de Electricistas (Mexican Electrical Workers Union) for two decades of militant resistance to privatization of a state-owned power grid. Then, President Felipe Calderón sent the army and police to occupy the generating plants and all other facilities, remove the union workers, and declare their union "nonexistent."[16] Various attempts to organize independent unionism in the maquiladora sector have also been crushed using similar tactics.[17]

The working classes bore the brunt of the crises of state capitalism and have been further decimated by the transition to semicolonized, free-market capitalism. Since the Bracero Program, bursts of displacement and out-migration of Mexican workers and peasants have corresponded to economic crises in Mexico and incorporation of their labor into the US economy. The transnationalization of the Mexican working class has produced two forms of superexploited labor: as workers in their own country oppressed by foreign capital that works with the Mexican state to constrain and suppress labor unionism and as displaced migrant labor that is criminalized once it crosses into the United States.

Due to the legacy of colonialism, combined and uneven capitalist development, and the tightening strictures of US imperialism, the Mexican government could not break out of perpetual social underdevelopment. Even at the height of ISI, when there were some assurances for employment, welfare subsidies, and land rights, it is estimated that only 30 percent of the population was actively participating in the formal economy.[18]

The collapsing of ISI, elimination of unionism, the influx of foreign capital and wealth transfer, devaluation and inflation, austerity, and privatization all impacted the Mexican working classes. These combined to shrink employment and the means of subsistence, lower wages and living standards, and squeeze the "excess" population into precarity, informality, and migration. By the early 1970s, these factors began to induce episodes of out-migration into the US—contributing the transnationalization of the Mexican working classes.

In the year after the 1973 crisis, the president of the Mexican Association of Industrialists estimated that the Mexican economy was producing one hundred and fifty thousand fewer jobs than needed to absorb the next generation of workers.[19] By 1979 unemployment reached about 50 percent of the population and only about 20 percent of the population could afford to consume goods and services produced domestically. Furthermore, it was estimated that between 1979 and 1981 about seven hundred and fifty thousand to one million workers entering into the labor force would be jobless.[20] Similar patterns followed the crisis of 1982, 1990, and 1994. For workers, the "real economy," i.e., the jobs-producing economy, went into decline, even as foreign direct investment increased—creating a distorted picture in GDP. The disconnect can be understood as real wealth being concentrated at the top of society and exported to the United States.[21]

Between 1970 and 2000, Mexico devalued the peso every six years on average—this in addition to the IMF-directed austerity measures.[22] The IMF-negotiated loan of 1976, for instance, required a host of austerity measures including a decline in public investment in health services, education, and public administration, amounting to a 60 percent cut in average annual funding between 1977 and 1983. Over that same period, the real value of workers' wages was cut by 50 percent when devaluation and inflation is taken into consideration.[23]

Like in 1982, another devaluation of the peso in 1995 hit the working classes with debilitating force. Between 1994 and 1996, the percentage of the population "with per capita income below the threshold needed to achieve minimum caloric intake" nearly tripled from 7.2 percent to 20.1 percent, or from 6.49 million to 18.63 million people.[24] Furthermore, the state downsized or dismantled its once formidable food redistribution system. Prices of basic goods were decontrolled, and government subsidies on food and basic services for workers and the poor were cut or ended. By 1999, CONASUPO, a system of state-run stores that sold basic food items like tortillas and milk at subsidized prices, had been closed.[25]

By the mid-1980s the suppression of authentic unionization became a paramount concern for the new ruling PRI fractions. They used the established mechanisms of control over labor as a means to degrade and devalue labor in order to increase foreign capital investment. The Confederación de Trabajadores de México (CTM) was unceremoniously kicked out of the inner circles of the party apparatus as the de la Madrid government altered the Mexican Constitution more than forty times—including the removal of corporatist provisions and references to labor as an official part of the state. Nevertheless, the changed guard of the party apparatus simultaneously utilized extant corporatist channels to apply pressures to suppress class struggle. Replaced and reoriented party bosses compelled the long tamed and transformed bureaucracies into compliance throughout the transition to free-market capitalism.

The dismantling of authentic unionism and the full conversion to either charrismo or protective antiunionism occurred between 1982 and 1994. The state-controlled CTM and other affiliated unions shifted their operational methods with the end of ISI. To avoid becoming irrelevant, and having collective contracts nullified by the new private owners, they signed off on all of the new pacts and formally pledged to support the transition. In doing so, they openly (or tacitly) agreed to abandon any pretense toward class struggle and abandoned strikes altogether.

> In the process, preserving the collective contract remained a basic goal; but compromise replaced strikes as the tool of choice to protect union interests, and syndicates grew more receptive to noncontrac-

> tual forms of compensation (job training, generous severance packages, community infrastructure projects) to help offset contract givebacks. As engagement patterns changed, compromise gradually displaced unyielding conflict, allowing both camps to preserve core interests and permitting later divestment rounds to proceed more smoothly.[26]

The core interests of the CTM leadership and bureaucracy fully transitioned away from the pretense of negotiating wages and working conditions in good faith or of representing working-class political interests in general. In order to remain relevant within the new order, they adapted their operations accordingly by becoming labor managers of a performance-based model. Their evolved role has been to ensure labor discipline in exchange for wage increases typically tied to productivity and profitability, while the most successful bosses continue to receive exorbitant pay and bonuses for their effort. In other words, their loyalty has shifted from the workers to the state to the company. For instance, tiny wage increases, typically between 1 and 2 percent, became tied to higher productivity rates that passed exponential value on to the owners.

The model of class collaboration with the new emphasis on "partnership" and "shared productive interests" mirrored the process of union decline in the US as well. As a Mexican labor historian Luis H. Mendez Berrueta describes: "Worn out, senile, and without an alternative to offer, these unions continued only because of inertia, and continued their decline as a useful tool to the system that no longer had any use for them."[27] The disintegration of authentic unionism, and the transposition of methods of labor management and control perfected in the maquiladoras into other sectors of manufacturing, began the process of full maquiladorization of the Mexican economy. Without substantial working-class opposition, the neoliberalization of the economy proceeded swiftly.

The phases of privatization and closures produced mass layoffs. In one burst, over half a million workers were laid off in the first quarter of 1986 alone. Union militants were dismissed and replaced because of widespread blacklisting. Older generations of workers with union and strike experience were replaced by a new generation without that history who entered into more overtly antiunion work environments.

The number of strike declarations dropped from 16,930 in 1982 to 7,007 in 1989, a 58 percent decline, while the actual number of strikes conducted fell from 675 to 136 over the same period, about an 80 percent decline.[28] With the administration of Carlos Salinas de Gortari—and the triumph and consolidation of the neoliberal capitalist reorganization of the party—the state increasingly declared strikes illegal.

Furthermore, the new owning class seized the tradition of charrismo and utilized it to convert nominally existent unions into antiunion protection rackets. In these cases, former union leadership became full-service muscle for employers against unions, arranging exploitative contracts with the bosses that rewarded them for keeping wages low by repressing workers trying to independently organize or collectively bargain.

This became a widespread practice in the maquiladoras to keep the largest sectors of foreign-owned manufacturing scrubbed of any real union organizing. When taking fake, company unions into consideration, the rate of paper membership increased substantially over this period, distorting and obscuring the actual decline of authentic unionization rates nationally.

Through these methods of union-busting, membership rates plummeted. Between 1978 and 2005, the unionization rate for manual labor jobs fell from 43 percent to 19 percent (with a 22 percent drop between 1993 and 2007 alone during the exponential expansion of maquiladora production). Over this same period, productivity overall doubled as managers implemented new speed-up techniques, while a commensurate decline in wages occurred. By 2002, for instance, wages for all manufacturing workers fell 14 percent below what they were in 1983.[29] The steepest plummets in wage drops overlapped with recurring economic crises. Between 1994 and 1998, during the 1995 recession, wages dropped by 16 percent overall, and manufacturing wages by nearly 20 percent, while inflation increased by 52 percent.[30] These occurrences created new, lower wage floors across the board.

In auto production, the largest of the foreign-dominated industrial sectors, productivity rates increased over 66 percent between 1990 and

1999, while real wages fell by an estimated 20 percent over the same period.[31] Shrouded in these statistics are the processes by which billions of dollars of have been transferred from Mexican workers to international capital. By 2019 authentic labor unionism had largely ceased to exist, except in name only.

## Privatizations Continue

Without unions and any other form of class-based representation or solidarity, the full implementation of the components of NAFTA and subsequent reforms between 1994 and 2008 thrust the majority of Mexicans further into economic hardship. The state continued on the path of privatization. In 1995, the Mexican government partnered with the World Bank to begin the process of full privatization of the federal old-age pension and social security programs. World Bank officials oversaw the process by providing funds and technical assistance to manage the transition.[32] Other privatizations followed. In 1995, thirty-four of the country's fifty-eight airports were partially privatized, allowing private-sector investors to control between 25.5 percent and 49 percent of shares in airport operations with fifty-year concessions.[33]

The minimum wage rate stagnated, becoming one of the lowest in the western hemisphere.[34] For instance, in 2000, Mexico's labor costs were 58 percent more expensive than Chinese labor, then considered the cheapest and most abundant labor available. By 2015, the average manufacturing labor costs in Mexico were pushed down to almost 20 percent lower than those in China.[35] A leading research firm even identified Mexico as one of sixteen "successor" nations to replace China as future centers of cheap labor for global capital, stating that the "era of Chinese development—pyramiding on low wages to conquer global markets—is ending simply because there are now other nations with even lower wages and other advantages."[36]

After seventy-five years of state ownership, the restored PRI government of Enrique Peña Nieto began the process of privatizing Mexico's oil industry. After again changing the constitution in 2013 over the cries of mass public opposition, the state opened the oil sector to foreign capital for new exploration and production, essentially turning over the nation's remaining untapped reserves. It also opened wind, solar, hydro, and geothermal energy production to privatization.

Oil is Mexico's main export and provides the state with over 33 percent of its total revenue to fund the nation's social services. From 1980 to 2019, the state oil company PEMEX produced an average of 1.5 million barrels per day, generating up to $50 billion per year in state revenues. Since 2014, the state has started the sell-off of the nation's oil, signing over one hundred contracts with multinational oil corporations worth a total capital investment valued at more than $160 billion.[37] In 2016, the state began the privatization of electricity generation and production, selling licensing rights to private companies to produce and sell electricity directly to the government.[38]

## Transnationalization of Mexican Workers through Migration

Migration became a response to the depression-like conditions experienced by Mexican and other workers in the region. Between 1960 and 2010, over thirty million Latin American workers crossed the border into the United States, following the transfer of wealth from their homelands into the United States. The largest share of migrants came from Mexico, whose economy was increasingly integrated as part of that of the United States, where wages were higher and opportunities more abundant. Furthermore, there had already been multigenerational experience of migration and an understanding that Mexican labor had long been essential to the US economy.[39]

Over this period, the US state granted legal authorization to about 60 percent of migrants, a rate that has been decreasing ever since. The decreasing rate of legal authorization corresponds to an increasing rate of migration *and* criminalization—especially of Mexicans crossing the border after the passage of NAFTA (and Central Americans and Caribbean people after 2005).

The total number of Mexican people living in the United States was 11,300,000 in 2017.[40] About 60 percent of this population has migrated since the passage of NAFTA, with the high point of two million workers entering the country between 2000 and 2005 alone.[41] By 2019, Mexico had ten million migrants living outside its borders, the second highest number in the world after India.[42]

Since the United States allocates fewer than twenty thousand work visas to Mexico each year—the majority of those going to skilled workers—most Mexican workers can only enter without official authorization. The majority of migrants, having limited resources to pay first-class smugglers, have to navigate an increasingly fortified border and hazardous terrain throughout the migrant corridor into the United States.

As part of labor market restructuring in the United States (i.e., state efforts to push down wages to assist in increasing capital accumulation for private owners) successive US governments since Jimmy Carter have intensified border enforcement efforts and closed off legal access to citizenship for a widening population of working-class migrants.[43] This has engineered the growth of an undocumented workforce. Instead of curtailing cross-border movement, US border militarization policies have criminalized migration. This has only made crossing deadlier and laborers more exploitable since they cannot attain citizenship and labor rights. For capitalists north of the border, therein lies the value.

# PART II

# The Transnational Working Class

*The farmworkers of the San Quentin Valley are done being invisible.*

—Fidel Sánchez, a leader of the 2015 berry strike in San Quintín Valley, Baja California, Mexico

# EIGHT

# The North American Model of Labor Exploitation

North American capitalism has had to reinvent itself by killing off outdated arrangements and constructing new ones, driven by an insatiable and compulsory need to accumulate, especially within a framework of imperialist competition and rivalry. Nevertheless, each revamping of the capitalist mode of production inevitably engenders new contradictions and heightened class antagonisms, as it is eternally contingent on labor exploitation regardless of form.

In the last three decades, the natural rights of capital have been encoded in the international agreements and enforcement agencies that define and regulate the operations of the global economy. Free markets are then aggressively promoted across national boundaries by states, transnational enterprises and organizations, armies of enforcers, and ranks of functionaries, intellectuals, consultants, and other frontline intermediaries.

Within the North American pole of the global system, US capitalism has reorganized and rewired a regional economy by facilitating, seeking out, and shifting production to nonunion and state-repressed workers across the southern border. US capital, while extending beyond its own national territory, maintains its primary production centers and investment zones near indispensable, US-based consumer markets.

Geographically, this has contributed to what David Harvey calls capital's "spatial fix," which refers to the structured mobility of capital to seek a "fix" for falling rates of profit where it is currently situated and toward new locations where it can operate more profitably.[1] Crossing into Mexico to take advantage of lower wages and evade unions is an example of this phenomenon.

Capital export into Mexico has also fueled geographic reorganization, internal economic displacement, and criminalized migration. It has contributed to the growth of concentrated industrial clusters and population centers along the border and into the interior, interconnected through international transportation hubs. This illustrates the one-dimensional form of current open borders, for capital, money, and products only, which has substantially transformed the relations of production within the region.

These features combine to create a North American model (NAM) of US-centric capitalist imperialism that contains some distinct and organic features. It has facilitated a type of segmented manufacturing process known as supply chain production, shifting US capital investment and resituating whole stages of production into Mexico (and beyond) in order to exploit cheaper labor inside these nations.

This process has destroyed and replaced local industry and has restructured economies based on creating systems of exploitation, extraction, and profit repatriation. Due to this arrangement, more jobs have been destroyed than created, leading to waves of out-migration corresponding to greater influx of US capital investment and wealth transfer. Migration follows the path of theft. Furthermore, the NAM facilitates the superexploitation of migrants as workers, creating a secondary means of accumulation as a superexploited reserve army of labor.

As one sympathetic study observing cross-border supply chain development reported in 1983:

> A modern form of this trade is the interchange of parts that are fabricated or assembled in different countries. Such offshore assembly activities emerged from growing worldwide competition in manufactures after World War II, as Western Europe recovered and Japan became a top industrial power. The United States faced the new competition first because of its relatively high wages. As labor-intensive production became increasingly uneconomic, US firms turned offshore, breaking up production into stages and carrying out the labor-intensive processes in countries where wages were low. Items assembled abroad

> have become an important part of the American supply of certain manufactured products, especially in textiles and electronics.[2]

A key point made here is that "relatively high wages" became "uneconomic" (i.e., undesirable).

Through the subdivision of production across borders, capital can intensify the rate of exploitation of all segments by lowering the wage threshold to the lowest possible denominator. This is made possible by reinforcing national boundaries, which in turn maintain the differentials between the two nations embodied in such factors as: balance of class forces, union density, extant forms of labor repression and control, and other factors that determine wage levels within any particular region or industry. Capitalists then use the differentials to ideologically divide the workers along national lines by making them compete with each other for jobs.

Through the forceful implementation of free-trade agreements, previously restricted capital markets in Mexico and Central America have been opened and saturated with US and other foreign investment. This massive influx of international capital has displaced and consumed state and domestic capital across the economies, evoking a semicolonial reality. This includes taking ownership over privatized industry, acquiring large tracts of arable land, subsuming local production centers, restructuring and segmenting production across borders, and dominating national markets for capital, financial, and consumer goods.

An unintended but welcomed by-product of this historical process has become the unprecedented amalgamation of the regional proletariat. Sections of the working classes of the United States and Mexico—as well as Central America and the Caribbean—have been fused into unitary, trans- and multinational production lines, interconnected supply chains, linked transportation, logistics, and distribution networks, and increasingly into common employment for the same multinational corporations and investment firms.

This exposes a sizeable contradiction for this model of capitalism. While it depends on the use of enforced border restriction, national economic differentiation, and the immobilization of sections of workers within national boundaries in order to maintain unequal wage differentials, it also lays the basis for new forms of cross-border solidarity, and transnational unionization. Understanding how the North American model has brought workers together—even as it works aggressively to divide them—illustrates how workers can begin to see themselves as having shared class interests and common cause.

As much as 40 percent of the value of US imports from Mexico actually originate in the United States. In other words, US companies send semi-finished products to their own subsidiaries in Mexico to finish products that are then exported back to the US.[3] This is an indication of the increasing integration of manufacturing supply chains on both sides of the border, and how exploitation of labor on the Mexican side of the border is a critical factor for cost saving in these arrangements.

From the point of view of capitalism, the maximum exploitation of labor within transnational and international production and finance requires borders and the constrained movement of labor. Nevertheless, the contours of labor integration across borders are also becoming more apparent and exposed, especially in supply chain manufacturing, multinational employment in the same firms, transborder logistics, and agricultural production.

Recent strikes in the maquiladoras, retail sector, agriculture, and the transnational automotive industries are cases in point. These illustrate the first stirrings and tremendous potential for class struggle to cross borders within the NAM.

The following chapter will look at some case studies that illustrate the transnationalization of labor and class alignments, how workers can shut down supply chains and whole industries across borders by going on strike, as well as the first significant stirrings toward unified class action across borders. These examples show the urgency of the need for transnational organization to facilitate class struggle against global entities, especially within the NAM.

## Decline of Unionism in Mexico

About 10 percent of Mexico's labor force carries union cards, but nine out of every ten members belong to secretive and undemocratic pro-business unions. According to recent estimates, the proportion of Mexican laborers who belong to authentic unions that negotiate on behalf of their members in good faith hovers at about 1 percent. This represents one of the lowest unionization rates in the world.[4]

Strikes had been on a steep decline in Mexico over the last three decades since the passage of NAFTA, under both PRI and PAN administrations. In the six-year presidency of Ernesto Zedillo (1994–2000) there were 283 strikes, in that of Vicente Fox (2000–2006), 267; Felipe Calderón (2006–2012), 111; and under Enrique Peña Nieto (2012–2018), a mere 22. In the latter, only five of those involved more than a thousand workers.[5]

Several factors explain the declining rate of class struggle. Capital mobility into Mexico has been predicated on the maintenance of low wages. The Mexican neoliberal model has ground down the welfare functions of the state and has simultaneously defunded its labor enforcement agencies while increasing its policing capacities.[6] For instance, since 2008, the US government has given the Mexican government nearly $2 billion to militarize the nation's borders and provide arms, training, and equipment to state and federal police forces and the Mexican military.[7]

Most significantly, the state has hollowed out the labor movement using various mechanisms at its disposal, including the manipulation of mandatory state and federal arbitration bodies. Under Mexican law, all labor conflict is subjected to government sanction. These highly corrupted bodies have become openly procapitalist instruments used to deny the legitimacy of strikes (inviting police repression) or gradually delay and suffocate strike movements through endless bureaucratic maneuvers. The state has also protected the framework of fake and charro unionism, which allows companies to use the existence of phony contracts, protection rackets, and entrenched, sellout leadership bodies to smash opposition or independent attempts to unionize.[8]

As one report studying organized labor observed in Mexico City, most union contracts exist only on paper. Where the semblance of protections and guarantees have existed for workers, these have been whittled down or dismantled in the last two decades under the approving eye of the capitalist state. Citing an example, the study reports the following:

> According to Federal District's Local Conciliation and Arbitration Board, there are 83,000 Collective Labor Agreements, in which only 27,000, at best, are even reviewed. . . . In the majority of cases the private interests take advantage and use the revision to mutilate the contract's industrial relations by preventing or at least limiting trade-union intervention in the labor market and reducing workers' organizations to simple instruments that communicate state rulings and industrial decisions back to the workers.[9]

Labor protections and guarantees enshrined in labor law have been denuded or go unenforced. The North American Free Trade Agreement has facilitated easy access for foreign capitalist investors to move freely into the Mexican economy to exploit labor and flee if and when markets become no longer profitable.

Through corruption, partnerships, and shared class interests, the ruling-class capitalist parties—especially the PRI and PAN, which have historically controlled the local and state governments in the maquiladora zones—have worked hand in glove with maquiladora owners and the fake charro unions to use various tactics to squash authentic labor movements to ensure a friendly environment for investors. Despite the success of this model, it suffered a mighty blow in early 2019, when more than thirty thousand workers carried out the largest wildcat strike wave in modern Mexican history.

# NINE

# The Maquiladora Strikes of 2019

The least-organized and most-exploited workers toil in the maquiladora sector, despite many heroic and persistent attempts at independent unionization.[1] Nevertheless, there has been a surge in class struggle in Mexico in recent years. The most significant independent union movement to emerge in decades has taken root in the northern border states where most maquiladoras are located and where a strike wave spread in the first three months of 2019.

Capital investment in Mexico grew precipitously after the introduction of NAFTA and exploded after the turn of the twenty-first century. Whole industries were restructured or created, with a substantial population of the Mexican working class transitioning into export-oriented capital production clusters or multinational firms. Between 2000 and 2014, the size of the labor force in Mexico that works in the NAFTA-zone export sector grew to 4.6 million, or about 11 percent of the total workforce, a figure twice the size of its US and Canadian counterparts.[2]

The maquiladora industry is the largest sector of this export-oriented manufacturing base. It comprises about 60 percent of the total manufacturing economy, with about six thousand registered maquiladoras employing between two and three million workers as of 2019.[3] With the transition of Mexico through the North American model of capitalism, manufactured goods have consistently dominated Mexico's exports, accounting for about 90 percent of total export value in 2018 and with 80 percent going north of the border.[4] The growth of this sector reflected a flood of investment, especially from the United States, to take advantage of Mexico's proximity to US markets, suppressed wages, high productivity, and virtual absence of real unions and successful strikes in recent memory.

## Raise in the Minimum Wage

Wages in Mexico had fallen so low that consumption rates began to collapse. Like in the United States, production for domestic consumption accounts for over two-thirds of the gross domestic product. Between 1992 and 2012, exports grew at 8.6 percent a year. While production *increased*, wages went into a tailspin. Between 2005 and 2012, for instance, real labor income per capita in Mexico fell 6 percent.[5] Falling wages and disinvestment pushed larger segments of the working class into poverty, and, along with them, rates of national consumption declined.

In January of 2019, the newly elected Mexican government of Andres Manuel López Obrador swept into power with a 63 percent majority vote, promising to raise wages, revitalize unions, and invest more in social development—all without disturbing the functioning of NAFTA. His newly created MORENA party was a reconstitution of the fragments of the old PRI that still cling to the idea of progressive capitalist development; which included increasing domestic consumption rates and mitigating the excesses of neoliberal integration. The working class widely embraced his campaign after nearly thirty years of free-market capitalism, believing there would be a change in course. Once in office, he issued a decree raising the minimum wage by 16 percent (from 88 pesos to 103 pesos per day, or $5.40), while doubling the minimum wage for workers in the border region (from 88 to 177 pesos per day, or $9.30).[6]

While this increase has benefitted the poorest workers by raising the abysmal wage-floor threshold, it fell below what the majority of maquiladora workers in the border city of Matamoros *already* made—which was only slightly higher than $10 a day.[7] The tepid reform by the incoming administration of López Obrador revealed the rudderless drift of Mexican economic nationalism. Once a devoted *priísta* functionary himself, López Obrador tried to revive the flagging brand of populism once situated on the center-left of the PRI state-party spectrum with the creation of the MORENA party in 2014. After previous failed presidential campaigns in 2006 and 2012, defeats, largely attributed to electoral fraud orchestrated at the state level, López Obrador moderated his rhetoric against the neoliberal transformation and focused on compartmentalized reforms within the new order.

In the context of the absolute collapse of popular credibility in the thoroughly neoliberal PRI and PAN parties, López Obrador and MORENA ran for president once again on a vague platform of economic nationalism. Along with his immense political popularity as a critic of neoliberalism, and with no remaining options this time around, the Mexican capitalist class openly supported his candidacy. This near universal support became a public campaign after a series of high-profile meetings between López Obrador and leading bankers and business associations where he pledged to preserve and expand NAFTA/USMCA, and to reject any notion of renationalization of the economy.[8] Since coming to power in December of 2018, López Obrador has focused on growing the Mexican economy and has factored in NAFTA/USMCA alongside state-led megadevelopment and extractivist projects as twin engines of growth. Raising the wage threshold has been part of a parallel project of increasing purchasing power, but subordinate to his vision of growth that minimizes the interests of workers to capital and foreign investment—in very much the PRI mold.[9]

Taking matters into their own hands, maquiladora workers in the state of Tamaulipas went on their own offensive against low wages in early 2019. In the state of Tamaulipas, there are 411 registered maquiladoras that employ about 257,000 workers. There are about 152 in operation in Reynosa, 111 in Matamoros, 33 in Nuevo Laredo, and 62 in other parts of the state. The industry in Matamoros has been booming for three straight years, especially through growth of the auto parts production facilities. Yet the benefits have only accrued to the expanding ranks of multinational investors and not to workers. Nevertheless, strikes have been rare in the industry and have become virtually nonexistent over the last decade.

The new wage law coincided with the annual renegotiation of forty-six maquiladora contracts, an industry-wide practice unique to the sector in Matamoros. Typically a formality in which representatives of the state and local government, the maquiladora owners, and the unions make arrangements over the heads of the workers, things changed this year.

The outcome of the contract proposal for the thirty-five thousand workers covered by the contracts proved less than satisfactory, especially as they believed their wages should increase in proportion to the minimum wage increase. Instead of a pay increase, the president of the Centro Coordinador Empresarial (CCE, the big business alliance of Matamoros that includes the maquiladora industry) announced that owners would instead agree to an adjustment in the ratio of employer-to-worker pay into their retirement plans.[10]

Some owners resisted any adjustments at all, using the minimum wage increase as an excuse to cancel productivity bonuses altogether. Others rallied behind statements made by Rogelio García Treviño, president of the Cámara Nacional de la Industria de Transformación (the main national maquiladora trade association). Fearing the national implications of wage increases in the maquiladoras in Matamoros, García Treviño pressured his regional counterparts to hold firm against pay increases and instead lay off workers, if necessary, to avoid increasing their overall annual budgets.[11]

## Wildcat Strikes

As the maquiladora owners rejected pay increases, workers at three plants took the initiative to walk out in a wildcat strike on January 10. Their call for a 20 percent wage raise and an increase in the annual bonus to 32,000 pesos (1,680 dollars) has been termed the 20/32 demand.[12] The workers determined that their pay should increase by 20 percent as a relative proportion to the doubling of the minimum wage. They also factored the pay increase into their annual performance bonus. For the first time, they called for the bonus to be universal for all workers under contract as a standard.

Facing the first instances of workers' confidence to strike and with pending production contracts now threatened, the maquiladora owners buckled in their efforts to stonewall. While publicly denouncing the initial labor stoppages as "premature" and "unnecessary," they frantically offered a 7 percent wage increase and a 3,373-peso bonus (worth 177 dollars) to head off further strikes.[13]

The president of the Sindicato de Jornaleros y Obreros Industriales y de la Industria Maquiladora (Union of Industrial Workers and Laborers in the Maquiladora Industry), Juan Villafuerte Morales, was put into the unprecedented position of having to represent workers taking independent strike action. He urged the owners to increase the proposal to 10 percent, which they did, but the workers rejected it.

Corrupt union leaders like Villafuerte Morales have historically functioned as a booster for the industry, seeing their role as supporting increases in jobs and facilitating labor peace to ensure profits and growth for the companies and big payoffs for themselves at the expense of the workers. This is reflected in the fact that workers' demands are also directed at the union leadership. In some cases, the workers have called for an end to or reduction of extortive union *cuotas*, or fees, deducted from worker pay to line the pockets of the union bosses.

Villafuerte Morales had worked closely with the maquiladora owners and municipal and state politicians to make Matamoros an ideal place for foreign investment by keeping wages and benefits constrained.[14] Each year, the union "renegotiates" the pay and benefits for the workers, without their input, and typically carries over contracts with little change. Charros are rewarded for keeping wages and benefits low, while more notorious union bosses go even further in systematically fleecing workers of their pay and benefits. In this case, Villafuerte Morales recognized the gravity of the moment, as the workers' movement quickly moved beyond his control.

In fact, on January 12, two thousand of the most militant workers from the struck plants marched on the offices of the union to demand Villafuerte Morales's resignation for failing to adequately represent them and their demands. According to one account:

> Amid booing, whistles, and cries of "Villafuerte out! Sellout!" and "Cacique!" [corrupt political boss], the workers arrived at the union headquarters. The leader opened the doors of the building and asked the workers to come in, but they refused and told him to come out onto the street to face them all directly.[15]

After Villafuerte Morales made a feeble attempt to blame others for his failed leadership, the workers shouted him down. They demanded that he immediately declare and organize a strike in the forty-five plants that had refused to concede. Even though he asked for more time to negotiate their demands and urged strikers to return to their jobs in the meantime, the workers persisted.[16] The following day workers shut down fifteen more plants, placing red and black strike flags (*banderas rojinegras*) across the gates of the struck companies.[17] The employers, many US-owned or backed operations, moved into action to clamp down with the support of local and state officials.

## A Massive Shutdown Begins

With each side refusing to concede at the conclusion of arbitration, workers demonstrated their strength on the morning of January 25 by coordinating a massive strike shutdown, placing their banderas rojinegras across the gates of all forty-five of the maquiladoras. At least thirty-five thousand workers were now out of the plants, bringing to a halt the manufacture of mostly auto parts for US automakers, but also electrical equipment, medical equipment, metal, plastics, and textiles across the industrial parks.

The walkouts coincided with a downpour of rain, yet workers gathered in throngs at the entrances of the factories, huddling under umbrellas and makeshift tarps to also maintain safety in numbers against any possible forms of repression—a specter raised when, on the first day of the strike, the military commander of the zone of Matamoros, Francisco Miguel Aranda Gutiérrez, sent in troops to occupy strategic areas across the city.[18] Not deterred, the strikers held their ground. Within two days, eleven of the companies conceded to the 20/32 demand.

Trying a different tactic, the owner of Autoliv, one of the struck auto parts plants, got a strike injunction issued by a sympathetic judge. When the Autoliv workers refused to return to work, Ricardo Monreal, a former PRI leader who is now president of the Senate for the ruling MORENA party, contacted Susana Prieto Terrazas, a Texas-Chihuahua-based labor lawyer supporting the workers. Prieto put the call on speakerphone in front of the workers, who heard Monreal characterize the strike as "illegal" and say that the workers should "return to their jobs." The López Obrador administration then dispatched several high-level functionaries from the office of the federal secretary of labor to Matamoros to participate in ongoing negotiations to end the strike.[19]

Meanwhile, the state governor Francisco García Cabeza de Vaca, affiliated with the right-wing PAN party, sent in state police to break up the Autoliv strike, but they were unsuccessful as they were faced down by several hundred workers and community supporters who blocked the entrance gate and refused to move. With the help of Susana Prieto, they were then able to get the injunction overturned.

As one of the workers commented to *La Jornada* on the experience, "They want to scare us, but they are not going to succeed. This [strike] is for my children, and they will have to listen to the workers of Matamoros: We have raised our horns."[20] By January 29, nineteen of the companies conceded to the strike, and by February 6, forty-four of the original forty-five plant owners had capitulated and agreed to the 20/32 demands.[21] Eventually, all of the owners conceded, and the strike spread to other maquila clusters.

The strikes won handily as workers remained united and confident, aware of the centrality of their labor in the supply chains of automotive production within the highly transnationalized industry. Their ability to shut down auto parts production threatened to disrupt operations on an international scale, a prospect that frightened investors and corporate executives. In an attempt to punish her and squash the efforts to build a new independent union in the maquiladora sector, authorities arrested Susana Prieto Terrazas and jailed her for nearly a month in the summer of 2020 amid another organizing campaign in the state of Tamaulipas.[22]

Their victory touched off a new period of militancy, class consciousness, and awareness of the transnationalization of labor and production that later spread into the other sectors of the industry.

# TEN

# Transnational Automotive Production and the 2019 GM Strike

Since the turn of the twenty-first century, Mexico has become one of the largest centers in world automotive production. Between 1998 and 2004, the total neoliberalization of Mexico's auto industry was completed. All import/export duties for auto-associated products were reduced to zero and the legal barriers for all foreign ownership in the industry were removed.

Asian, European, and US automakers have shifted production and exported capital to Mexico on an enormous scale. US investors especially have focused on extending auto parts manufacturing south of the border as a strategy of supply chain reorganization. By the end of 2018, automotive production became the largest manufacturing industry in the nation, accounting for 20.7 percent of Mexico's total GDP. Exports of automotive products amounted to $142.18 billion, while imports were $59 billion, creating a surplus of $83 billion in 2018. Automotive exports are the single largest source of foreign income reserves for the Mexican government, generating more than oil exports, tourism, and migrant remittances combined.

Between 2009 and 2018, international capital has invested $124 billion in North American automotive production, with 20 percent going into Mexico (the remaining 73 percent to the United States and 7 percent to Canada), averaging about $2.5 billion per year. In the years 2016 and 2017 alone, there was a total investment of $49.2 billion in the Mexican auto industry. Automotive production in Mexico doubled between 2007 and 2015 from two million to four million vehicles. It is poised to reach six million by 2022.[1] This would propel Mexico forward as the fifth-largest auto producer in the world with $92 billion in revenues annually and the second-largest in North America, roughly half the size of the US market. Around 88 percent of the vehicle production in Mexico is devoted to exports with the remaining 12 percent destined for the domestic market. The lion's share of exports, 84.9 percent, goes to the US.[2]

The primary reason for the influx of international capital to Mexico is to increase profit. The exploitation of Mexican labor reaps substantial reward. Labor costs for automotive assembly are approximately 80 percent lower in Mexico than in the United States, taking wages, benefits, and other forms of compensation into account.[3] By 2015, suppressed wages in Mexico's manufacturing sector fell almost 20 percent below those in China.[4]

Through the construction of free-trade agreements (i.e. freedom of movement for capital export), investors found a way to further increase profits by decreasing the threshold for wages and working conditions by crossing the border. The corporations relied on mobility to first shift production from higher-wage to lower-wage areas within the United States. This advantageous approach to increasing labor exploitation was observed in the *Washington Post*:

> Back in the 1980s, the US auto industry went through a major upheaval. Foreign automakers started opening up more and more plants in the South, taking advantage of the region's weaker unions and lower labor costs. That, in turn, undercut the historically dominant position of Detroit and the Midwest.[5]

They then pursued mechanisms through the state to facilitate the permeability of national borders for capital, looking directly at Mexico. As they moved operations into Mexico through the aegis of state-negotiated trade regimes, they effectively redefined and pushed out a new set of international boundaries for the free movement of capital and for the rich. Nevertheless, the physical border and the repressive architecture of migrant labor enforcement remains intact.

Furthermore, Mexico's neoliberal trade law and practices are riddled with generous pro-corporate incentives and tax exclusions, and they exclude technology transfer requirements. These embed a multitude of benefits which transfer an even larger share of the value of production from the domestic population to the owners of capital. Another major factor is the close proximity and reduced logistics and transportation costs to the United States, which is the largest market for automobiles and auto parts in the world.

The Mexican government maintains unusually high interest rates for capital investment, invests in workforce development and training programs, subsidizes energy costs, and maintains an array of tax incentives and benefits for capital. It has extended free-trade zones (FTZ) into all areas of the economy, providing tax-free benefits for exported products. State governments are allowed to establish their own FTZ arrangements, turning the country into a multilayered investment zone with various overlapping privileges and exemptions for international capital.[6] Additionally, the declining value of the peso against the US dollar means that the manufacture of vehicles and parts in Mexico is less expensive relative to the United States. Lastly, Mexico collects the least amount of taxes of all thirty-six of the member countries of the Organization for Economic Cooperation and Development, making it a virtual tax haven for US investors.

This set of highly lucrative arrangements for capital has resulted in the construction of a matrix of transnational production zones and supply chains that crisscross a unidimensional open border. Through and across this matrix, the NAM has also situated a highly condensed and clustered workforce that assembles and produces the same finished products and typically for the same capitalist firms. The immense workforce on the Mexican side cannot cross freely, although the products they create and the value generated by their labor have that right.

International capital investment poured in through this portal for accumulation. Auto assembly plants in Mexico more than doubled from 11 in 2004 to 25 in 2020.[7] The number of auto parts production facilities (maquiladoras) increased from 187 in 1990 to 313 in 2006—and then more than quadrupled to over 1,300 factories in 2019. US investors own a third, or about 750, of these plants, followed by Mexican, European, and Asian capital. Much recent investment in Mexico has been in current technologies and equipment, making the production interchangeable with that of its North American, European, and Asian counterparts.

All major international automotive corporations now operate interconnected and interdependent automotive assembly, production, logistics, and distribution supply chains across North American borders. As one US Federal Reserve study notes:

> By 2020, all of the 11 carmakers operating in Mexico will have other production facilities in North America. They tend to run their North American operations in a geographically integrated fashion. This applies especially to their respective supply chains, which extend across national borders in North America.[8]

Mexican workers are central to the whole operation of North American auto production. Mexico has about 900,000 auto manufacturing workers (over 90 percent in parts and component production), accounting for 45 percent of the North American total auto production workforce and 15 percent of the total industrial labor force in the country. By comparison, the US has slightly over one million autoworkers (49 percent of North American auto production workforce), and Canada has 125,000 workers (6 percent).[9]

The movement of manufactured goods through transborder supply chains also links workers in other ways. An estimated 80 to 85 percent of motor vehicles assembled in Mexico for US and Canadian markets are transported by rail, directly linking production centers with northern markets.[10] This is a legacy of how US-invested industry in Mexico over the last century was constructed to extract and repatriate Mexico's wealth and resources north of the border. The remainder are moved by shipping, linking Mexican and US ports. Taken together, the logistics of this system are contingent upon rail workers and dockworkers on both sides of the border.

From the point of view of the US and Mexican capitalist states, it is imperative that the NAM retain its differentiated national character through the regional immobilization of labor. This is in order to keep Mexican labor subordinated and wages artificially depressed, even as the economy becomes more directly integrated through the transnationalization of capital—and as the transnational working class has become more interconnected and interdependent. The criminalization of migrant labor once it crosses national boundaries serves as an instrument to maintain the segregation of labor along racial and national lines. Mexican workers are paid less for the same work—even when working for the same employer or within the same transnational industry. Migrant workers are also segregated, ensuring they are paid less for the same work than their "citizen" counterparts. The organization of transnational unions, cross-border labor solidarity, and coordinated strikes are the only ways to upset this predatory framework—and to lay the basis for overturning the antiworker, repressive border regime that criminalization depends on.

## Workers Shut Down Transnational Auto Production

Strikes in the supply chain across the US-Mexico border in 2019 showed the power that workers have within the NAM and why it is necessary to organize common unions and strike demands.

More than thirty-five thousand workers in more than forty-eight mostly auto parts production and assembly plants in the Mexican state of Tamaulipas launched simultaneous, consecutive, and rolling wildcat strikes over the course of a month and a half in early 2019. The workers were affiliated with four different charro unions. Like in other instances previously mentioned, the leaders of these so-called unions are corrupt, bought off, and used to discipline their workers and prevent labor stoppages to protect profits for the company in exchange for payoffs and occasional concessions to the workers that are trivial or symbolic in nature. Because of these arrangements, workers in the Mexican auto industries get paid about one-tenth of what their counterparts make in the United States.[11]

Despite the official opposition of the charro leadership, the workers coordinated their own strike actions and won against disproportionate odds and asymmetrical opposition. The contending forces extended from paid thugs to the police to the state government, and also a constellation of local, statewide, and national business federations and their political enforcers at every level of government.

Parts buyers in the United States and Mexico were hit with immediate shortages, disrupting their just-in-time deadlines. Because of the high level of solidarity between the workers and significant disruption of the auto supply chains, which caused an estimated loss of at least $50 million per day, the companies were forced to quickly settle and concede to the strikers' uniform 20/32 demands.[12]

That same year, GM workers affiliated with the United Auto Workers union conducted a forty-day strike, the longest strike by the UAW in more than fifty years. The strike shut down thirty-three manufacturing plants and twenty-two parts distribution warehouses across nine states. It had similar multiplier effects in Mexico and Canada. Initially, the corporation compelled its Mexican plants to speed up production to pick up the slack, but it was ultimately forced to shut them down as the strike continued. About 49,000 GM workers in the US, over 6,000 in Mexico, and an equal number in Canada were idled during the GM strike. Another 25,000 of GM's staff and an estimated 75,000 auto parts workers across the borders in the supply and production chains were stalled. All told, according to one estimate, over 150,000 North American workers were affected by the strike.[13]

For example, GM workers at two assembly plants located in Oshawa and St. Catharines, Ontario, Canada, had to down their tools or stay home after a ripple effect of the strike disrupted their places along GM's transnational assembly lines. Parts coming into the plants dried up, while demand for the essential components further down the chain (such as drive trains destined for US manufacturers) was abruptly cut.

GM was eventually forced to stop its operations in Mexico. It halted production workers at its plant in Silao, Guanajuato, after necessary components coming from the US ran out. This further rippled through the Mexico-based part suppliers, triggering further shut-downs. If the strike had persisted, it could have also had deeper reach, hindering the procurement of replacement parts for an estimated thirty million GM vehicles on the US roads.

All told, GM was dealt $1.1 billion in lost income—at least 165,000 fewer cars and trucks were produced. The strike disrupted steel and aluminum sales, cutting demand for an estimated 1,820 tons of steel and 340 tons of aluminum. The total multiplier effects added up to an estimated $3 billion overall loss to the economy, with proportional multiplier effects in Mexico and Canada as well.[14]

The GM strike took place on the heels of efforts by Mexican autoworkers to build new, independent unions across the automotive industry. Organizers and workers who led the successful strikes in the auto parts maquiladoras in Matamoros launched an independent and militant union called the Sindicato Nacional Independiente de Trabajadores de Industrias y de Servicios /Movimiento 20/32 to challenge and replace the corrupt CTM-led charro unions. There have also been attempts to organize independent unions in the auto assembly plants. In fact, there has been a surge of new union organizing campaigns across Mexico.

Even though GM is the largest auto manufacturer in Mexico, workers are not part of the UAW and have no authentic union representation. Unlike in Canada, where the United Auto Workers union crosses the border, they have no relationship to Mexican workers. GM Mexico relies on protection rackets and phony unions to police, discipline, and punish workers who step out of line.

In fact, Mexican autoworkers have been consistently clamoring and organizing for independent union representation in different capacities since the 1970s.[15] In GM's Silao plant in Guanajuato, workers had been organizing an independent union on the shop floor to evict the corrupt CTM-affiliated union. In the weeks before the GM strike, the company and the CTM collaborated to fire a group of eight worker-organizers at the plant. The company conducted a "random" drug test that was applied to those identified as organizers and sympathizers, and then fired them after falsely claiming they tested positive.

## Opening the Border Means Transnational Labor Solidarity and Organization

Despite their victimization in the lead-up to the strike, the Silao organizers went on to build and lead an international solidarity campaign for their striking US counterparts. They called for the strike to spread across the borders to GM plants in other countries in order to prevent GM from increasing production internationally to weaken the US-based strike. They also called for the international strike as a collective action to stop GM's "restructuring plans." Announced in 2018, this downsizing project included the planned closure of seven manufacturing plants worldwide, five plants in North America, and two others elsewhere, with the goal of eliminating fourteen thousand jobs. This overture is especially meaningful and prescient coming from the Mexican autoworkers, as the closure of US plants as production increases in Mexico indicates that the company will likely shift even more operations to Mexico in the coming years.[16]

According to one report, they

> promoted assemblies where workers from the Silao plant in Mexico, Brazil, and Canada, communicated their support for the Americans. Their intention is to globalize the conflict, because if production is forcibly increased elsewhere, the effect of the strike is lost and with it the ability to stop the company's intention to close seven plants globally.[17]

Despite the show of solidarity and evident logic of the Mexican call for at least attempting to expand the strike across the borders, the UAW leadership did not even consider it. They contained the strike, achieving only minimal gains for its vastly shrunken membership, which has dropped from 1.5 million in 1979 to about three hundred and ninety thousand today.[18] Adding to this decline, the new contract language concedes the company's main demand: its plan to proceed with multiple plant closures.[19]

The effort led by Mexican autoworkers demonstrates an alternative to the union politics of defeat and decline demonstrated by the UAW leadership. It shows the capacity and potential for autoworkers across borders to issue joint demands, prevent the company from playing one against the other, and lay the foundation to create a genuine international union movement responding to and challenging twenty-first-century neoliberal capitalism.

## ELEVEN

# NAM Transnational Retail and Logistics Operations

On the heels of the 2019 maquiladora strikes, militancy spread into the retail sector. On February 3, workers affiliated with the Sindicato de Casas de Comercio (Retail Workers Union), based in Matamoros, began their own campaign for wage increases and restoration of bonuses that had previously been eliminated.

Workers from Centro Comercial Smart and Centro Comercial Chedraui walked off the job to begin the strike. These were followed by a wave of shutdowns at the Soriana department stores across Matamoros. Twelve hundred workers walked out of six stores on a wildcat strike after their union failed to represent them in negotiations.[1] Shortly after that, workers began a walkout and threatened a national strike at Walmart.

On March 20, 2019, Walmart workers threatened to go on strike across Mexico. Like in the United States, Walmex (Walmart in Mexico) is the largest private employer in the nation, employing over 200,000 workers at 750 stores in 2018 and generating estimated revenues of over $35 billion. About 60,000 workers in Mexico are covered by the charro union Confederación Revolucionaria de Obreros y Campesinos (CROC, or Revolutionary Confederation of Workers and Farmworkers). Like in Matamoros after the successful maquiladora strikes, the initiative of the workers pushed the conservative, company-aligned union to have to put themselves at the front. Thirty thousand other workers were covered by other phony union contracts, while 118,000 other workers were not covered by any contracts.[2]

Workers at stores in Matamoros began to walkout in early February 2019 as the maquiladora strikes spread. Walmart labor stoppages then spread to two other states. Over three thousand Walmart, Super Center, and Bodega Aurrerá workers followed suit in going on strike in Baja California Sur and Colima.[3] The workers demanded a revised contract that included a 20 percent wage increase, a 4 percent sales commission, and an end to various types of problems workers face on the job such as harassment and withheld overtime. The demands then went national.

The strike movement initially involved sixty thousand Walmart workers covered by a union contract, while potentially drawing in the other 118,000 nonunionized workers. According to the CROC union president more Walmart sites affiliated each day leading up to the national strike call.

Walmart had experienced four straight years of 6 percent growth without raising wages. It operates under the names Walmart, Sam's Club, Superama, Bodega Aurrerá, Bodega Expréss, Bodega, and Mi Bodega.[4] Other national retail chains also facing strikes, such as Chedraui (whose workers in Matamoros originally walked out as well) granted wage increases of 16 percent nationally to avoid similar walkouts.

The victory by the workers in Mexico shows how one of the world's largest, most powerful, and most antiunion multinational corporations can be defeated. This serves as an example for the over one million Walmart workers in the United States, whose most militant sections have been trying to organize a union for over a decade.[5]

## NAM Transnational Logistics

Since 1998, much of Mexico's state-owned infrastructure associated with the logistics involved in transportation, infrastructure, and distribution has been privatized. The construction and operation of highways, airports, maritime and land ports, and railroads have been partially or wholly privatized.[6] This has allowed US-based capitalist firms and investors to shift large-scale investments into Mexico to shape and integrate logistics, distribution, and transportation into a North American-wide system that supersedes borders. This allows US capitalists to exert greater control over production and distribution chains within the NAM. In regards to logistics, methods of moving Mexican-based production to US and international markets, there has been increasing investment in the last two decades to facilitate a growing level of cross-border integration. Concurrently, workforces within transnational logistics operations are growing and becoming more synchronized across borders.

For instance, the value of the trade between the United States and Mexico has been increasing each year since the era of NAFTA. From 1994 to 2000, trade grew by 16 percent per year, amounting to about $100 billion in 1994 to $248 billion in 2000. The total volume of trade more than doubled again to $671 billion in 2018, amounting to about $1.8 billion in freight crossing between Mexico and the US daily.[7] The relationship is highly disproportionate, with about 80 percent of Mexico's exports destined for US markets, while the US provided 46 percent of all imports into Mexico (these constitute about 16 percent of total US exports, with Mexico being he United States' second-largest export market in 2018).[8]

The North American model depends heavily on modern logistics infrastructure, including freight transportation and distribution networks (railroads, highways, ports), warehousing, communications, border and customs processing and clearance procedures, payment systems, and other supporting systems. Funding to upgrade these systems has grown over the last decades in proportion to the level of capitalist integration. For instance, US capitalist firms spent a record $1.64 trillion on logistics investments in 2018.[9] In Mexico, the government spent half a trillion dollars on logistics investments between 2006 and 2018.[10] This investment directly benefits the large transnational capitalist cartels, groups, and consortiums that have developed from the womb of the NAM and can rely on their respective states to invest public monies alongside private investors to facilitate their increased profitability.

The most important method of transportation is trucking, which accounts for 70 percent of all freight within North American Logistics, followed by rail, air, water, and pipeline, respectively. The growth of these industries in proportion to increasing trade has also led to an attendant increase and transnational alignment of NAM-based workforces: truckers, air-shipping workers, dockworkers, port workers, warehouse workers, and other integral and aligned groups.

For instance, industrial real estate development in Mexico has been booming in recent years. According to one study,

> The national vacancy rate for industrial real estate in Mexico fell to 4.4 percent at the end of 2018, down from 4.9 percent a year earlier, as the average rent for space ticked up to $4.95 per square foot, from $4.77 in 2017, according to CBRE [real estate firm Coldwell Banker Richard Ellis]. That market tightening occurred as developers were creating about the same amount of new space in both years: 23.3 million square feet in 2017 and 23.9 million square feet in 2018.[11]

Similarly, warehouse space has also been reaching capacity. From 2014 to 2018, the vacancy rate reached a near record low of just over 4 percent while annual effective rent growth ranged between 3.5 percent and 6 percent. Investment in new space has been rising and will likely continue to rise into the foreseeable future.[12]

Recent auto strikes have shown how cross-border supply chain production and distribution can be disrupted. Struggle or disruption of logistics by workers on either side of a border distribution node has also been a factor impeding the movement of goods.

## Trucking

An estimated 80 percent of total goods moved across the border from Mexico to the US each year are moved by trucks. In Mexico thirteen thousand companies operate with over eight hundred thousand truck drivers.[13] Most of these truckers move goods within Mexico and can only cross within three- to twenty-five-mile "commercial zones" inside the United States.[14] Only twenty-five Mexican carriers have long-haul authority in the US across the border, allowing for US trucking companies to expand operations into Mexico.

In the United States, trucking, an estimated 700-billion-dollar industry, moves about 70 percent of all freight and employs more than 7.7 million people, of which 1.7 million are truck drivers (accounting for nearly 6 percent of all the full-time jobs in the country).[15] About 180 US-based trucking companies move about 70 percent of US-bound Mexican freight from the Mexican border to markets within the United States.[16]

The number of trucks crossing the US-Mexico border has been increasing over the last decade, passing through eighty-eight commercial lanes of highway at twenty ports of entry. Two-thirds of the total volume pass through three ports of entry alone: at Laredo and El Paso, Texas, and Otay Mesa, California. Commercial truck crossings climbed 29 percent from 2009 through 2015, when the figure hit 5.5 million.[17] By 2018, there were 6.3 million truck crossings from Mexico to the US, an increase of nearly 17 percent over the previous five years. Trucks hauled a cargo totaling $424 billion across the US-Mexico border in 2018, comprising the largest percentage of NAFTA-based trade.

This has put pressure on the governments to invest in expansion in trucking logistics and for the trucking operations to expand. The penetration of US trucking companies into transborder trucking has been increasing. The Mexican government even privatized road building in Mexico so that private companies can build and directly own highways within their production and distribution zones.[18]

This means that trucked freight is the pulsating arterial node that is the lifeblood of NAFTA/USMCA. Circulating transborder trade (increasingly under the same corporations such as General Motors, Walmart, Home Depot, etc.) is interconnecting and aligning tens of thousands of Mexican and US truckers into one integrated transportation system.

This is also illustrated by the fact that migrant workers from Mexico now comprise a sizeable minority of the US-based trucking workforce in the US, many as members of the International Brotherhood of Teamsters. Between 2013 and 2017, Mexican and immigrant truckers in Los Angeles led fifteen strikes against working conditions and for other rights in the ports of Los Angeles and Long Beach, California.[19]

## Ports

Mexico has 117 ports with enough port capacity to move 530 million tons of goods a year.[20] Much of the operations within ports have been privatized. One port, in Acapulco, is wholly privatized, while the rest have increased the privatization of operation. For instance, private companies typically manage multimodal and container terminals and shipping processes in the port zones.[21]

Between July 2014 and May 2015 over fourteen thousand International Longshore and Warehouse Union workers and the Pacific Maritime Association, the operators of the shipping industry on the Pacific coast, were locked in struggle over intense contract negotiations. There were lockouts and slowdowns over the course of the year, periodically slowing or shutting down all twenty-nine of the ports, which typically handle nearly half of the nation's maritime container trade each year.[22] This is estimated to amount to over $1 trillion a year.[23]

The fear of a strike and shutdown scared the capitalist class, which began to look for both short- and long-term solutions. Most significantly, they considered shifting West Coast unloading to Mexican ports. As one journal reported, "The 2014 to 2015 US West Coast labor crisis reawakened shippers' interests in using Mexican ports as a hedge against disruption north of the border, but the distance, along with inconsistent rail service, from border states have prevented diversions from cementing."[24]

"Inconsistent rail service" also refers to strikes and blockades in Mexico (discussed below), which shows a converging interest between dockworkers and other logistics workers to be conjoined into the same unions, with a common strategy of opposing the use of borders to divide workers against each other.

## Railroads

The privatization of Mexico's railroad infrastructure in 1998 has allowed US operators to extend their control of a growing share of that nation's rail freight system. This has led to an increasingly integrated rail system, in which US operators control the movement of goods across borders. According to one report,

> The network of the smallest Class I railroad in North America connects to the other six Class I carriers, allowing shippers to access sunny Mexican factories from frigid Canada. The railroad has seen high dou-

> ble-digit quarterly intermodal growth, as makers of automotive, white goods and other products have shifted production to Mexico.... The 1,000-plus Mexican manufacturers and roughly 900 Mexican carriers certified under C-TPAT are less likely to be inspected by US Customs, allowing agents to focus their scrutiny on higher-risk cargo movements.[25]

Three major railroad companies control about 94 percent of total freight movement in Mexico. These are Ferromex, a joint partnership between Mexican-based mining conglomerate Grupo México and the US-based Union Pacific, which holds a 26 percent stake (and makes up 46.62 percent of Mexican rail movement); The US-owned Kansas City Southern de México (KCSM) (32.26 percent); and Ferrosur, also owned by Grupo México but operated as a separate entity (14.91 percent).[26]

Ferromex, Mexico's largest railroad operator, moves freight across 8,500 kilometers of track nationwide, and dominates the transport of cars and auto parts from Mexico to US and international markets. For instance, they moved two million cars in 2018, transporting 72 percent of the production from the Chrysler, Ford, General Motors, Honda, Mazda, Nissan, Toyota, and Volkswagen assembly plants interconnected with their network.[27]

For its part, KCSM works with the Mexican Transportación Marítima Mexicana (TMM), a large, Mexico-based, for-profit logistics corporation that operates in twenty-one states and integrates rail and shipping transport and warehousing. KCSM operates 4,238 kilometers of rail lines that transport freight between Mexico City and the northeastern border cities of Nuevo Laredo and Matamoros. Furthermore, KCSM also owns 25 percent of the shares of Ferrocarril y Terminal del Valle de México (Ferrovalle), the largest dry port and intermodal terminal in the country.[28] The railroad company now generates one-quarter of its revenue moving parts and finished goods across the border.

Since 2012, there has been a boom in railroad logistics, especially in relation to auto production. KCSM, for instance, has built the first intermodal network between the two countries. It also operates the only road lines that directly connect the port of Lázaro Cárdenas, Michoacán (the largest and fastest growing port in North America in terms of containerized cargo movement) to the interior of the United States. By 2012, cross-border freight generated one-quarter of its $1.67 billion in revenue, and total volume increased in double-digits between 2012 and 2015.

Union Pacific's cross-border carloads tripled to 9 percent of total freight movement in 2011 and continued on a similar scale the following year. By 2012, transborder freight produced over $1.5 billion in revenue (of a total $15.6 billion that year), a rate that increased each year since 2007.[29]

Increased revenues and profits are a result of the expansion of US ownership and operations deeper into Mexican territory. Other US service companies have followed the rail giants. Progress Rail, a subsidiary of the Caterpillar multinational corporation, is the main railroad supplier and maintenance service provider for the Mexican railroad system, with locations in twenty-nine cities and sixteen states in the country.[30]

The transnationalization of the rail system has brought into alignment over one hundred and ten thousand workers in Mexico and the United States, many of whom work for these same US-based companies. That includes over ninety thousand working north of the border and twenty thousand working to the south.[31]

The importance of logistics to the functioning of the North American capitalist model was demonstrated during a strike of Mexican teachers in 2019. Teachers affiliated with Section 18 of the Coordinadora Nacional de Trabajadores de la Educación (CNTE) in Michoacán went on a month-long strike from December 2018 to January of 2019. The teachers shut down schools across the state and also occupied at least thirty different city halls and camped outside of the government palace in the capital city of Morelia. They demanded the payment of unpaid salaries, benefits, retiree pensions, and the funding of *normalistas* (teacher training schools) going back a year. That amounts to over 5 billion pesos. The teachers and their supporters blocked all major railroad lines extending from the port city of Lázaro Cárdenas. This blockade paralyzed the movement of 180 trains and stranded thousands of containers with more than a million tons of goods valued at 10 billion pesos.[32]

The potency of the blockades had a significant disruption on the economy and sent secondary shockwaves through the supply chains. As one panicked market research company reported:

> The Michoacán teachers' strike will disrupt trade flows and negatively impact growth. . . . Current estimates of lost economic output vary,

> but losses are well into the billions of Mexican pesos. Rail companies and businesses are warning of potential shortages in staple food crops and inputs needed by factories, including auto and steelworks, should rail lines remain shut. While there was a partial lifting of blockades on February 1, amid ongoing negotiations between the union and Michoacán state officials, rail companies continue to report that the bulk of traffic remains halted.[33]

After thirty-five days, the CNTE won their main demands: fully restored pay to some categories of teachers who had their salaries cut (eliminating "tiers"), full payment of annual bonuses for all teachers, and a commitment to dismantle the "education reform" law initiated nationally under the administration of Enrique Peña Nieto, which was designed to break the militant CNTE union.

## TWELVE

# Transnational Agricultural Labor

Migrant labor has become a growing proportion of the workforce in a number of industries in the US economy. Agriculture has historically been the sector most dependent on migrant workers, employing up to three million people per year in the United States. For over a century, the US state has intentionally structured and reproduced populations of undocumented laborers to allow for the maximum rate of exploitation by agricultural capital.

Various forms of labor control have been used to suppress unions, to keep wages depressed, to make work fragmented, temporary, and contingent, and to minimize investment in overall worker safety. Contract labor, braceros and other forms of temporary or seasonal worker-importation programs, and undocumented workers are variations of state-sanctioned disenfranchisement of farm labor.[1]

Most farmworkers are born outside of the United States, primarily in Mexico but also in Central America and the Caribbean. Over half of the workforce is undocumented, although many have lived and worked in the US for over a decade. Agricultural production has become highly concentrated, capitalized, and profitable. The exploitation of a highly skilled, undocumented workforce is the cornerstone of accumulation for this industry and increasingly in others.

Regionally concentrated agro-industrial production and export zones in the United States now dominate national markets and export to international markets. For example, a cluster of producers from five regions in central Washington State supply more than two-thirds of the nation's apples and export about 30 percent of their product internationally.[2] Furthermore, some of the biggest capitalist firms, like the California-based berry company Driscoll's, have transnational operations and produce for international markets. The multinational company sources its products in twenty-one countries and sells them in forty-eight.[3] A large portion of Driscoll's berries, for instance, are produced and picked in the San Quintín Valley of Baja California, Mexico, to take advantage of lower wages—and then exported back to US markets.

## The Opening of Mexican Agriculture

Beginning in 1986, the Mexican government began the process of dismantling the system of price controls, licensing fees, and tariffs and restricting foreign direct investment in agricultural production.[4] This started with the replication of the Border Industrialization Program (BIP) for agriculture, with the intention of creating new agro-industrial export zones in the states of Sinaloa and Baja California to provide for US markets. This maquiladorization of the fields was expanded after NAFTA removed tariffs on agricultural products and deregulated foreign capital operations in Mexico.

As borders became more restricted for migrants and Mexican labor more accessible, some capitalist firms began to shift production south of the border. Borders were first opened for agricultural capital in the 1980s. Part of this process was the government-sanctioned abolition of the ejido system, which eventually incorporated large quantities of relatively less expensive agricultural land into the private market, while the promulgation of NAFTA opened up these markets to foreign capital. The influx of foreign capital investment in land, along with implantation of cutting-edge technology and access to transnational distribution networks and credit lines, eventually pushed out smaller growers and allowed a smaller number of capitalist firms to consolidate and dominate. This rapid liquidation of state protectionist regimes created the space for large grower-shipper companies to penetrate Baja, and eventually regions across Mexico, to partner with local growers in a vertically integrated production chain or supplant them altogether.[5]

By 2007, twelve large agricultural firms (part of the Western Growers Association representing agricultural capital in California and Arizona) expanded operations in Mexico covering forty-six thousand acres and employing eleven thousand workers, primarily in Guanajuato and Baja California.[6] According to a study by the Wilson Center's Mexico Institute,

> Per capita US consumption of fresh fruits rose 30 percent from 1970 to 2010, and consumption of fresh vegetables rose 20 percent. About half of the fresh fruit available to Americans is imported, as are a quarter of the fresh vegetables. . . . About half of the fresh fruit and three-fourths of fresh vegetables imported to the United States are from Mexico.
>
> Mexico exported fresh produce to the United States worth $10.6 billion in 2016, about half fresh fruit and half fresh vegetables. In 2016, Mexico provided 45 percent of US fresh fruit imports (excluding bananas) and 70 percent of fresh vegetable imports.[7]

Furthermore, transnational integration has also seen increased agricultural export across both sides of the US-Mexico border. For instance, US agricultural exports to Mexico grew 48 percent from $12.9 billion to $19.1 billion between 2008 and 2018, comprising about 14 percent of Mexico's total agricultural products. This adds another dimension to the transnationalization of production, as migrant workers in the US, alongside Mexican and migrant Central American labor in Mexico, are at the center of the international production and export complexes. This has become apparent in a number of industries, especially in berries.[8]

Between 2002 and 2017, the value of Mexican berry exports increased 125-fold. The tonnage of Mexican berry exports increased by 130 percent between 2010 and 2017, but the value of Mexican berry exports rose by 230 percent.[9] In Baja California, on Mexico's Pacific coast, a small number of transnational companies, most notably Driscoll's berries, have established an important link in their global commodity chain. They have invested in a berry production system that relies on the exploitation of a large and migrant workforce to pick and pack fruits to then be shipped across the nearby border to US markets. The lack of significant regulation, cheaper land and labor costs, and the state-supported suppression of labor unions have turned the region of San Quintín into a fiefdom for Driscoll's.

## Migrant and Transnational Workers Strike

Over the last decade, there has been increased strike activity along the transnational migrant corridor stretching from southern Mexico to the Pacific Northwest of the United States. The twenty-first-century capitalization of hyperindustrialization of farm production has advanced alongside the maintenance of late nineteenth-century labor relations. Agricultural workers have always resisted superexploitation in the United States and have borne the brunt of some of the most brutal episodes of state and grower repression.[10] The transnationalization of production, and of Mexican migratory labor, has created new conditions for the rise of cross-border agricultural strikes.

Whether agriculture is undertaken by US or Mexican transnational companies, contract farmers or independent growers, berry production in Baja for international markets relies on a labor management system that treats workers as seasonal labor with limited if any labor benefits. Along the North American Pacific coast, this workforce has become comprised largely of Indigenous Mixtec, Triqui, and Zapotec workers, extending from Oaxaca to Sinaloa and from Baja California to Washington state.

Driscoll's poured heavy capital investment into techniques of agricultural superexploitation: speedups through changing day wages to piecework, the measurement of performance through productivity cards, traceability technology to hold individual workers accountable for error, increased surveillance by increasing the rate of supervisors to workers, and shifts to more difficult sheltered production. Most importantly, the company relied on the state government and the existence of charro unions to maintain protection contracts.

This scheme rests on the symbolic construction of Indigenous laborers as migrant workers that is often used to exclude them from access to health insurance and other basic labor benefits as mandated by the law. The workers typically made about $8 a day by 2014, a significant decline and deterioration of wages akin to the maquiladoras. These conditions framed the backdrop to one of the largest agricultural strikes in modern Mexican history.

In March 2015, thirty thousand mostly itinerant and Indigenous farmworkers from Oaxaca went on strike at the massive fifty-mile agro-industrial complex in the San Quintín Valley of Baja California, Mexico. The target was a collection of corporate berry growers called BerryMex, who produce for the US-based Driscoll's, the largest berry distributor in the world.

As one report describes:

> Like modern agribusiness corporations that operate on a global scale, the new labor movement capitalizes on the transnational social and political connections farmworkers and Indigenous organizations have built across the Mexico-US border to advance their claims and cultivate the support of consumers in the United States. The labor strike of 2015 marked a new threshold in the history of farmworkers' labor resistance, resituating the struggle from a regional to a transnational political arena.[11]

These workers had not been passive amid the deteriorating conditions of the reorganization and transnationalization of North American agriculture. There were significant strike movements in 1998, boycotts, and other forms of resistance sustained through kinship networks and relationships developed from previous strike experiences in other regions and through short-lived organizations.

In the San Quintín strike of 2015, they demanded: higher wages, access to a national healthcare system, the end of sexual abuse of women workers by field bosses, and the abrogation of charro union contracts. They formed strike committees in the *colonias*, developed a strategy to get national and international attention, marched to the border, blocked the transpeninsular highway, and built solidarity and support through Indigenous ethnic associations, community mobilization and mutual support, and by establishing contact with social movements in US to call for an international boycott of Driscoll's.

Amid the strike, a new union was formed and a new model used. In this model, union leaders had to be workers, term limits were instituted, relations and connections were developed with migrant worker unions in the US (same workers, same struggle) like the Familias Unidas por la Justicia (FUJ) strike against Sakuma farms, which also grows for Driscoll's (a struggle described in further detail below).

The Alianza de Organizaciones por la Justicia Social, a network of grassroots groups, including Indigenous networks, neighborhood associations, and left-wing political parties, served as the organizational infrastructure for the strike mobilization. Emerging strike leaders were transnational migrants who drew from their experience in the US labor movement. For instance, one central leader of the union named Fidel Sánchez Gabriel had been a participant in the farmworker strikes in Immokolee, Florida.[12]

During the strike, workers blocked major transport hubs, had running battles with police during violent episodes of repression, and faced targeted arrests. The three-month shutdown disrupted berry markets across North America and forced the landowners and the Mexican government to the negotiating table, leading to a raise from 120 to 200 pesos per day.[13]

The newly formed Sindicato Independiente Nacional Democrático de Jornaleros Agrícolas (SINDJA) union ultimately won significant gains in the form of a government-brokered, fourteen-point labor agreement that set new benchmark standards for wages, benefits, and housing rights. Nevertheless, the growers and government immediately backtracked on full implementation of the accords, leading the union to remotivate the call for an international boycott of Driscoll's. Boycott campaigns against the purchase of berries have been conducted from Ensenada to San Diego to Seattle. Meanwhile, SINDJA-organized drives have been extended into several other Mexican states.[14]

The Indigenous Mexican farmworker diaspora across the border in Washington had taken on another Driscoll's supplier, Sakuma Brothers Farms, only two years prior. In 2013, three hundred Indigenous families formed a network among the larger migrant workforce, calling themselves Familias Unidas por la Justicia. After painstaking organizing efforts over four years, including successful boycotts, lawsuits, and walkouts over wages and working conditions; the FUJ constituted itself into an independent union and won a contract in 2017. It has established new benchmark standards for pay, working conditions, and collective bargaining rights in agriculture in the state. Like in San Quintín, they are now spreading their model, showing a path of advance for transnational class struggle.

In 2020, another series of seven strikes broke out among apple packers in the Yakima Valley of Washington State spanning the month of May. The region is one of the largest agro-industrial export zones in the nation, situated at the northern column of the backbone of the same transnational migrant labor corridor stretching up from Mexico. The fruit companies supply multinational corporations that operate internationally.

Yakima County growers produce and export over a billion dollars' worth of fruit each year.[15] Yakima County is the largest apple producing county in the country, providing 60 to 70 percent of apples consumed in the United States. There are over sixty fruit companies in the county, employing over sixty-five thousand workers, including H-2A visa workers, many of whom work and live in poor and highly exploitative conditions.[16]

The strikes were led by a core of highly skilled and experienced agricultural workers who formed strike committees at each location and also coordinated through FUJ. As one newspaper covering the strikes reported, workers at the different plants coordinated solidarity campaigns to build mutual support through integral interethnic networks:

> Hundreds of strike supporters showed up Thursday morning, traveling on foot or by vehicle between plants in a pack that workers started calling "the caravan." They had painted their vehicle windows with messages of support in Spanish. They honked and waved as they drove by. Strikers waved back, held their protest signs higher, and quietly said "Thank you" to each passing vehicle. Rosalina Gonzales was one of those strikers. She's worked at Columbia Reach Pack for 19 years. She does the physically demanding work each day to provide for her children and family, she said.[17]

Many of these workers have lived and worked in the industry for over a decade, aware that their labor not only feeds the nation but has underwritten huge profits for multinational corporations. A breaking point came when the packing shed owners forced the workers to continue at their jobs with inadequate protections and without hazard pay during the COVID-19 pandemic. As one report noted:

> Since Yakima County's first reported case of COVID-19 on 8 March, the region has had the most cases per capita among west coast states. By the end of July, the county had recorded more than 10,000 cases and more than 200 deaths in a population of not much more than 200,000 people. The clusters have been concentrated among health care workers, and in manufacturing, food processing and agriculture, the region's largest employer... Latinos account for 51 percent of confirmed cases.[18]

When the companies refused to recognize and negotiate with the workers over conditions in the sheds, they walked out. The first coordinated job action began at a company called Allan Brothers, and hundreds of others followed suit at Mason Fruit, Jack Frost Fruit, Monson Fruit, Columbia Reach, Madden Fruit, and Cold Storage. The workers had tried to unionize before, but faced fierce opposition from the owners, who had come to exploit the undocumented status of many workers to keep them in line.

Edgar Franks, political director of Familias Unidas por la Justicia, observed that Border Patrol and ICE agents had been used to police workers in the region and prevent them from unionization. As he reported in an interview:

> The threat of repression and deportation is always on the minds of undocumented workers. . . . Because of the racial profiling that goes on, and how aggressive and violent the state is generally, even workers who are citizens live in fear. When we visit the undocumented workers in their homes or in the "labour camps," we need to make sure we don't attract the wrath of the authorities and get workers deported.[19]

Over the course of the four weeks, workers received solidarity and support from the Washington State Labor Council, which raised strike funds, provided legal support, and helped financially sustain FUJ organizers in the region for the duration. As another account described:

> When growers proved recalcitrant despite the pressure, workers increased it by going to the state capitol in Olympia on May 26. There they delivered 200 complaints against Allan Brothers to the Department of Labor and Industries, and held a noisy rally outside the home of Democratic Governor Jay Inslee. "The companies thought they could contain this," [organizer Edgar] Franks explained, "but it put a lot of pressure on them and made the strike a statewide issue."[20]

The companies eventually caved and agreed to negotiate with the workers, who then began the process of consolidating their gains into a formal union drive.

# PART III

# Immigrant Workers: Unionization vs. Criminalization

*They're no longer afraid of la migra; that's a major factor.*

—Ventura Gutiérrez, secretary and organizer with the United Packinghouse Workers Union, quoted in 1989

# THIRTEEN

# New Union Movement Built out of 1986 Amnesty

On November 6, 1986, the US Congress and President Ronald Reagan passed a monumental piece of immigration law known as the Immigration Reform and Control Act (IRCA). This law had two major features. First, it conferred citizenship to about 2.7 million undocumented workers. This partial amnesty extended to those who had lived continuously in the United States since January 1st, 1982, or who worked in the fields for more than ninety days within the two-year period prior to the passage of the new law. The paradigm that informed the bill's passage is captured in a Senate report: "An increase in the immigrant labor force would benefit the owners of those resources that are complements with low-skilled labor."[1]

Even though designed to benefit capital by providing a more stable and long-term workforce, some sections of the capitalist class were concerned about the secondary effects of the implementation of legalization. As the *Wall Street Journal* reported amid IRCA negotiations, "The same [employers] that fear amnesty often fear more the loss of cheap, docile labor provided by the illegal workers." The Journal quoted then-Texas Democratic governor Mark White saying, "'I don't know many businessmen that want it.'"[2] Agricultural capitalists especially feared that amnesty would allow mobility for farmworkers to leave the fields for urban occupations or feel more confident to unionize. The chairman of a major fruit and vegetable grower actively opposed amnesty, lamenting that he feared the "influx of alien, socialistic views" with unchecked immigration (i.e., unionization).[3] Another farm operator said he was "holding his breath" that the amnesty would be struck down so as to keep "his" workers in the field.

To assuage the concerns of businessmen, IRCA also initiated the federal criminalization of labor migration by requiring for the first time that workers show proof of citizenship in order to obtain work in the United States. This seemingly contradictory combination reveals an incipient pattern underlying future policy: the correlation between the control of labor flows in a period of changing transnational economics and the ability for capital to increase the rate of exploitation of deterritorialized labor. This reveals a continuity: from bracero labor to undocumented workers to the state-led construction of an "illegalized" section of the working class.

Two significant features emerged from the IRCA and have shaped the trajectory of immigration politics ever since. The amnesty opened up a period in which hundreds of thousands of immigrant workers joined unions, while the "illegalization" component has led to an incessant escalation of state repression of those without documents.

The passage of the law was proceeded by a period of protest and hardening political divisions over the question of undocumented immigration. It also took place in the context of the North American Free Trade Agreement, which began the process of opening borders for capital and the construction of the North American model of open-market capitalism.

Labor unions were instrumental in the passage of the IRCA, supporting both components of amnesty for existing immigrants *and* criminalization of future crossers. This contradictory position has to be untangled in order to understand both the promise and the failure of rebuilding the labor movement in the twenty-first century.

The national AFL-CIO had opposed immigration since its foundation in 1955 and had called for an anti-immigration law. By 1986, it maintained enthusiastic support for employer sanctions and border enforcement, but it had also begun to support the call for amnesty in previous years. Its opposition to immigration aligned with reactionary and racist forces and policies while business interests were turning to undocumented workers. Its disastrous support for migrant labor criminalization and border closure positioned it directly against the fastest-growing segment and most inherently prounion sector of the working class. Mexican and Central American migrant workers typically had more experience with unions in their homelands and were more likely to be sympathetic and willing to join than their US-born counterparts.[4] In fact, undocumented workers were taking different forms of worksite action beginning in the 1970s, including organizing walkouts and wildcat strikes, but were made vulnerable because of noncitizen status. As one newspaper report noted, "National labor law allows illegal immigrants to participate in union campaigns, but gives them no protection against deportation. Immigrant rights attorneys say employers try to dampen union drives by threatening to report illegals to immigration authorities."[5]

Nevertheless, divisions within organized labor began to emerge in the late 1970s, as migrant workers began to increase as a proportion of the working class, especially in the southwestern states. Undocumented workers had become integrated into various industries over the course of the decade. A series of studies focusing on border cities showed high rates of participation in agriculture, manufacturing, commerce, construction, and service.[6] In response, labor leaders in this region pressured the national AFL-CIO to invest in organizing undocumented workers. Their efforts led to the creation of the Labor Immigrant Assistance Project, which assisted in the formation of immigrant workers' organizing committees.

The California Immigrant Worker Association, for instance, was set up as a kind of proto-union that recruited and cultivated thousands of worker-leaders who then formed a core of operatives that organized in the different jobsites. Other unions, like the International Association of Machinists (IAM), also sent eight full-time organizers into the Los Angeles barrios after undocumented workers organized and led eight hundred of their coworkers on a four-day wildcat strike at an aluminum manufacturing plant in the spring of 1990. Capturing the mood of militancy among the workers, the IAM told reporters, "These people had this thing won before they found us."[7] The successful vote to affiliate brought over a thousand workers into the IAM local. It was one of the largest union representation elections held in the United States in 1990, and the biggest in Los Angeles over several previous years.[8] Wildcat strikes involving immigrant and undocumented workers became more frequent, attracting further attention.

As the *Los Angeles Times* described in a November 1979 article:

> Organized labor, once the nemesis of the illegal alien, has shifted its stance in recent years. A number of unions, including the ILGWU [International Ladies Garment Workers Union], the United Steelworkers, the Teamsters, and the United Auto Workers have begun taking undocumented workers into their ranks. Joe Donahy, the ILGWU's national coordinator, also said that his union advocates amnesty for all illegals in the United States.
>
> "They came here illegally, but so what? [. . .] I don't think the people on the Mayflower had papers either." [. . .] A similar call for amnesty came this past summer from Douglas Fraser, president of the United Auto Workers, who also urged increased efforts to organize the undocumented workers.
>
> George Meany and the man who is expected to succeed him, Lane Kirkland, [also] agreed on the need for amnesty for most undocumented aliens now residing in the United States.[9]

Unions had been suffering serious setbacks over this period. From the Reagan White House to the rise of highly capitalized union-busting law firms to the formation of right-wing think tanks churning out ideological broadsides, ruling-class antiunionism was on the march. Concerted action of the part of the capitalist class to upend and root out unions, coupled with the inherent failure of the AFL-CIO's "business unionism" to defend, workers took at devastating toll.[10]

The rate of unionization has spiraled downward in the United States since the 1980s, from about 30 percent in 1970 to 20 percent in 1980 and to 14.1 percent by 1990, with the private sector suffering the brunt of loss. This decline trend affected all unions except those that positioned themselves to recruit legalized immigrants. In Los Angeles County, which had the largest concentration of undocumented immigrant workers in the nation (estimated at one million in 1987), unions such as the ILGWU (forerunner to UNITE-HERE) and the Service Employees International Union (SEIU) were at the forefront of immigrant inclusion.

As one report detailed:

> Desperate to replenish their ranks, a handful of unions are making unprecedented efforts to recruit urban workers—the fastest growing segment of the workforce—regardless of whether the immigrants are

> here illegally. Los Angeles . . . has become an unofficial organizing laboratory, where new hypotheses are being tested by aggressive, bilingual union organizers. These organizers believe they are participating in the beginning of a national labor resurgence.[11]

Those unions directly rooted in immigrant worker–dense industries or regions took the lead in organizing undocumented workers and to call for an amnesty.[12] They advocated for the broadest scope of inclusion in the legalization and vocalized opposition to the criminalization components of the law. They allocated and mobilized resources and staff to organize within communities to support undocumented workers and their families in advance of the law's passage. These included providing workshops and legal advice, translation, and other necessary steps to prepare for the application process.[13]

For example, the United Food and Commercial Workers Union set up information hotlines and legal consultants for its members, including over four thousand mostly undocumented packinghouse workers.[14] As previously mentioned, the Los Angeles County Labor Federation set up the Labor Immigrant Assistance Project, which included six different centers in different locations in the county located at union offices. These included union halls for the Amalgamated Clothing and Textile Workers, the ILGWU, the International Brotherhood of Electrical Workers, the Laborers' International Union, United Brotherhood of Carpenters, and the United Food and Commercial Workers.[15] Union staff and legal professionals counseled over ten thousand undocumented workers through the amnesty process. They also set up English as a Second Language classes, job training programs, provided legal services and multilingual materials, and offered membership in the California Immigrant Worker Association.[16]

Organized labor also led the campaign to block the agricultural capitalist-led plan to reintroduce the discredited, antiunion Bracero Program into agriculture.[17] At a time when unions had more leverage within national politics, they successfully pressed for the amnesty to be extended into fields instead of a misnamed "guest-worker" program. The United Farm Workers led the campaign to shift public opinion against the ploys of the growers to exclude farmworkers from the amnesty.[18] They filed lawsuits on workers' behalf and assisted farmworkers through the legalization process by setting up statewide centers in proximity to the rural communities where farmworkers were concentrated.[19]

The legalization of the status of these workers increased their mobility, negotiating power, and ability to collectively bargain. The civic components of citizenship do not guarantee labor rights, but they do remove the threat of arrest and deportation. In the years following the amnesty, unions like the ILGWU set up organizing offices in different garment districts across the country, including Los Angeles and San Francisco, California, El Paso, Texas, and Brooklyn, New York, in order to "declare war on sweatshop conditions."[20] In LA, for example, they increased their organizing staff and set out to lay the groundwork to organize the hundred thousand mostly immigrant workers who were the backbone of the city's $6 billion apparel industry.

SEIU launched Justice for Janitors, a nationwide campaign to organize janitorial workers across fifteen US cities. Legalized workers tended to join unions because unions played a role in advocating for their legalization and supporting them in the workplace, and because their legal status made it more likely that they could engage in class struggle activity and collectively bargain with the threat of arrest and deportation removed.

In 1986, the Hotel Employees and Restaurant Employees union launched a multiyear campaign to organize hotel workers in the a densely clustered zone of over 150 hotels that ring the popular theme parks and convention centers in Anaheim, California. They began by sending bilingual organizers to canvass in the Latino neighborhoods where most of the workers resided. After lengthy campaigns that combined boycotts, pickets, and protests at the homes of hotel executives, the union was able to organize master contracts covering all workers.[21]

The boom in unionization was the result of strikes led primarily by immigrant workers who won sizeable gains and demonstrated class power against seemingly insurmountable odds. From 1987 to 1982 a strike of four thousand mostly Latino and undocumented dry-wall workers broke out and spread through Orange, Riverside, San Bernardino, and San Diego counties. A worker-organizer and spokesperson named José Valadez told the *LA Times* in 1987 that a year prior, "organizing the drywallers would have been impossible because many refused to speak out for fear of deportation by the Immigration and Naturalization Service."[22] The wildcat strike called for a pay increase and union recognition.

During the strike, some owners called in the INS but were notified by the agents that their hands were tied because the amnesty grace period had led to a moratorium on raids and sweeps. Without immigration agents to break the strike, the resolve of the construction companies' management crumbled. Construction bosses across the region conceded or offered wage raises to their workers to head off the walkouts at their own companies. This surge of union drives in this period led wages across the board to increase, in some cases doubling or tripling.[23]

The SEIU-led Justice for Janitors campaign won several contracts covering 90 percent of custodial workers across Los Angeles by 1992. By 1995, the SEIU had become the fastest-growing union in the country, with over 300,000 of its 1.1 million members at that time in California alone. The SEIU's rapid growth was also the result of a militant, class-struggle approach and rank and file organizing within the union pushing forth new leadership and strategy. As one observer noted:

> The SEIU's techniques . . . are reminiscent of the 1930s. The Justice for Janitors campaign, for instance, has been marked by street protests and an infamous Century City march in 1990 in which demonstrators were beaten by police.[24]

A surge of post-amnesty strikes also swept through other parts of Southern California as immigrant workers joined into the ranks of organized labor in large numbers. In 1994, strikes and union recruitment campaigns led by the Teamsters and the hotel and restaurant employees union were conducted among mostly immigrant workers at recycling plants, hotels, and manufacturing companies.[25]

Wages and working conditions improved significantly, bolstering industry standards for all workers.[26] There were also significant gendered impacts. For example, 42 percent of the recipients of amnesty granted through the IRCA were female. According to one study, all categories of Latinas experienced wage increases after legalization, from those with little formal education to those with college degrees.[27]

The majority of those who were legalized through the 1986 amnesty were concentrated in three regions representing the relative concentration and regionalization of the undocumented workforce in those years. The largest number were those working in six major cities, four of which are located in Southern California: Los Angeles, Anaheim, Riverside, San Diego, Chicago, and Houston. An additional 150,000 legalizations occurred in agricultural areas of California, and another 135,000 took place in smaller towns and agricultural areas of Texas. This also reflects the fact that the employment of undocumented workers was heavily concentrated in four industries: agriculture, garment manufacturing, hotel work, and the service sector (custodial and landscaping). In those large clusters, the IRCA was followed by substantial increases in unionization rates, even as the overall rate of unionization across other economic sectors continued to plummet.[28]

Since 1986, the number of undocumented workers active in the economy has grown to an estimate of at least eleven million, while tens of millions more have other variations of noncitizenship status.[29] Furthermore, their employment has extended into over a dozen industries and dispersed geographically across the nation, including substantial concentrations in nine of the twelve largest state economies in the US.[30] The history of this trajectory of undocumented workers toward unionization after legalization; the growth, expansion, and profitability of criminalized labor since 1986; and the reconfiguration of the North American economy around borders and migration controls have combined to inform capitalist class opposition to any further legalization or border demilitarization.

# FOURTEEN

# The Political Construction of Illegality

In the mid-1970s, high-ranking officials of the US government began to sound the alarm about the effects of neoliberal capitalist restructuring in Latin America and the likelihood of increased migration. In 1975, Immigration and Naturalization Service (INS) commissioner Leonard Chapman warned of "a vast and silent invasion of illegal aliens."[1] In 1978, former CIA director under presidents Richard Nixon and Gerald Ford and dedicated Cold Warrior William Colby identified crisis-induced Mexican labor migration as a perilous threat to the United States. He said,

> At present, the number of Mexicans illegally in the United States in search of the jobs they cannot find at home is estimated between 5 and 8 million. Among the additional 60 million who will be present by the year 2000 it is obvious that a substantial portion will make their way to the United States. Our border and immigration services will be helpless before this flood, dwarfing the flow that already overwhelms them; the resulting social tensions between the Spanish and English-speaking communities will produce violence, misery, and turmoil.[2]

As the US government helped orchestrate the smash-up of state capitalism in Mexico, Colby then expressed concern that further waves of austerity and unemployment-driven migration posed an even greater threat to the United States than did the Soviet Union.[3] His policy recommendations included a call to increase trade and capitalist investment in Mexico and a labor registration process to channel displaced migrant workers into low-wage sector jobs in the US economy, especially agriculture. By 1982, the

INS was being positioned to increase interior enforcement with an emphasis on policing immigrants in workplaces across a dispersed geographical range across the nation. According to a testimony given on behalf of INS Commissioner Alan C. Nelson,

> Mr. Chairman, we are considering numerous factors involved in our interior enforcement, particularly that which addresses area control. I think all factors have to be considered in the total spectrum, such as the percent of aliens that are currently residing in geographical areas, the unemployment rate in geographical areas, the types of industries that are currently existing in those areas, the lead that our investigators do have on employed aliens in area control. We will have to look at the totality of the circumstances, and then we will direct our resources to an appropriate area. Those are some of the areas that we are looking at."[4]

US military personnel also had a direct role in advising a state restructuring of undocumented migration. In 1983 the Naval War College at the Department of the Navy issued a report titled *Illegal Immigration to The United States: A Growing Problem for Law Enforcement*, which included calls for "employer sanction laws prohibiting hiring of illegal aliens [that] seem the only reasonable approach to true long-term effectiveness . . . [and] a carefully managed temporary foreign worker program to meet the [labor] shortfall."[5] Interestingly, the report also concludes that one possibility to discourage low-wage labor shortages that were filled by undocumented workers was for US businesses to increase wages and improve working conditions across the board, a suggestion brushed aside by policy makers.

While certainly not the first bursts of anti-Mexican racism and anti-immigrant hyperbole emanating from within the US state, these very public fusillades signified a shift in ruling-class orientation coinciding with processes of neoliberal capitalist restructuring in the late 1970s. Beginning with the administration of Democrat Jimmy Carter, the state initiated and incrementally institutionalized a now four-decades-long project of criminalizing labor migration as a method for increasing capital accumulation.[6]

## Free Markets Depend on Unfree Labor

The persecution of migratory workers has now become a permanent and perpetually augmented function of the US state dedicated to migrant and refugee repression, which will be referred to here as the migra-state. The function of this apparatus is the use of law enforcement agents and the border regime and the power these transmit to owners of capital to increase their control over labor. Illegality denies workers basic rights to organize unions, collectively bargain, petition for grievances, or in any way leverage their class power for higher wages, better working conditions, or their political rights. In effect, it also makes them permanent "at-will" workers. Under these conditions, owners deny undocumented workers seniority, promotions, and other benefits of longer-term employment and are not held accountable if they do not comply with labor code or other legal or civil rights when hiring or firing. Over time this constructs a type of unfree labor contained in sectors of the economy where working conditions deteriorate and descend into superexploitation. When workers have virtually no means to resist conditions of exploitation under capitalist relations of production, employers will increase the rate of exploitation (i.e., push wages lower, increase working hours, pay less into workplace protections) to below the point where workers can sustain themselves economically or even physically. Not just the value of their labor but also their health, lives, and family economy are extracted in the process.

The conditions of superexploitation establish wage floors that are so degraded they are typically confined to other undocumented workers. These relations of superexploitation have been structured into and throughout the lower echelon of the economy through the manipulation of immigration policy and enforcement. The state assists the owners of capital in accessing and accumulating substantial amounts of value from undocumented workers. It also allows employers to leverage unfree labor against unions and free labor, serving as a drag on all wages and working conditions. Since undocumented workers have demonstrated their willingness and readiness to engage in class struggle, the migra-state serves as a full-spectrum carceral system, built up over the last four decades to keep transnational workers unfree.

Under the Reagan-Bush administration, the amnesty component of the Immigration Reform and Control Act was a negotiated concession to allow for the introduction of sweeping immigration restriction policies that lay the groundwork for mass criminalization. This included the illegalization of employment and the increase of resources dedicated to border enforcement. As the research and reporting reveal, the way employer sanctions were implemented and enforced had a qualitatively different effect than what was stated. Instead of reducing undocumented employment, it shifted enforcement power to the owner. This gave tremendous power to bosses over their workers, including the ability to police them, threaten them, and fire them at will.

The IRCA also contained a provision that funded the expansion of INS operations and a doctrinal shift of enforcement focus to those crossing the US-Mexico border. Between 1986 and 1995, the budget doubled from $577 million to $1.5 billion.[7] This significant transition initiated the process in which criminalization was extended from the point of employment to the illegalization of presence anywhere within the national territory. This was followed by the expansion of border walls and constant budget increases ever since. This opened the door to an unprecedented build-up of the migrant repressive apparatus and subsequently increased profits through the superexploitation of migrant labor and the creation of secondary industries associated with the criminalization of their presence.

The way repressive measures have been structured and enforced lay bare the class content of immigration enforcement under capitalism. While the benefits of a particular law or policy bestowed upon capitalists in the course of enforcement may not have been intentional in their first iteration, they become guarded and reified once implementation provides evidence of reward. For example, the 1986 IRCA requirement that all workers show proof of citizenship as a condition for employment did not stop undocumented labor migration or prevent employment. In practice, employers, managers, and contractors learned to use the lack of papers as leverage to pay these workers lower wages, eventually restructuring whole industries around the preferred hiring of undocumented labor.[8] Even though the implementation of law may not have the intended effect, the incidental outcomes may still prove beneficial for the economy. In this case, the political representatives of capitalists formalize and maintain these as policies, and state bureaucrats and police agents enforce them accordingly. All aspects of immigration policing, from the border wall to operations of ICE to the construction of detention camps and prisons, fall into this category of failed—yet beneficial—policy. They do not stop migration, but they make it profitable in different capacities.

Throughout the literature analyzing immigration enforcement, researchers constantly characterize failure to achieve stated goals (i.e., stopping undocumented immigration). This conclusion is misguided, as it takes the stated aims of such policy prima facie. Dysfunctionality becomes functionality if you observe the practice from a different angle. After the experience of legalization diminishing employer advantage through loss of control, while criminalization incrementally increased it, owners gradually shifted and aligned their preferences for increased criminalization without a new legalization or comprehensive deportation. Failure became the best option, and, therefore, it became institutionalized as a practiced norm.[9]

Undocumented workers were not collectively ejected from the country or prevented from crossing the border, but rather the value of their labor was stigmatized and degraded through the construct of illegalization. As researcher James Massey understood this historic transition, "discrimination against [undocumented workers] was mandated by federal law." Furthermore:

> Paradoxically, IRCA seems to have yielded the worst of all possible scenarios: undocumented migration persists despite the new law, while wage exploitation and illegal employment practices proliferate. Instead of stemming the tide of undocumented immigrants, IRCA may simply have pushed undocumented migration further underground. Even though it may have increased the penalties to undocumented labor in the United States, many who pay the price are the people least able to afford it.[10]

Legalization also pushed more undocumented workers away from agriculture, which was initially saturated with legalized workers, and into the urban industrial economy.[11] Owners within a range of low-wage and nonunionized industries incorporated this new flow of workers. Since these were newly established relationships under the conditions of illegalization, different industries have replicated the process of leveraging wages downward. With the growth of the undocumented workforce, alongside the restructuring of whole industries that standardized the hiring of undocumented workers, saturation and competition again allowed employers to leverage down wage rates, even to the point of falling below those of agriculture.[12]

The IRCA began a new phase of labor control and repression by shifting enforcement mechanisms to the workplace, granting owners the right to hire and fire undocumented workers thereafter according to their own needs. Employers did this by building opacity into the enforcement process that favored them over their workers. Owners were required to check for proof of citizenship as part of the hiring process, and reporting on undocumented workers was required by law on paper—but voluntary in practice. As William B. Odencrantz, western regional counsel for the Immigration and Naturalization Service (forerunner to ICE), reported at a meeting to the Merchants and Manufacturers Association: "Basically what we are looking for is good faith . . . if you act in good faith . . . you'll probably not have a problem."[13]

Workers were threatened with up to two years in prison if the management reported them. This effectively transferred enforcement into owners' hands, giving them the means to regulate workers based on their status, and it initiated a trend in which employers reported or threatened to report. The act also contained language that allowed the employer to favor citizens over noncitizens in hiring practices, thereby setting up informal instruments for labor control. As one immigrant rights attorney observed, "Employers have the idea that because of IRCA, these people are not supposed to be working anyway, and therefore, they can treat them anyway they want to."[14]

Most significantly, employers were given a potent tool to prevent workers from joining or organizing labor unions. As one report from the period explained:

> The new law adversely influences the ability of unions to organize and protect undocumented workers. If undocumented workers sign union cards, they may be fired but have no recourse. Prior to the IRCA, this would have been an unfair labor practice. Post-IRCA, the union is defenseless: the employer, after all, cannot be asked to reinstate a worker who cannot lawfully work. Thus, employers will continue to hire the undocumented as long as it is suitable—at a low wage—and discharge them when it becomes inconvenient.[15]

The law bound a residual, ineligible population of between 1 and 2 million undocumented workers to their employers, many of whom were hurriedly recruited by opportunistic owners before the passage of the law.[16] The IRCA stipulated that previously employed undocumented workers were not to be subjected to investigation, nor could their employers be sanctioned for their hire. Only if workers tried to change to new jobs would their status be checked.

The sorting out of a segment of legalized workers left a large pool of disqualified immigrants whose ranks continued to grow through an unprecedented surge in undocumented migration in the years after the IRCA.[17] According to one study, an estimated four million people crossed the border in the two years following the amnesty, with most choosing to reside permanently.[18] According to a US Census Bureau report, an estimated 3.3 million undocumented workers were living and working in the country by 1990.[19] The number increased incrementally with an average of up to half a million people crossing the border and entering the workforce each year and an estimated 7 to 8.5 million undocumented migrants in the United States by 2000.[20]

This population incorporated into the workforce through a loophole in the IRCA permitting employers to accept any document that "reasonably appears on its face to be genuine." This enabled the use of easily prepared fake documents and induced the rise of a new industry of labor contracting middlemen. Subcontractors thrived and fanned out through the economy. Employment through their "services" generally cost workers up to a quarter of their (already depressed) wages, paid as a cut for assuming risk.[21]

These practices became normalized in the architecture of post-IRCA practice, and they absolved the owners of responsibility for employing undocumented workers, while also allowing them to fire them at will with no legal recourse. With so many undocumented workers entering into the ranks of the working class, employers felt no pressure to offer better terms of employment and instead leveraged them downward. Without the freedom of movement, workers became trapped in their existing jobs or pushed into irregular and more exploitive jobs.

In practice the law did not stifle continued migration, it only established a back-channel method to police it. It opened an underground economy for undocumented labor and delivered absolute control over employment into the hands of the bosses. Under these conditions, workers were made vulnerable through a confluence of factors: increased state repression of undocumented workers and a trend toward owners exploiting their criminalization to decrease their wages, compensation, and working conditions. According to researchers, the impact became apparent quickly. Workers who migrated between 1983 and 1986, for instance, earned wages 11 percent lower than those migrating before 1983; while those migrating after the IRCA earned wages that were 19 percent lower.[22] This was happening in the larger context of attacks on all workers' wages and benefits. By repressing migrants more forcefully, politicians could justify their actions as being in defense of citizens—a spurious claim that allowed them to suppress wages and working conditions for all workers. This trend worsened in the following years.

## Criminalization Undercuts Labor Conditions for Undocumented Workers

Before 1986, there was no penalty for hiring an undocumented worker. Previous immigration policy was carefully crafted with an eye toward guarding access for capitalists to this population of workers.[23] After the passage of the IRCA, owners began to systematically lower undocumented workers' wages. The leveraging of illegality led to decreased labor costs, higher profits, and, therefore, an expanding market and internally driven competition to hire as much undocumented labor as possible. This reached a point where whole industries, tiers, and subdivisions emerged in the economy comprised of degraded migrant labor.

While there was some risk attached to companies that knowingly hired undocumented workers through skeletal and scarcely deployed enforcement regimes, the benefits far outweighed the costs. Furthermore, increased savings in labor cost and profits compelled other competitors within an industry to follow suit in order to remain viable. Massive cuts to labor costs, the single largest expense for any firm that relies on labor exploitation, and the lowering of wage thresholds for other categories of legal employment, provided a generalized benefit for capitalists.

Undocumented labor was rendered the cheapest, less costly than citizen labor, legalized workers, and even captive guest-worker labor. Furthermore, the systematic superexploitation of migrant labor became a factor of accumulation within the North American model, sprouting secondary and tertiary markets tied to both employment and enforcement.

Criminalization expanded through the implementation of hundreds of laws, the fortification of borders, introduction of war-zone technology and military theoretical modeling, and the multiplication of armed immigration police from the border into the interior.[24] In the workplace, it has included episodic raids and audits that have led to arrests, detention, and deportation.

These measures neither stanched migration flows, nor did they lead to increased wage benefits for US-born workers. Instead, they degraded the value of migrant labor upon entrance into the economy.[25] One study even observed how actual enforcement levels periodically dropped when demand for migrant labor increased, even as funding for the machinery of enforcement was increasing overall![26] The 1986 law began this process and inaugurated the ritualized practice of increasing and augmenting border enforcement and immigrant repression every year since.

Militarization proceeded with the implementation of Operation Blockade in 1993 and Operation Gatekeeper in 1994. These led to the expansion of the physical border wall, the deployment of military technology and battlefield strategy, and more extreme and lethal acts of violence and repression.[27] The passage of the Illegal Immigration Reform and Immigrant Responsibility Act in 1996 increased funding and personnel for the Border Patrol, allowed for deportation of migrants without judicial review (expedited removal) and incorporated police into immigration enforcement.

Other policies focused on depriving immigrants of access to social services and benefits, further defining the state-directed process of illegalization. The Personal Responsibility and Work Opportunity Reconciliation Act of 1996 (a component of the Welfare Reform Act) restricted undocumented workers from accessing any federal programs or benefits. The Antiterrorism and Effective Death Penalty Act of 1996 declared any immigrant to be retroactively subject to deportation if they were charged with a crime and significantly expanded the range of crimes requiring mandatory detention. This set off the construction boom that spawned the private, for-profit detention industry.[28]

After the attacks of 9/11, the US Congress unanimously passed the USA PATRIOT Act, which allowed immigration agencies the power to deport immigrants without requiring a hearing or any evidence if they were deemed a national security threat. Subsequent laws have further built up and financed an immense immigrant repressive apparatus, including: creation and expansion of agencies such as ICE (the Homeland Security Act of 2002), extending the border wall (the Secure Fence Act of 2006), and further exponential growth funded through budget allocations.

If the intention was to curtail migration, these measures failed. Migration rates continued to rise and only waned during the Great Recession of 2007 to 2009, when the US economy experienced its second-deepest contraction in its history.[29] Net migration flow from Mexico to the United States in 2010, for instance, reversed, with more leaving the country after facing unemployment.[30] Economic crisis and the lack of jobs discouraged and decreased border crossings, illustrating the correlation between available work and patterns of migration.

Instead, the main impact of the policies shifted to the workplace. In proportion to the criminalization of migrant labor, employers increased the rate of exploitation. The findings of researchers Douglas Massey and Kerstin Gentsch looked at census data to show wage divergence between "native-born Mexicans" (US-born citizens of Mexican descent) and "foreign-born Mexicans" (immigrant workers, documented and undocumented) in relation to increasing criminalization of cross-border migration:

> [The] wages of both native and foreign-born Mexicans [in the US] rose steadily and in parallel from 1950 to 1970, with both series roughly doubling in real value over the two decades. After 1970, however, the two curves began to diverge. Whereas the real wages earned by native Mexican Americans rose by 11 percent between 1970 and 1990, those earned by foreign-born Mexicans fell by 20 percent; and when wages began to rise more rapidly for native-born Mexican Americans during the boom of the 1990s, the earnings of Mexican immigrants remained flat, thus widening the gap. . . . By 2000 the differential [between the groups] was 62 percent, and on the eve of the Great Recession in 2007 it stood at 78 percent.[31]

This widening gap had no correlation to productivity, quality of work, or other factors intrinsic to the workers themselves, but rather "this shift in the structure of US labor was driven by changes in US immigration policy, which criminalized hiring of undocumented migrants while accelerating both border and internal enforcement."[32] In fact, comprehensive research has shown that the productivity of migrant labor even contributed to the wage increases of native-born workers when the two groups worked together in similar jobs.[33] While the high productivity of immigrants can translate into wage increases, when combined with existent racial and immigrant-status discrimination, the benefits incidentally skew disproportionately toward US-born workers. Immigrant workers have also been more willing to unionize, which, when it occurs, will typically push up the wage floor across a whole industrial sector for all workers, regardless of nationality or status.

Criminalization crystallized a new algebra of exploitation into the class relations of the workplace, based on the maintenance of a state of permanent repression and the psychology that it inevitably engenders in both benefactors and victims.

Immigration enforcement has normalized into a low-intensity conflict. In practice, it amounts to the perpetual targeting of a small percentage of selected populations to establish fear of detention and deportation as a real and credible threat for all undocumented people. This renders two symmetrical conditions that are optimal for exploitation. First, in the face of full-spectrum policing, fear of arrest, deportation, and family separation, undocumented workers learn to police themselves as a self-preservation mechanism. They modify their behavior, minimize their movement, and lower social expectations in the face of a pervasive and omnipresent threat. In a workplace setting, owners parlay this inflicted vulnerability into a relationship of control and degradation.

Working conditions decline as undocumented workers experience a wide range of discriminatory practices inside the workplace, including wage theft, reprisals for a range of otherwise legal actions, absence of necessary protective measures and equipment, denial of collective bargaining and rights to join a union or to petition for grievances, predatory subcontracting, unpaid overtime, erratic scheduling, denial of worker's compensation or benefits, refusal of breaks, and a host of others. As one researcher explained, the conditions of criminalization logically lead to abuse:

> If the person who seeks to take advantage of the migrant understands this dynamic, he or she can feel relatively assured that the migrant will not report his crime to any law enforcement authority. Thus, there are four steps in the deportation threat dynamic: (1) an unauthorized migrant seeks, and often finds, employment; (2) a person, such as an employer... assumes the migrant is unauthorized; (3) the person takes advantage of the migrant by committing wage theft or another workplace violation,... (4) the migrant does not report the crime to law enforcement... [E]ach step in the process is guided by a logic informed by the threat of detection, arrest, and deportation of the unauthorized migrant.[34]

Illegalization has created the lowest wage floors within labor markets, concentrating undocumented workers into economic sub-tiers in and across industries and geographies. The models of repression push undocumented workers out and away from most locations of the legal, formal economy and the public sphere, encouraging concentration in those areas least policed and within industries that have since refashioned themselves to be dependent on migrant labor.

This has created a semi-formalization of their employment and coincides with patterns of diminished enforcement and normalization. One study shows how the rhetoric of aggressive enforcement was replaced with a model of "conciliatory regulation" and eventually "cooperation," as the INS redirected its enforcement efforts away from employers and toward immigrants.[35] Enforcement of the sanction regime decreased as undocumented workers increased as a percentage of the workforce. "The level of enforcement tapered off, falling to about 2,000 cases completed in fiscal year 2002, down considerably from the almost 8,000 in fiscal year 1998."[36] Meanwhile, the number of deportations skyrocketed.

Over time, immigrant workers have become increasingly subdivided and isolated from other sections of the working class where they compete with each other for work.[37] Within these marginalized economies, employers benefit from disarticulated labor. Without mechanisms for collective self-defense, conditions for superexploitation flourish.

Capitalist firms have since combined to create political alliances to lobby for legal means to access steady pools of controllable labor under these demonstrable conditions, even as immigration repression has incrementally increased in society as a whole.[38] In this way, immigration policy proposals have evolved into wide-ranging laundry lists based on different sectoral needs of the capitalist class. These interests even become contradictory within the sprawling complex of migrant repression, for instance, as the profiteers from labor repression jockey for position with and against those looking for access to cheap labor.[39]

Immigration policy and practice along these lines have created observable and distinct centers of production cynically referred to and understood as being "immigrant jobs." These include agriculture, landscaping, construction, domestic work, in-home care, hospitality, food service, cleaning service, meat production, light manufacturing, and various informal economies.

Another consequence of fortifying the border was to increase permanent immigrant settlement. Temporary or "shuttle migration" diminished, and the representation of women and children in the migratory flow increased as families reunited north of the border in larger numbers.[40] This began the establishment of larger working-class communities. It also spurred the growth of mixed-status families, with parents working decades without papers while their children received birthright citizenship. Furthermore, migrants began to migrate to nontraditional destinations. With enforcement concentrated in the US-Mexico border region, many migrants moved out of the Southwest and into different parts of the country.[41]

Undocumented immigrant workers settled and raised families, grew in numbers and dispersed across the country. They were ensconced in the political and economic realities of being part of the working class in the United States, while also facing a harsh parallel reality of being persecuted by the state through a recently constructed regime of illegalization. In the decade after the amnesty, many hoped to follow in the footsteps of their predecessors by gaining citizenship and joining unions, replicating the conditions that existed for the last amnesty and surge into organized labor. As one study observed:

> as the settlement process progresses, a community develops among migrants in the country in which they work, leading to an extended time horizon. Settlement lengthens the shadow of the future, increases social networks in the location of work, and increases the availabil-

> ity of information for migrants—factors that facilitate organization. Unions may view migrants as sociopolitical actors and potential union members at that stage when the settlement process sets in for migrants and a shadow of the future in the country of work develops.[42]

By the late 1990s, it appeared that this was on the cusp of happening. The national AFL-CIO reversed course in opposing unauthorized immigration and concluded its long arc toward immigrant justice. The labor federation shed its age-old hostility and repositioned itself to support and incorporate several million more undocumented workers through the call for a new amnesty.

# FIFTEEN

# The Deformation of Immigration Politics

In supporting the repressive aspects of the IRCA, the union leadership believed the state would be neutral and that criminalization and border enforcement would stem the arrival of further migration and protect their jobs. They were wrong on all fronts. The politicians within both parties prioritize the interests of the capitalist class and therefore were more responsive to their long-term needs, even while appearing to be responsive and judicious in crafting the language of the laws. Through implementation over time, where public scrutiny recedes, we can observe the class basis of the practical application of law in how it favors the interests of one class over another.

In the case of the IRCA, the biased practice reveals an emerging consensus within the owning class in favor of keeping the channels open for migrant labor flow into different industries, even while rhetorically clamoring for the need for more border enforcement. This duplicitous approach pushes the opposition, in this case the union leadership and liberal sympathizers, to unwittingly stake out even more right-wing and harsh positions calling for more restriction, when it appears the current regime is failing.[1]

The state's adroit and biased approach distorts the issue and creates toxic and self-defeating political alignments, with organized labor and far-right xenophobes forming the opposition to open borders. Meanwhile big business and capital, the beneficiaries of labor criminalization, get to shape their own version of "open borders" by maintaining access to undocumented labor while simultaneously undermining the conditions for solidarity and unionization. The capitalist class learned an important lesson about the relationship between amnesty and unionization from the IRCA, namely, that legalized immigrants join unions. This explains why any further considerations for amnesty disappeared from later immigration reform proposals.

The restructuring of US labor markets took place in a context in which neoliberalism became the governing orthodoxy within both political parties during the full implementation of the North American Free Trade Agreement. The radical top-down reorganization of capitalism and the beginning of the North American model created a transnational and criminalized migratory working class while opening borders for capital in a way that produced unprecedented profit margins. Organized labor and its liberal-minded attachés remained beholden to an outdated mode of national capitalism, even as capital internationalized. So while the amnesty component of the IRCA opened a path toward union expansion and provided a model for the benefits of class unity and international solidarity, it also contained the seeds of organized labor's further decline and sidelining within the political battles that lied ahead.

Immigrant inclusion advocates within the AFL-CIO pushed forward, calling for another amnesty in the late 1990s. At their 2000 convention, their efforts culminated with a resolution calling for a second amnesty, full labor rights for people regardless of immigration status, *and* the full enforcement of employer sanctions against companies that knowingly hired undocumented workers. This glaring contradiction was captured at the convention in the muddled words of then-president of the Hotel Employees and Restaurant Employees union, Jon Wilhelm: "We have not called for open borders . . . [but] . . . everyone understands that this is a different world than it was years ago."[2]

Even as the state was transforming the border into an open portal for the free movement of capital, while reinforcing it only as an instrument for migrant labor control and repression—a process that contributed to the decimation of unions on both sides of the border—these leaders continued to accept migrant criminalization. This left them blinkered and disarmed in the face of what was about to come.

By 2000, it was estimated that between 6.5 and 8.5 million more undocumented workers had crossed into the United States, creating an even larger pool of workers than before the last amnesty.[3] The previous experience of legalization leading to new infusions into organized labor and gaining higher wages and more negotiating power led the owners of capital to make a hard turn against another amnesty. Instead, they called for policies to procure access to controllable, unfree, less mobile, and disposable labor with no access to citizenship. This was the culmination of lessons learned, a consolidated, class conscious reaction, and a direct response to the AFL-CIO's call for a new amnesty beginning in 2000.[4]

After the election of George W. Bush in November 2000, the Republicans now opposed a new "blanket amnesty" in favor of a "labor path to citizenship" through an expanded guest worker, or neo-bracero, program. Through various iterations in congressional committee process, this approach further whittled down access to legal status to fewer recipients—who only qualified after years of work. By the end of the year, Democrats in Congress retreated from and abandoned support for a new amnesty and moved into line behind Republican calls for a guest worker approach.[5]

Now in the driver's seat, Bush and congressional Republicans scrapped plans for "a path to citizenship" altogether, opening the door to wide-scale criminalization of those undocumented workers already in the country. In July 2001, for instance, State Department spokesman Richard Boucher said that the Bush administration was aiming a guest worker program at Mexicans to assure "safe and orderly migration," and that any talks on changing the status of illegal workers already in the United States would come later. Mr. Boucher denied the administration would consider "some kind of 'ollie, ollie in come free' amnesty."[6]

This period of transition toward creating and maintaining permanent sections of criminalized labor also coincided with the astronomical growth and consolidation of power of finance capital in the neoliberal period. For instance, investment bankers like Warren Buffet began buying up industrialized sectors of the economy whose profitability was reinvigorated by migrant labor in the 1990s. His firm, Berkshire Hathaway, Inc., began investing in carpet mills in northwest Georgia, a $12 billion industry in a region known as the "carpet capital of the world," after thousands of Mexican migrants replaced an aged-out, mostly white workforce. This process of "Mexicanization" of the workforce followed by patterns of capitalist reinvestment "spread from the meat processors of Kansas, to the poultry centers of Arkansas as three million Mexican workers . . . swarmed over the border to fill gaping labor shortages."[7] The death knell of amnesty was signaled later in the year after the attacks of 9/11 and the hard right-wing and xenophobic shift in US politics.

Four days before the attacks of September 11, 2001, the AFL-CIO officially announced a broad call and movement for a second amnesty. The call kicked of a national campaign to replicate the symbolism and language of the civil rights movement, in what was called the Immigrant Worker Freedom Rides. This campaign gained momentum at the same time that sectors of the ruling class seemed open to negotiation for some kind of regularization of undocumented labor. For instance, in his 2004 State of the Union speech, then-president George W. Bush even proposed granting three-year renewable work visas to the estimated 8 to 10 million undocumented immigrants currently living and working in the United States.

The Bush administration, which initially entertained support for a second partial amnesty in exchange for a new Bracero Program, instead retreated and reversed course as the US ruling class and state abruptly changed direction after 9/11. After the attacks, the US government shifted the state to war footing. While the invasion of Afghanistan was being orchestrated abroad, the Department of Homeland Security was quickly engineered into existence as the juggernaut of domestic repression—from migrants and refuges to political dissidents.

Muslim and Arab migration was curtailed, and those in the country were scrutinized, arrested, and deported.[8] These practices were followed by expansion of the detention system, the extension and further militarization of the US-Mexico border wall, and the arming and unleashing of ICE across the country. The trajectory of brutal repression reached an apex with the introduction of the Sensenbrenner–King Bill, which would have elevated undocumented migration to the status of a felony-level crime.

The introduction and passage of this bill by the House of Representatives in December 2005 was meant to defeat and disperse the second pro-amnesty movement but failed. Instead, it provoked a six-month immigrant worker uprising and outpouring of opposition. Between January and May 2006, several million workers and their families and supporters carried out massive protests, strikes, walkouts, and boycotts. The entrance of the immigrant working class into the fray of class struggle sent shockwaves across the US political system. Facing the new surge in immigrant rights movement—which could potentially grow beyond an amnesty into a revival of class struggle against the neoliberal project—the state went on a brutal offensive.[9]

The Bush administration turned ICE loose against the workers' movement, and it carried out several months of military-style raids at hundreds of workplaces across the country in a highly orchestrated and publicized campaign. Subsequently, the war on immigrant labor that began under Bush was intensified and expanded under Obama and Trump, signifying the consensual end of amnesty as a negotiable political idea for the US capitalist class.

In the face of a xenophobic and anti-immigrant onslaught shrouded in the rhetoric of ongoing war and national security, the AFL-CIO leadership buckled and retreated from its call for amnesty. As the brutal raids were actually *accomplishing* the act of repressing undocumented workers in the workplace and the movement for another amnesty—something the unions had been actively calling for—the leadership remained quiet and abandoned the immigrant workers as they were being rounded up and deported around the country.

Claiming to support migrant workers while also continuing to call for their exclusion ultimately bound and gagged organized labor. By accepting and defending the toxic logic of labor illegalization, the union leadership was caught flat-footed and effectively sidelined as the state responded to the greatest and most important upsurge of working-class struggle in recent history.

This fatal flaw opened the door to the unprecedented expansion of the state repressive apparatus, a deadly border wall, austerity, and a reactionary right-wing lurch in politics that has paved the way for the reinvigoration of a neofascist right on a national scale. Coincidentally, it also paved the way to the continued decline of unionization into the third decade of the twenty-first century.

## Criminalization as a Pillar of US Capitalism

Rather than retreating in the face of globalization, the state has become a more naked instrument of class rule by aggressively suppressing labor mobility and closing off access to citizenship for millions of people to maintain an artificially high rate of exploitation of their labor. Through the normalization of illegalization, the state has also created opportunities for capital to construct and profit from a secondary set of extractive industries tied to migrant repression. After three decades, the US state has brought into existence the most elaborate, formidable, and authoritarian regimes of repression in modern history.

At the core of the NAM is the ability of the capitalist class to extract more surplus value from labor by increasing the rate of exploitation through the criminalization of migration. Within full-fledged neoliberalism, in which all can be privatized and commodified as an appendage to state policy, criminalization has spawned secondary and tertiary industries and markets, which has further spurred investment capital to seek out and make rational further possibilities to profit at the intake, detention, and expulsion points of migrant repression.

The largest, richest, and most powerful sectors of capitalism are now invested directly or indirectly in the illegalization of labor at the point of production through the maintenance of illegality. Auto production, agriculture, meat-packing, construction, hospitality and other forms of service, and manufacturing are only some of the industries that have restructured their productive capacities or employment practices to access and exploit undocumented labor.

Furthermore, the high profit margins emanating from this form of labor exploitation has attracted and led finance capital to invest large sums into newly generated industries that have emerged as outgrowths of criminalization, including defense industries, information and technology, surveillance, and detention construction. Criminalization has spawned products and services now circulating through national and international markets.

A recent study documents the unchecked and towering growth of the immigrant repressive apparatus in the United States.

> Budgets have more than doubled in the last 15 years and increased by more than 6000% since 1980.

> This has created a seemingly limitless market for border-security corporations. . . . [It is projected] that this will be a $52.95 billion market by 2022.[10]

According to an estimate based on this data, the border security industry will have more than doubled in value from approximately $305 billion in 2011 to $740 billion in 2023.[11] This unchecked behemoth infrastructure with over sixty thousand armed agents and support personnel now extends from the border into every corner of the country.[12] These are also assisted by thousands of police officers from eighty-nine police jurisdictions across twenty-one states that currently have 287(g) agreements allowing for their participation in ICE operations.[13]

These forces hunt, retrieve, detain, and deposit people into a sprawling complex of at least 637 known detention centers spread across the country and an unknown number of black sites.[14] A report by the Economic Policy Institute concludes, "A comparative analysis of 2018 federal budget data reveals that detaining, deporting, and prosecuting migrants, and keeping them from entering the country, is the top law enforcement priority of the United States."[15]

Rapid and aggressively implemented changes have produced an observable qualitative shift in national priorities toward securitization, resulting in authoritarian impulses, technological shifts toward social control, and enhanced capacities for repression—all under the rubric of "national security." According to one comprehensive study,

> Since 9/11, the United States has gradually moved away from nationality-based policies toward a redesigned immigration enforcement machinery that is conceived, driven, and funded with the central goal of advancing national security. It has resulted in the creation of a new Cabinet agency, the Department of Homeland Security; the creation or expansion of vast databases for the collection and analysis of information; new life for long-authorized but languishing initiatives; and the growth of a new generation of cooperative relationships between federal, state, and local law enforcement agencies.[16]

In a relatively short period of time, we have seen exponential growth in migrant enforcement industries. The fastest growing branch of capitalism, the tech industry, has become a major player in the criminalization industries. As of 2018, ICE had established contracts with over two hundred tech companies, including the giants Microsoft, Amazon, and Dell.[17]

As one recent report revealed,

> Companies that sell ICE access to vast amounts of data collect this data about people from a variety of sources. These sources include electoral registers, the census, local, state, and national online newspapers, sex offense registries, web cookies, email trackers, smartphone apps and third-party trackers, companies you interact with online and offline, social media sites, online quizzes, surveys, prizes, financial companies, other data companies, and many other sources. Analytics companies market their ability to make sense of large data sets and to "see the people behind the data."[18]

In one example, the software corporation Palantir received $1.5 billion in federal government contracts for developing an "Integrated Case Management System," which accumulates, stores, and integrates large data sets to help ICE agents in the field become more efficient and effective in identifying and deporting undocumented people.[19]

There has also been a boom in capitalist investment in border enforcement, including a boom in contracts for technology and equipment from defense industry corporations such as Lockheed-Martin, Boeing, Defense Support Services, General Dynamics, and General Atomics. Major universities across the country provide studies and research, AT&T, Comcast, and Konica Minolta provide telecommunications and photo equipment and services, and over a thousand other capitalist firms offer "an array of goods and services including vehicles, food, furniture, housekeeping, video recording equipment, and leasing" to the US Customs and Border Protection.[20] These examples illustrate the scale of growth of the migra-state and how deeply intertwined migrant repression of workers has become with the operations of US capitalism in the twenty-first century. That this whole edifice teeters on the backs of migrant labor, and further depends on the stratification, segregation, and weakening of organized labor as a whole, shows how vulnerable it can become when workers unite against it.

**PART IV**

# Opening the Border through Class Struggle and Solidarity

*Immigrant workers have always been... part of the labor history of the United States, the new blood, the replaced spark plugs, the fresh air that reignites the energy of a conservative and exhausted worker's movement.*

—Mexican labor historian Arturo Santamaria Gómez

SIXTEEN

# The New Movement against Borders

There are multiple crises facing working people internationally, including unprecedented social inequality, waves of global pandemic, economic recession, climate crisis, the reemergence of fascist movements, the rise of walls and anti-immigrant regimes, and the perpetuation of war. In the United States, there have been the reemergence of strikes, a Black Lives Matter uprising that has reverberated internationally, and the emergence of a movement against border walls and immigrant repression. All of these crises, and their negations, intersect at the point of class struggle.

Capitalism is undergoing multiple crises, and its state managers can only respond by intensifying methods of exploitation, violence, and conflict in order to maintain accumulation. The international criminalization of migration—at its most defined and systematic form in the United States—results in the superexploitation of transborder people through legally sanctioned repression, detention, and terrorization by an expanding wing of the repressive state apparatus—the migra-state.

This refers to an expanding public-private complex of migrant repression: The Department of Homeland Security, Immigration and Customs Enforcement, Border Patrol, the physical and virtual walls, an array of surveillance technologies, checkpoints, databases, detention centers, prison camps, and affiliated local police. The complex has been underwritten and nurtured by both political parties in the United States and executed by the state regardless of which party has been in power, thereby representing its instrumental role within the functioning of capitalism.

The movement against state violence is being drawn into closer proximity to the reality of this system. In recent years, human and worker rights activists have seen how the scale of repression has transmogrified into barbarism: agents killing migrants and refugees at the border with impunity, whole families held in detention centers or forcibly separated and locked into makeshift prison camps and made to endure torture, forced medical procedures, and psychological abuse.[1] In cities around the country, agents terrorize communities, disappearing people from the streets, homes, and workplaces.[2] People are snatched from hospital beds; kids are left abandoned without support. Furthermore, state agents routinely target workers attempting to organize in the workplaces, community activists, and political dissidents. The propensity and scale of violence has produced a qualitatively different reality for noncitizen society, one that shares some characteristics of state violence experienced under fascism.[3]

Therefore, the issue of labor migration has become bound up into two contradictory components of one whole: the future of organized labor is dependent on expanding rights for migrants, while the future of capitalism is dependent on curtailing them. Both cannot proceed in parity but only in conflict with the other. At the present, these forces are greatly imbalanced, with state repression expanding into a twenty-first-century behemoth and the organized labor movement at one of its lowest ebbs in history.[4]

Nevertheless, the depth of the crisis and recurring eruption of working-class struggle, and the rise of a new socialist consciousness and movement in the United States, shows the potential to shift the poles. The abolition of the migra-state and the rebuilding of a new labor movement, one with transformative politics and a class-struggle orientation, will require the conscious building up of social forces and organizational capacity to achieve its goals. This will require new formations of a socialist left that work directly in existing unions (or by organizing new ones), in the working-class communities, and in the streets to provide the critically needed ranks that can aggregate and coalesce the social forces necessary to open the border.

While there is no precise equation for opening the border, the process will need to develop and evolve across three dimensions: organizing campaigns to overturn and abolish the multifarious regimes of migrant repression, building labor solidarity within and across borders, and forming political organization that is ideologically equipped to coalesce and direct working-class power through social movements and political campaigns against the pillars that uphold the capitalist mode of production—including bordered capitalism.

## Opening the Border Means Dismantling the Migra-State

The fight to open the border unequivocally supports the free movement of poor, working-class, and refugee peoples across borders, as well as the guarantee of all attendant rights currently restricted to territorially based citizens. It rejects the embedded reactionary logic that migrants are an inherent threat and challenges the unquestioned rights of capital embedded in misnamed free-trade agreements (FTAs) by recognizing their destructive impact on unions, wages, and working conditions for workers on an international level.

Like FTAs do for capital, the movement for open borders seeks the extension of universal rights across national boundaries. In the case of labor migration, it means full and equal transborder human rights, labor rights, and democratic and civil rights.

Decriminalizing labor migration requires the overturning of the regime of laws and policies and physical structures that sanction state violence. It necessitates the delegitimization and demolition of the apparatus that has been constructed solely to obstruct, disrupt, oppress, and control a stratum of the working class who are denied the legal means to cross borders.

The machinery of state violence has to be dismantled. This begins with the demilitarization the border, the removal of the walls, checkpoints, and other antihuman technologies aimed at transborder populations. It necessitates the abolition of the assemblies of armed agents of the Department of Homeland Security and the barbaric complex of detention centers and concentration camps.

Furthermore, abolition must then extend into the architecture of segregation and labor repression that holds hostage millions of disenfranchised workers within the economy. A growing number of industries and workplaces have been sub-tiered with immigrant labor through the state-sanctioned suppression of their wages, conditions, and employment options, creating what are now commonly believed to be "immigrant jobs." These have been further structured with the introduction of employer-empowering checks and controls such as E-Verify, I-9 audits, and other antimigrant data-collection, surveillance, and other information-gathering systems. Opportunistic capitalists and managers originally mastered the use of these tools for labor superexploitation compelled their competitors to follow suit, carving out whole sectors and geographies of the economy.[5]

Opening the border requires the eradication of these regimes and other explicitly antiworker and union-busting methods and the extension of the rights to unionize and collectively bargain. This is something immigrant workers have shown a propensity to support, and that is imperative for the advance of US unions and the labor movement. The US legal and justice system cannot be relied on to achieve these goals, as they have been designed and ingrained by centuries of practice to function under the premise of the sanctity of capital accumulation and profit over labor. From the district attorneys to the judges, and from the legislators to bureaucratic appointees, policy makers and policy executors operate under the premise that the functioning of capitalism, i.e. (the exploitation of labor in all legitimated forms), is the "normal affair of things."[6]

As migrant labor has been functionally necessary for the US economy as a form of labor reproduction, the perpetuation and maintenance of disenfranchised labor demonstrates its political function. There is precedent for creating legal pathways to citizenship for migrant workers, for example, amnesty and other methods to attain legalization. These have historically led to worker integration, democratization, and unionization, which in turn increase workers' negotiating power and shifts the balance toward increased class struggle as workers go on strike to retain a larger share of the value they produce.

As a result of its essential function, bordered capitalism no longer accepts labor integration as a permissible option or negotiable item. Migrant labor criminalization has become an objectified and operational branch of capitalist accumulation, such that the state has become the full-time manager of its reproduction to sustain capitalism. Under the system of capitalism, "freedom" for both capital and labor mobility cannot coexist, as this model of accumulation is dependent upon explicit and legalized forms of labor repression, control, and disorganization. This existential contradiction means that labor can only free itself through struggle, ultimately by abolishing the capitalist mode of production and replacing it with workers' democracy and socialism. Therefore, reforming the migra-state while the capitalist mode of production is intact *is not possible*; so dismantling and abolishing the migra-state requires full-scale confrontation with the capitalist mode of production itself.

In recent years, we have seen the emergence of abolition movements. The Black freedom uprising has produced and reinvigorated movements to defund and abolish the police along with the prison industry. There has also been a surge of support behind a nationwide campaign to abolish ICE and to close the detention centers and refugee concentration camps. This historic reckoning with state violence through policing and incarceration—that disproportionately target Black and brown working-class people—exposes the racist and class nature of the state and the capitalist system. It also shows the intersection points of struggle that can unite the larger ranks of the working class behind these movements. As one observer notes of the recent uprising and role of immigration police:

> Indeed, ICE and CBP [Customs and Border Protection] have reinforced police attacks on protesters. Their participation in police violence reminds us of the tight connections between domestic policing and immigration enforcement, and why organizers pushing to dismantle policing and defend Black lives also demand that we #AbolishICE and #AbolishCBP. The webs connecting ICE, CBP and police show that policing is not just about official police departments. Policing is a means of social control over a society defined by structural inequalities—by race, class, gender, immigration status and more. From its deep roots, policing grows multiple branches that extend in all directions, forming an entangled system of immigration, militarism and domestic state violence.[7]

## Abolish ICE

Immigration and Customs Enforcement is a central pillar and notoriously brutal face of the migra-state. ICE was created as part of the Department of Homeland Security in 2003 as a domestic arm of the "War on Terror." This refers to a generational plan by the US government to reorder the imperialist system following 9/11 through aggressive reassertion of US military power, especially into areas formerly contested during the Cold War: the Middle East, South Asia, Eastern Europe, and Latin America.

Over eight hundred thousand people have died as a direct result of US invasions, bombings, and other attacks, while 21 million people have been displaced due to this violence.[8] Since 2001, the United States has spent an astonishing $5.6 trillion conducting wars of invasion and covert actions in eighty countries on several different continents. As part of this project, there has been a commensurate militarization of domestic law enforcement and its repositioning as if on war footing as well.

ICE operates in a qualitatively different manner than other enforcement agencies. It is a special body of repressors created to fight a domestic war through the elaboration of national security doctrine and has been made permanent and deployed against general populations, including against the Black Lives Matter protests in 2020.[9] Furthermore, its organizational mission has evolved and morphed over the years of its existence.

ICE's first directives were to locate and document Arab, Muslim, and other Middle Eastern people with expired visas between the years 2003 to 2006, leading to an opaque and arbitrary detention and deportation system for selected populations.[10] After mass protests for immigration legalization swept the country in 2006, ICE agents were turned loose on migrant workers across the country. For over a year, they conducted hundreds of workplace raids, from bakeries to factories to large meatpacking plants.

Several thousand undocumented workers were arrested and deported, effectively smashing the workers' movement for unionization and legalization.[11] The function of ICE agents as strikebreakers was reflected again in 2019, when they raided several poultry-processing plants in small towns outside of Jackson, Mississippi.[12] About 680 workers were targeted in a chain of plants where workers had won a union-facilitated lawsuit against rampant workplace violations a few years prior.[13] In other words, ICE has become the preferred gendarme of migrant labor control, an instrument of capital accumulation through the function of labor repression and atomization of immigrant labor organizing. It is the police, FBI, and the

Pinkertons all in one—specifically targeting the more politicized migrant section of the workforce. What Border Patrol has historically done to keep agricultural fieldwork unorganized, ICE is now doing across industries.[14]

Under the Trump-led state, ICE was further politicized, given free rein to conduct operations against political leaders within the migrant population. ICE powers have again been expanded to investigate and arrest undocumented political activists in highly specific operations. More than twenty known immigrant rights organizers in different parts of the country were targeted and arrested for non-criminal offenses since 2017 alone.[15]

By 2019, twenty thousand ICE agents operated out of twenty-four Enforcement and Removal Operations regional command centers and "field offices" and seventy-nine "fusion centers," spread over every state and some US territories.[16] In the fusion centers, ICE, local and state police, other federal agencies, and private contractors share information and coordinate action against migrants and refugees. By 2013, the US government was already spending more on armed federal immigration enforcement than on the FBI, DEA, Secret Service, and all other federal law enforcement agencies combined.[17]

Reflecting the policing of migration and transnational mobility on a global scale, ICE operations have fanned out across borders and along the nodes of global transportation, with seventy-eight overseas offices in more than fifty-two countries. Its growth overlaps the expanding zones of US capital mobility and investment.[18]

ICE strategy and tactics are developed out of counterinsurgency doctrine, a military-honed means of policing people during a time of "low-intensity" war, specifically guerrilla warfare in Latin America during the Cold War.[19] This includes the building of paramilitary bases within and around population centers, developing elaborate methods of surveilling, tracking, and extracting people from a subject population while not upsetting the overall social and economic functions. ICE's political nature, paramilitary structure, and operational impunity make it a protofascist instrument: it is shielded from external oversight, its agents are given exemption from oversight, it engages in racial targeting and profiling, and it has become politicized and overtly subservient to ideology.[20]

One study found that during the administration of George W. Bush, from 2003 to 2008, 73 percent of the nearly 100,000 people arrested in "fugitive recovery operations" had no criminal record or pending charges.[21] ICE removal operations in Obama's first year led to the deportation of 389,834 people, of which 253,491, or 65 percent, were "non-criminal immigration violators." Obama earned the ignominious moniker of "Deporter-In-Chief" as the total number of deportations and removals surpassed three million during his eight-year tenure, a number greater than during any other presidential administration.[22]

Under pressure from the young undocumented activists of the Dreamer Movement, which disrupted and protested Democrats at all levels during Obama's last years, his administration was forced to introduce "prioritization memos" which de-emphasized the detention and removal of non-criminal offenders. Trump rescinded the prioritizations and replaced them with his own.

In 2017, ICE Enforcement and Removal Operations carried out a total of 226,119 deportations, a 30 percent rise from fiscal 2016. The agency also overtly manipulated its own reporting mechanism to create a false narrative of criminality by padding its numbers and lumping together those charged with overwhelmingly civil, non-criminal immigration violations with the very few "criminal offenses."[23] Under Trump, ICE established a new priority of targeting immigrants in the country with final orders of removal. This status refers to a population of over a million people who have standing deportation orders or pending removal proceedings that have resulted from non-criminal, civil circumstances, such as collateral arrests, rejected green card or refugee applications, and dozens of other scenarios.[24] Trump also attempted to strip all protections from the seven hundred thousand recipients of the Deferred Action for Childhood Arrivals (DACA) program, and used ICE to track and detain the youth around the country.[25]

## Movement Takes Shape

In 2017, a national campaign to abolish ICE took shape. Activists in Los Angeles, San Francisco, and San Diego, California; Detroit, Michigan;

Columbus, Ohio; Portland, Oregon; McAllen, Texas; Atlanta, Georgia; New York City, New York; Washington, DC; and other cities temporarily occupied or blockaded strategic entrance and exit points at ICE detention centers in order to effectively disrupt operations.[26]

Since the election of Donald Trump, over 475 counties (about sixteen percent of all counties in the country) have implemented sanctuary-city policy protections which instruct local agencies and officials to not comply with ICE operations or officials. Furthermore:

> More than 700 counties have declined to hold people on ICE detainers, and another 196 counties have stopped notifying ICE each time they release someone with an ICE detainer. An ICE detainer is a request from ICE to a local jail to notify ICE when someone in local custody will be released and to detain them for an extra forty-eight hours so ICE can come take custody. At least 240 counties have instituted policies limiting ICE agents' ability to interrogate people who are detained in local custody. More than 160 counties have prohibited officers from asking people their immigration status at all. And many more localities have taken other steps not reflected in our data, such as ending data sharing agreements with ICE, preventing ICE from entering municipal facilities without a federal warrant, and reducing arrests and prosecutions by linking local criminal justice and policing reforms.[27]

ICE also functions as a profit-procuring arm of the for-profit detention industry. ICE agents spend most of their time arresting and feeding detainees into a network of corporate prison complexes distributed across the interior of the country, and are also responsible to provide their own "oversight."

## Close the Detention Camps

The immigration policy regime is opaque, labyrinthine, and purposefully dysfunctional. A steady stream of executive orders, constant internal policy shifts, insular Department of Homeland Security operations, lack of meaningful oversight, conflicting jurisdiction purviews, congressional inaction and impasse, and the virtual autonomy and impunity of armed agents combine to create a sense of chaos for those who have to navigate it.

The US government, under both Democratic and Republican administrations, have built up a detention regime that has grown in parity with the criminalization of migration, especially since the Clinton administration (1992–2000). The Bush, Obama, and Trump administrations have added new depths of depravity to this trajectory, authorizing the DHS to begin incarcerating whole families and children between 2007 and 2014.[28] The practice exploded under Trump. As of Trump's time in office, all forms of migration became criminalized or restricted through border policy.[29]

From April to June of 2018 Trump introduced the first "zero-tolerance" family separation policy through executive order. This order required the prosecution of all adult migrants and refugees apprehended trying to cross the US-Mexico border, and the separation of all children who were turned over to state custody. Over this period, more than 5,500 children, including babies and toddlers, were separated from their detained and sometimes deported parents, and moved through the detention-to-shelter process within the United States. By October of 2020, the whereabouts of the parents of 545 children still remained unknown.[30]

Unionized flight attendants at major US airlines took a public stance against Trump's policies, refusing to work flights that transported immigrant children to "relocation" sites after being separated from their families. Illustrating this coordinated defiance, one flight attendant wrote a union-endorsed public letter declaring:

> I have made a decision that if I'm ever assigned to a flight with children who've been separated from their families, I will immediately remove myself from the trip due to the nature of this unconscionable act by my government and my employer's complicity.[31]

The spread of this sentiment and coordination across the Association of Flight Attendants–CWA union led six major airlines to publicly declare their opposition to migrant transfers using their carriers.[32] American Airlines publicly declared that the government must "immediately refrain from using American for the purpose of transporting children who have been separated from their families due to the current immigration policy."[33]

Tech workers have also taken a stand against migrant repression. A group of Amazon workers published an open letter taking a position against collaboration between the company and ICE.

> We refuse to build the platform that powers ICE, and we refuse to contribute to tools that violate human rights... We call on you to: 1. Stop selling facial recognition services to law enforcement. 2. Stop providing infrastructure to Palantir and any other Amazon partners who enable ICE. 3. Implement strong transparency and accountability measures, that include enumerating which law enforcement agencies and companies supporting law enforcement agencies are using Amazon services, and how.[34]

Another group of over a hundred workers at Microsoft also wrote a public letter, calling for the company to cancel all contracts with ICE.

> As the people who build the technologies that Microsoft profits from, we refuse to be complicit. We are part of a growing movement, comprised of many across the industry who recognize the grave responsibility that those creating powerful technology have to ensure what they build is used for good, and not for harm.[35]

Tech workers at Google, Apple, Facebook, Palantir, Salesforce, and GitHub also publicly organized and manifested their discontent toward collaboration with ICE.[36]

Public opinion registered this discontent, with two-thirds of the population opposing the policy.[37] In June of 2018, Trump was forced to rescind the "zero tolerance" policy of family separation amid fuming public outrage. Instead, he mandated that the Department of Homeland Security detain all migrant and refugee families and incarcerate them together pending a hearing on their status proceedings.[38]

To do this, the Trump administration changed the rules to the asylum process along the US-Mexico border. International treaties and federal law require the government to evaluate a claim for asylum from anyone who enters the United States, regardless of method—through a port of entry or by crossing the border and being apprehended. Historically, more than 75 percent of asylum seekers have passed the first screening as having a "credible fear" and been allowed into the country pending a review.[39] In a deliberate act of cruelty, Trump administration guidance memos ordered ICE and Border Patrol officials to refuse to release any asylum seekers into the country and instead confine them into mandatory detention to punish them for trying.

Migration rates had not increased to a higher point than in the past, but rather criminalization and long-term forms of detention led to a surge in migrant incarceration within existing capacity, resulting in the rapid degradation of conditions.[40] This rapid expansion of detention has not included additional funding to facilitate the additional incarceration of hundreds of thousands of people or any increase in funding for the legal bureaucratic process of administering asylum cases. All facets of detention capacity are swelling, which along with the erosion of rights, protections, and oversight, has turned these institutions into centers of neglect, abuse, and violence levied to dehumanize people.

The incarceration of asylum seekers rapidly increased the number in detention. By the end of 2018, an average of 51,379 men, women, and children were incarcerated daily. Roughly 138,000 were detained in the last three months of the year, and they were held for an average of forty-four days.[41] In the first six months of 2019, more than 274,798 migrants and refugees had been put into makeshift detention camps.[42] Between May and June 2019 alone, the Border Patrol apprehended 133,000 refugees, including 84,000 as families, 36,000 single adults, and 11,500 unaccompanied minors. By the end of the year, a total of 851,508 people had been detained (76,000 unaccompanied children, 473,683 people in family units, and 301,806 single adults; while 126,001 people were deemed "inadmissible").[43] While the exact number of detained asylum seekers who were deported from this population is not attainable, by the DHS's own data, only about 3-7 percent of asylum cases were approved in 2019 from Mexico and Central America.[44]

Eyewitness reports found conditions at Border Patrol stations along the border appalling:

> A chaotic scene of sickness and filth is unfolding in an overcrowded border station in Clint, Tex., where hundreds of young people who have recently crossed the border are being held, according to lawyers who visited the facility this week. Some of the children have been there for nearly a month.
>
> Children as young as 7 and 8, many of them wearing clothes caked with snot and tears, are caring for infants they've just met, the lawyers said. Toddlers without diapers are relieving themselves in their pants. Teenage mothers are wearing clothes stained with breast milk.
>
> Most of the young detainees have not been able to shower or wash

> their clothes since they arrived at the facility... They have no access to toothbrushes, toothpaste or soap.[45]

In other cases, people housed in open-air camps faced extreme temperatures. One notorious encampment was created near the international bridge in El Paso, Texas. According to *Texas Monthly* magazine, "CBP [US Customs and Border Protection] previously detained people under the bridge in March and early April but moved the detainees to enclosed conditions after a public outcry over reports of children and pregnant women sleeping on gravel and being bombarded with pigeon droppings."[46]

Later, it still functioned under squalid conditions after women and children were moved to a separate facility:

> one hundred to 150 men behind a chain-link fence, huddled beneath makeshift shelters made from mylar blankets and whatever other scraps they could find to shield themselves from the heat of the sun. "I was able to speak with detainees and take photos of them with their permission," [an eyewitness] said in an email. "They told me they've been incarcerated outside for a month, that they haven't washed or been able to change the clothes they were detained in the entire time, and that they're being poorly fed and treated in general.[47]

Under federal law and court rulings, families and unaccompanied children who seek asylum may not be detained for longer than twenty days, but the Department of Homeland Security ignored legal requirements, keeping children and families incarcerated for up to a month at a time in the camps. It is under these conditions that at least six children, Jakelin Amei Rosmery Caal Maquín, Felipe Gómez Alonzo, Juan de León Gutiérrez, Carlos Gregorio Hernández Vásquez, Wilmer Josué Ramírez Vásquez, and Darlyn Cristabel Cordova-Valle, have died in custody inside the facilities.[48] Another three children died shortly after being released.[49]

Border Patrol agents have repeatedly demonstrated their contempt for the plight of migrants and refugees at the border. Agents were recorded laughing and joking as children were crying after being separated from their parents.[50] It was recently revealed that half of the entire force (about 9,500 agents) participated in a secret Facebook group that joked about the deaths of migrants, referred to them as "subhuman," and made violent and misogynistic threats against Latina legislators.[51] In fact, the Border Patrol is an extremely violent organization, with agents killing ninety people since 2010.[52] According to a report from the American Immigration Council:

> Agents of the Border Patrol (a component agency of CBP) are known for regularly overstepping the boundaries of their authority by using excessive force, detaining people under inhumane conditions, and using coercion and misinformation to remove people from the United States. Not only do alleged abuses occur with regularity, but they rarely result in any serious disciplinary action . . . 95.9% of the 1,255 cases in which an outcome was reported resulted in "no action" against the officer or agent accused of misconduct.[53]

Public opinion held firm against Trump's policies, with 65 percent of the population expressing opposition to all forms of family separation by mid-2019.[54] In response to public opposition, Trump continued to shift his approach.

Beginning in January of 2019, the Trump administration then moved to effectively end the established legal practice of allowing migrants and refugees to seek asylum at US ports of entry through the implementation of the Migrant Protection Protocols, commonly known as the "Remain in Mexico policy." Through this order, Trump closed the border altogether to further incoming asylum seekers. This required refugees to wait on the Mexican border while their case was reviewed and processed, forcing people to reside in squalid open-air camps, over-crowded shelters, and in the streets.[55] Trump then directed the DHS to limit asylum eligibility, deny legal aid, and to wind down the review process.[56] The Mexican government under López Obrador was complicit in this persecution, deploying six thousand National Guard to reinforce its southern border and another fifteen thousand soldiers and National Guard to the north of the country to "control immigration" and prevent people from crossing into the United States.[57]

By early 2020, the closing of the border had produced atrocious conditions. According to one report, about 60,000 mostly Central American people have been forced to cluster at seven ports of entry on the Mexican side the US-Mexico border to wait in unsafe conditions for months at a time. Those denied entrance include 16,000 children and 500 babies.[58] There have been over eight hundred public reports of violence against the refugees, including murder, rape, kidnapping, sexual assault, child trafficking, torture, and other violent attacks against asylum seekers returned under this policy.[59] Trump announced the policy shift by openly mocking Central American refugees, crassly stating at a press conference that, "They are coming like it's a picnic, like 'let's go to Disneyland.'"[60]

## Children in Detention

Existing immigration policy asserts that unaccompanied children have to be moved out of these camps and put into shelters within twenty days. These shelters are managed by the Health and Human Services Department (HHS), which works with ICE to contract for-profit and dubious "nonprofit" services.

In reality, the spike in unaccompanied child refugees has given rise to a shelter industry, the main site of which is called Southwest Key Programs, which has emerged as the largest player and beneficiary. This company began as a conglomerate of for-profit businesses, but grew massively by landing federal government contracts to run a "nonprofit" shelter operation.[61]

After it received lucrative contracts from the Obama administration during the first phase of migrant family incarceration, Southwest Key then reinvested in these operations as detention became a growing and profitable enterprise.[62] What began under Obama massively expanded under Trump. Southwest Key now operates across several states including all of the border states and has pulled in over $1.7 billion in federal contracts in the last decade (over $600 million under Trump) for housing up to fourteen thousand child refugees at one hundred sites.[63]

This "nonprofit" functions as a money-making operation for its top executives and industry partners. The CEO of the nonprofit, Juan Sánchez, earned a salary of $1.5 million before retiring abruptly while under federal investigation. Southwest Key paid seven other people more than the legal federal salary cap for nonprofit operators of $187,000, including the chief financial officer Melody Chung, who was paid $1 million, and Juan's wife Jennifer Sánchez who earned $500,000 as a vice president.[64]

Furthermore, it uses money from government contracts to make sizeable profits for crony investors. The company has loaned tens of millions of dollars to real estate developers and investors, who then purchase properties to establish more shelters. Southwest Key then "rents" the shelters from those same developers and investors. According to one investigation:

> Over the past five years, a group based out of Mesa, Ariz., has earned more than $28 million in rent for properties that cost roughly $16 million. Others who benefited included a former New Mexico state cabinet secretary, a former adviser to a Mexican presidential candidate and two brothers who ran gas stations in Matamoros, Mexico.[65]

"Children's shelters" are a misnomer for these profitable cages, which are pushed to and beyond capacity, are understaffed, and have virtually no government oversight. Public investigations have shown instances of violence and abuse, sexual assault and molestation of children across multiple sites.[66] Several shelters have been shut down as a result.[67] Instead of investing in better conditions for the children, the managers have created a cash cow for connected investors, and factories of abuse and sexual exploitation for the children.

In government-administered child camps, the Trump administration applied measures of cruelty to directly punish the children. The Office of Refugee Resettlement, which is the arm of Health and Human Services charged with caring for an estimated forty thousand unaccompanied migrant children in government custody, recently scaled back or cancelled activities at the shelters.[68] These measures included cuts in education programs, legal services, and funding for recreation.

Six months into the Biden administration, many of the Trump-era policies have persisted intact or with only minor modifications. The administration refused entry of most adult asylum seekers and has continued the practice of holding children in detention centers. By the summer of 2021, this included holding over 21,000 children within an opaque network of over 200 facilities (including reactivated Trump-era camps) in over two dozen states, includes several mega-centers with more than 1,000 children packed inside.[69]

## ICE Detention: Profit and Abuse

The interior complex of ICE-managed detention centers held on average about 53,000 people daily in 2019.[70] Over 70 percent of the over six hundred detention centers are privatized, with little operational federal oversight, and with a sordid history of corruption. Furthermore, about three-quarters of all detention capacity are owned and run by two major corporations:

GEO Group and CoreCivic.[71] In 2019, GEO Group reported $2.4 billion in revenue (from public money) and CoreCivic reported $1.98 billion.[72]

This has been abetted by the close relationship between high-ranking government officials and detention companies. A review by advocacy groups of five years of ICE inspections of detention centers, between 2007 and 2012, found that ICE failed to properly inspect facilities under its jurisdiction and shrouded their operational methods in secrecy.[73] According to a report:

> Over the past decade, dozens of Immigration and Customs Enforcement agents and contract guards responsible for the detention and removal of undocumented immigrants have been arrested and charged with beating people, smuggling drugs into detention centers, having sex with detainees, and accepting bribes to delay or stop deportations, agency documents and court records show.[74]

Under these conditions, at least 196 people have died while in ICE custody since 2003, many under suspicious circumstances.[75] Furthermore, between January 2010 and July 2016, the Office for Civil Rights and Civil Liberties (an oversight agency within DHS) received over thirty-three thousand complaints of sexual assault or physical abuse against children, women, men, and LGBTQ people in detention by DHS agents, mostly from ICE. The inspector general, the office in charge of looking into complaints, investigated less than 1 percent of these cases.[76]

ICE detention centers have also become forced labor sites. Kevin Landy, a former ICE official in the Obama administration said, "Contractors save a lot of money by using detainee labor because they're performing work that would otherwise have to be performed by paid employees."[77] That work includes cooking and cleaning for as little as a dollar a day, or even for nothing, in some cases.[78]

GEO Group, the largest immigrant detention center contractor in the nation revealed in a 2017 financial report that 64 percent of its revenue came from detention and correctional facilities operations, and 22 percent from providing privatized health and educational services to detainees within their facilities. ICE is GEO Group's and CoreCivic's largest customer.[79]

In the run-up to the 2016 election, GEO Group donated $475,000 to a Trump-supporting Super PAC and for Trump's inauguration festivities.[80] CoreCivic, the other major private prison contractor in the US, gave

$250,000 to support Trump's campaign and inauguration. In the first year after Trump's election, GEO Group's stock price rose 63 percent, and CoreCivic's rose 81 percent.[81] They are seeing their investment pay off.

The DHS and ICE now function as a means to accumulate profit, a direct interface between capital and the state to administer large-scale transfers of public wealth to private, for-profit institutions and investors. This is reflected directly in the diminishing lines of demarcation between the heads of the detention industry and the DHS and ICE itself.

GEO Group's deals with ICE, for example, have steadily grown since 2012, when it hired David Venturella, ICE's former head of deportation and detention operations under the Obama administration.[82] In July 2017, GEO Group then hired Daniel Ragsdale, the former second-in-command of Immigration and Customs Enforcement.[83]

Scott Sutterfield was Immigration and Customs Enforcement's top official in the South, overseeing operations in several states. When Trump came to office, he ran ICE operations in the region like a fiefdom, ignoring basic human rights and legal rulings and keeping migrants and refugees in hellish conditions for indefinite terms of detention.[84] He gained notoriety after being the manager of the only field office to deny parole to 100 percent of asylum seekers. Between 2018 and 2019, the number of detainees within the New Orleans region increased from 2,400 to 10,000. After arranging an ICE contract for eight new detention centers in Louisiana and Mississippi with a for-profit prison corporation called LaSalle Corrections, he was hired on by the company. He is now a "development executive" who advises the company on how to secure more ICE contracts.

Former secretary of homeland security Kirstjen Nielsen, who held the office from 2017 to 2019, was appointed right out of the for-profit, border security sector. Before becoming secretary, she ran a series of shady security consulting firms called Homeland and National Security Solutions, Civitas Group, and Sunesis Consulting. On her resumé she boasted about,

> our expertise in national security, homeland security, and government services markets and policy domains and direct experience as senior government officials allows us to advise our clients at the unique intersection between policy making and profit generation.[85]

Nielsen was followed by Kevin McAleenan, who after a short stint as director left to form Pangium, a for-profit company seeking government contracts for installing airport security technology and data-processing products.[86] He was followed by Chad Wolf, who was previously the senior director of Wexler & Walker, a bipartisan lobbying firm, where he developed specialized experience

> working in the defense, homeland security and transportation sectors. With an intimate knowledge of security budgets and programs, Chad has represented defense and homeland security contractors, major system integrators and small entrepreneurs.[87]

The list goes on.[88]

## The Close the Camp Movement Grows

The detention, surveillance, transport, and policing of immigrants are profitable growth industries.[89] For Trump, the centering of racism, bigotry, and xenophobia in his presidency allowed him to cultivate a political base within society. He rallied this base to mobilize against his opposition on all fronts, allowing him to impose reactionary divides within society that mask the astronomical inequality between the rich and the rest of the population. Due to the complicity of the Democratic Party in building up the apparatus of migrant criminalization, their "opposition" became inherently muddled, half-hearted, weak-kneed, and then splintered.

This was followed by a surge of protest and civil disobedience coming from activists and rights groups. Japanese American survivors of the World War II US concentration camps took direct action at Fort Sill in Lawton, Oklahoma, a site where they had been detained and that was being considered for reactivation for Central American refugees.[90] Thousands of Jewish protesters and allies with Never Again Action and #JewsAgainstICE participated in a wave of militant disobedience actions across the country at ICE detention centers and offices. The campaign highlighted the historical memory of concentration camps and why reemergent forms taking shape in the twenty-first century need to be shut down by all means.[91]

Other activist groups responded to Trump's family separation policies and mass incarceration of refugees. National coalitions of human rights activists developed and called for the termination of the policy and release of refugees and migrants. Several coalitions formed by the summer of 2019: Coalition the Close the Concentration Camps, No More Concentration Camps, Close the Camps, and Lights for Liberty organized mass protests between July and October that brought out tens of thousands directly to detention centers, ICE and CBP offices, and other locations across the country.[92]

At the height of organizing national rallies, more than five hundred workers at the Boston headquarters of the online furniture company Wayfair organized a one-day wildcat strike to oppose their employer's contract to furnish a detention center for migrant youth in Carrizo Springs, Texas. The strike was successfully organized in twenty-four hours and received broad public support, even without them being part of a union.[93] In a public letter, they declared their action in solidarity with detained peoples:

> The US government and its contractors are responsible for the detention and mistreatment of hundreds of thousands of migrants seeking asylum in our country—we want that to end.[94]

It will take mass organizing and mobilizations, persistent campaigns over time, and the need to push the whole political establishment from below to close all of the detention camps.

In August of 2019, Whole Foods workers, through their union organizing committee called Whole Worker, protested against their parent company Amazon, demanding the corporation break all ties with ICE and Palantir. Workers held protests in front of several Whole Foods locations in New York City.

> We as Whole Worker stand with our co-workers inside Amazon AWS demanding Jeff Bezos cease all business with Palantir and any other company involved in the continued oppression of marginalized groups. . . . We also stand firmly with our co-workers in calling for Amazon to end the sale of its facial recognition software, Rekognition, to law enforcement. The software has already been proven to be racially biased, and the last thing an increasingly fascistic law enforcement culture needs are further tools for mass surveillance.[95]

In October of 2019 workers at Chef, a software automation company, went into company systems and deleted code in software products used by ICE as a form of protest, compelling the company to announce it would not renew the contract.[96] In November, GitHub workers set up a giant cage outside a company conference to protest its business with ICE, presenting a letter signed by a group of 150 GitHub workers calling for GitHub to cancel its contract with ICE.[97]

Public sector workers have also engaged in forms of class struggle that incorporate demands against the migra-state. In Los Angeles, with the nation's second-largest school district, thirty thousand teachers went out on their first strike in over thirty years in 2019. The demands of their largely student-centered strike included: more librarians, counselors, nurses, and mental health professionals for their schools, smaller class sizes, reduced standardized testing, and a host of other gains. In a district that is comprifed of 73 percent Latinx students and 43 percent Latinx educators, many come from migrant or mixed-status families who face the impact or threat of arrest, detention, and deportation on a regular basis. Many of the teachers were once youths who participated in protest movements against anti-immigrant policies in the 1990s. As one magazine reported:

> Rodolfo Dueñas, an L.A. native and public-school teacher who is picketing, describes this burgeoning movement as a natural next step for the many Latinos like him whose activism can be traced back to the mid-1990s, when thousands of Latino teens staged a school walkout in opposition to an anti-immigrant state-ballot initiative known as Proposition 187. For many like Dueñas in the "187 Generation," those experiences eventually drove them into teaching. And Dueñas's generation has been following in the footsteps of the Latino education activists who came before them, during the 1968 walkouts known by some as the Mexican Student Movement.[98]

ICE repression sows terror into the communities and traumatizes students. In recognition of this social injustice and the way it impacts the learning environment, the union incorporated a demand that the schools provide "immigrant defense support" through a dedicated hotline and an attorney for immigrant families to provide free counsel on immigration-related matters.[99] The teachers' picket lines stayed firm and were bolstered by a massive show of popular support from the immigrant and Latinx communities, leading the school board to concede after one week.[100]

## Opening the Border Will Take Class Struggle

Polls taken during the 2018 election cycle showed that 25 percent of voters already supported ICE abolition, while another 21 percent weren't sure. Nearly half, 43 percent, of Democrats supported abolition. This was influenced by the protest movement, before the presidential election cycle was in full swing. In the electoral arena, Alexandria Ocasio-Cortez and other Democrats were elected into congress on a platform that reflected leftward-moving sentiment, including ICE abolition.[101] Democratic Party candidate for governor of New York Cynthia Nixon called ICE "a terrorist organization" that should be abolished.[102]

Responding to this tide of opposition, congressional Democrats Mark Pocan, Pramila Jayapal, and Adriano Espaillat introduced the Establishing a Humane Immigration Enforcement System Act into Congress in the summer of 2018, a bill to ostensibly shut the agency down.[103] "President Trump has so misused ICE," explained Pocan, "that the agency can no longer accomplish its goals effectively."[104] The lack of "political will" for the Democrats to get behind "Abolish ICE" became apparent when the same Democrats who introduced the bill to abolish ICE quickly collapsed their efforts.

They introduced the bill only to curry favor with the immigrant rights movement and get ahead of changing public sentiment in the lead-up to the 2018 elections, knowing full well it would never pass a Republican-controlled Congress without a fight. When Republicans called their bluff, threatening to quickly bring the bill to a vote on the House floor, these same Democrats announced they would not vote for their own bill.[105]

The growing calls from politicians to defund and dissolve ICE have pushed the conversation forward. But there are limitations to the electoral path, which shifts the initiative to elected officials working inside parties largely financed and controlled by the same corporate interests they seek to confront.

Public sentiment continued to shift even further against ICE, changing the character of the presidential campaign. By 2019, two Democratic presidential candidates supported the abolition of ICE (Sanders and DeBlasio) while seventeen others campaigned on the need to "restructure the agency."[106] All of these politicians actually stood *in favor* of the migra-state prior to 2019 and helped construct and fund it directly or indirectly, which shows how much they gauged the changing terrain around the issue. Most of the candidates also rhetorically stood for decriminalizing undocumented immigration, opposing the expansion of the border wall, and reducing deportations.

The election of Joe Biden and the return of a Democratic majority in Congress in November of 2020 contained the possibility for realizing the promise for a new amnesty and the dismantling of the migra-state. Despite Biden's campaign rhetoric and repeated promises to restore a "fair and humane" policy, the Democrats quickly retreated on the issue. Many of Trump's four hundred executive orders and guidance memos designed to inflict punishment and cruelty on migrants and refugees have so far remained in place. The promise of legalization, even in a "labor path to citizenship," has already been shelved in favor of the status quo. The radical rhetoric of self-described progressives and social democrats calling for the abolition of ICE and the DHS and the closure of the concentration camps under Trump has since faded into conspicuous silence.[107]

The volatility of bourgeois politics reflects class polarization but offers no solution. The bipartisan consensus in favor of migrant repression as a form of capital accumulation, even if temporarily modified in form, cannot resist the gravitational pull back to servicing the needs of the capitalist class. That is why even the most left-wing reform campaigning within the Democratic Party is still framed in terms of *reorganization* and not *abolition.*[108] By containing the discussion in the framework of continuity, right-wing positions for *increased* repression are legitimated and given greater weight within the spectrum of "acceptable solutions." This is especially the case when working within a system that has already been physically structured and ideologically conditioned *for* repression. Similar dynamics have played out in the movement against migrant detention.

At the core of the migra-state is labor repression. It is precisely designed to repress that labor power among immigrant workers—who have shown their capacity to be the leading edge of a new generational surge in union-building—and to foster racism and divisions among their nonimmigrant coworkers and neighbors. Ultimately, it will likely take the reemergence of a militant workers' movement to open the borders, which is a precondition to rebuilding a labor movement within and across boundaries. That is why the opposition movement is emerging from below, especially by working people taking the struggle into the workplace.

The call for the free movement of labor lays the basis for a universal working-class consciousness and a vision of solidarity. This is especially urgent as ruling-class demagogues and their fascist followers try to blame immigrants for the deepening and recurring crises of capitalism. Their only response is to amplify reactionary nationalism to facilitate division and foster racism and xenophobia at a time of economic deterioration for all workers. It ultimately instills a sense of impotence and powerlessness as it conveys that workers themselves cannot change their declining conditions, but instead must align with their own oppressors to defensively cling to an ever-shrinking share of the pie. Breaking with the appeal of these ideas is made easier by the changing contours of class formation and coordination within the NAM, where the working class has become more increasingly integrated and transnational.

Workers can only strengthen their position through class struggle that can overcome the divides within national boundaries, and along the nodes of transnational capitalism that cross borders. Building cross-border networks that fuse militant and class-conscious workers, and that can facilitate coordinated and joint action, can lay the basis for new leadership and rank-and-file movements capable of aligning the large sections of workers who are already situated in the same workplaces and industries or are interconnected through transnational supply chains and employment for the same multinational employers.[109]

Solidarity on this level can create a foundation for further organizational capacity building, which can lead to common demands and universal contracts, coordinated strikes and other job actions, and the construction of international unions and affiliation. Building class power along these lines can begin to shift the balance of class forces and toward the equalization of rights, strengthening of workplace democracy, raising of wages, and improvement of working conditions within industries and across borders. Ultimately, this trajectory could also create the basis for exerting class power on an economy of scale capable of bringing down altogether the migrant repressive apparatus.

Trump's budget shutdown of early 2019 illustrated the power of organized labor to defeat the migra-state. His attempt to force increased budgetary funding for an expansion of the border collapsed in the face of working-class resistance. When the funding wasn't forthcoming, Trump ordered a month-long federal government shutdown, effectively idling over eight hundred thousand workers nationwide. Ostensibly designed to rally public support behind his campaign promise to "build the wall," his plan backfired and instead stoked the wrath of workers in the airline sector.

A day after the second missed monthly payday of the shutdown, air traffic controllers organized a sick-out from work, temporarily grounding all flights at New York's LaGuardia airport and causing flight delays across the East Coast. As news of the delays spread, the fifty thousand flight attendants at twenty airlines who form the Association of Flight Attendants-Communication Workers of America threatened to walk out and strike as a "suspension of service" action due to safety concerns.[110] This was accompanied by several other unions issuing ominous warnings about the declining ability to operate the aviation sector with integrity and safety amid the shutdown. When Trump continued to hold out, AFA-CWA international president Sara Nelson announced at an AFL-CIO press conference that the flight attendants would call for a general strike of all aviation workers together if Trump didn't back down on funding for the wall.[111]

As she said in an interview, "We're mobilizing immediately. . . . If air traffic controllers can't do their jobs, we can't do ours." The threat of a general strike and shutdown of the nation's airports, and the implication of a revolt of labor directly against Trump's much vaunted border wall expansion, brought the administration to its knees within hours.[112] Trump quickly conceded and ended the shutdown the next day. A source inside the White House "told CNN Friday that the flight delays were a 'contributing catalyst' to the hasty deal."[113] A telling public opinion poll a week later showed that 60 percent of the US population was against the border wall expansion, exemplifying how demonstrations of workers' power can change public discourse quickly.[114]

These few but potent examples of the power of organized labor to stand against migrant repression and border walls show the tremendous potential for workers to bring down the migra-state. They illustrate that the material necessity of working-class people to organize toward justice leads them to oppose borders and migrant repression in the context of class struggle and consciousness.

The Black Lives Matter uprising has raised and popularized demands to defund and abolish police departments. Immigrant rights campaigns have taken similar approaches to defunding and abolishing ICE, closing detention centers and prison camps, and giving full and equal rights to all people. These demands have emerged from below and against direct opposition and push back from the two ruling-class parties, the state, and even the police and immigration agencies themselves.[115] Through the sheer weight of mobilization and confrontation, these movements have pushed abolition demands into the political arena, by exposing the problems to the wider public, presenting solutions and alternatives, and by giving confidence to others to act.

These movements should also push these demands into electoral campaigns outside of the two capitalist parties that can expose their complicity in funding and arming state repression. Nevertheless, it is important to recognize the limits of this strategy. The US electoral system as it is currently composed will not allow for capitalism to be dismantled through democratic means. During the pandemic and subsequent economic crisis, some sections of the US ruling class made it clear that maintaining the flow of profit was more important than preserving human lives or majority will. Politicians and reactionary protest movements forced the reopening of the economy and return of people back to work amid spreading infections and a rising death toll claiming the cost of death was worth it.[116]

Class polarization and the growth of different forms of class struggle in the absence of a workers or socialist party in the US has enabled the ruling politics the be led by the farthest-right sections of the class. This is reaching the point of convergence with fascist movements that are gaining more confidence in the streets. Open collaboration between police and far-right militants has come out into the open, while evidence continues to pile up of neo-Nazi and other white supremacist groups actively integrating into and recruiting from within police departments and other armed state agencies.

Therefore, the dismantling of state repressive power will be inevitably bound up with other forms of working-class struggle at the point of production. This will have to also extend against the repressive state apparatus that legislates and enforces unequal relations of production. To fight to open the border and abolish the repressive state that upholds it will necessitate culmination into revolutionary struggle and social transformation.

The recent episodes of struggle against migrant repression and border walls demonstrate the power and illustrate social forces necessary to abolish the migrant repressive apparatus and, by necessity, the system of capitalism as a whole. This will also require a convergence and reintegration of socialist politics as a guiding framework of the class struggle, rooted in internationalism and a concrete vision for building working-class unity within and across borders. This requires the commitment of organizers to do the work inside unions and in social movements to build the capacity and strengthen working-class social forces already demonstrating the power to confront the state. The growth of a new and generational socialist and anticapitalist left, rooted in working-class struggle and broad support for the necessity to replace capitalism with socialism, shows the possibilities for envisioning and realizing a world without borders in our lifetimes.

# Acknowledgments

I would like to especially thank my partner Norell Martínez and my parents Don Akers and Naedine Chacón for their love and support. This book was also made possible with help and assistance from Sol Martínez, Anthony Arnove, Ashley Smith, Nisha Bolsey, Héctor A. Rivera, Maya Marshall, Sylvia Lizárraga, Héctor Reyes, and Rachel Cohen.

# Notes

## Introduction

1. Central American and Caribbean states also fit within this framework to varying degrees, though this book will focus primarily on Mexico as the model of neoliberal transformation that has since been exported to other countries.
2. Profit, or "return on investment," refers to the value added to a product or service by labor, which is then expropriated by the capitalist through their ownership and control of the means of production. Profit is therefore the accumulated wealth created through the process of labor exploitation, i.e., paying a worker less than the total actual value of wealth they produce through their labor. Capital, the root of the term capitalism, which is the global economic system, describes the process in which the capitalist reinvests profit into expanding the means of production to employ and exploit more labor with the intention of accruing even more profit. See Karl Marx, *Capital*, vol. 2 (Hertfordshire: Wordsworth Classics, 2013), Part 2, and Karl Marx, *Capital*, vol. 3 (London: Penguin Classics, 1991), Part 1.
3. For a full discussion, see Karl Marx, "The Production of Absolute and Relative Surplus Value," part 5 of *Capital*, vol. 1 (Hertfordshire: Wordsworth Editions Limited, 2013).
4. For a theoretical description and overview of the development of state capitalism in Mexico, see Sergio de la Peña, "Proletarian Power and State Monopoly Capitalism in Mexico" *Latin American Perspectives*, Vol. 9, No. 1, Mexico in the Eighties (Winter, 1982), pp. 20-35.
5. Adam David Morton, *Revolution and State in Modern Mexico: The Political Economy of Uneven Development* (Lanham: Rowman & Littlefield Publishers, 2013), 35.
6. For a comprehensive class analysis of the Mexican Revolution, see Adolfo Gilly, *The Mexican Revolution* (New York: New Press, 2006).
7. For a comprehensive overview and class analysis of the period, see Art Preis, *Labor's Giant Step: The First Twenty Years of the CIO: 1936–55* (New York: Pathfinder Press, 1972). See also Rhonda F. Levine, *Class Struggle and the New Deal: Industrial Labor, Industrial Capital, and the State* (Lawrence: University Press of Kansas, 1988).
8. Marx, *Capital*, vol. 2, 137.
9. Jake Johnson, "'Eye-Popping': Analysis Shows Top 1% Gained $21 Trillion in Wealth Since 1989 While Bottom Half Lost $900 Billion," *Common Dreams*, June 14, 2019, www.commondreams.org/news/2019/06/14/eye-popping-analysis-shows-top-1-gained-21-trillion-wealth-1989-while-bottom-half.

10. Larry Elliott, "World's Twenty-Six Richest People Own as Much as Poorest 50 Percent, Says Oxfam," *Guardian*, January 20, 2019, www.theguardian.com/business/2019/jan/21/world-26-richest-people-own-as-much-as-poorest-50-per-cent-oxfam-report.
11. Based on the metric: "Percentage of Persons Living with Less than 50% of Median Equivalized Disposable Income," Calculated and published by the OECD, information available at "OECD Income Distribution Database (IDD): Gini, poverty, income, Methods and Concepts," www.oecd.org/social/income-distribution-database.htm.
12. Emmie Martin, "The Government Shutdown Spotlights a Bigger Issue: 78% of US Workers Live Paycheck to Paycheck," CNBC, January 10, 2019, www.cnbc.com/2019/01/09/shutdown-highlights-that-4-in-5-us-workers-live-paycheck-to-paycheck.html; Amanda Dixon, "A Growing Percentage of Americans Have No Emergency Savings Whatsoever," Bankrate, July 1, 2019, www.bankrate.com/banking/savings/financial-security-june-2019/.
13. Americans for Tax Fairness, *Billionaire Wealth Grew by $845 Billion, Or 29%, as America Struggled through First Six Months of Pandemic*, September 20, 2020, americansfortaxfairness.org/billionaire-wealth-grew-845-billion-29-america-struggled-first-six-months-pandemic.
14. Linda Lobao, Mia Gray, Kevin Cox, and Michael Kitson, "The Shrinking State? Understanding the Assault on the Public Sector," *Cambridge Journal of Regions, Economy and Society* 11, issue 3 (November 2018): 389–90.
15. For a comprehensive, historical analysis of the anti-democratic origins and character of neoliberal capitalist ideology, see Quinn Slobodian, *Globalists: The End of Empire and the Birth of Neoliberalism* (Cambridge: Harvard University Press, 2020).
16. For an overview of Mexico's free trade agreements, see M. Angeles Villarreal, *Mexico's Free Trade Agreements*, Congressional Research Service, April 25, 2017. https://fas.org/sgp/crs/row/R40784.pdf.
17. *World Migration Report 2020*, International Organization for Migration, www.un.org/sites/un2.un.org/files/wmr_2020.pdf
18. Dennis C. Canterbury, *Capital Accumulation and Migration* (Chicago: Haymarket Books, 2013), 4–5.
19. Canterbury, *Capital*, 4–5.

## PART I

Report cited in Marvin D. Bernstein, *Foreign Investment in Latin America: Cases and Attitudes* (New York: Knopf, 1966), 157.

## Chapter 1

1. For examples see Walter R. Echo-Hawk, *In the Courts of the Conqueror: The Ten Worst Indian Law Cases Ever Decided* (Golden, CO: Fulcrum Publishing, 2012).

2. For a full discussion see Patrick Wolfe, "Settler Colonialism and the Elimination of the Native," *Journal of Genocide Research* 8, no 4 (2006): 387–409.
3. For an in-depth exposition of this historical process, see Edward E. Baptist, *The Half Has Never Been Told: Slavery and the Making of American Capitalism* (New York: Basic Books, 2016).
4. Karl Marx, "Genesis of the Industrial Capitalist," chapter 31 in *Capital*, vol. 1, www.marxists.org/archive/marx/works/1867-c1/ch31.htm.
5. For an overview of this historic process, see Rachel St. John, *A History of the Western US–Mexico Border* (Princeton: Princeton University Press, 2012).
6. Cuba gained nominal independence in 1903, while the rest are still colonies of the United States.
7. Phil Gaspar, ed. *Imperialism and War: Classic Writings by V. I. Lenin and Nikolai Bukharin* (Chicago: Haymarket Books, 2017), 101–2.
8. Rudolph Hilferding, *Finance Capital: A Study of the Latest Phase of Capitalist Development* (Boston: Routledge & Kegan Paul, 1981), 326.
9. For further analysis of this history, see Sidney Lens, "The War Before the War (I)," chapter 14 in *The Forging of the American Empire: From the Revolution to Vietnam: A History of US Imperialism* (Chicago: Haymarket Books, 2016).
10. Smedley D. Butler, *War Is a Racket: The Antiwar Classic by America's Most Decorated Soldier* (Port Townsend, WA: Feral Press), 2003.
11. A number of historians have addressed the specific role of the exploitation of migrant labor as a facet of capitalist accumulation and expansion in US history. For instance, see Lucie Cheng and Edna Bonacich, *Labor Immigration under Capitalism: Asian Workers in the United States before World War II* (Berkeley: University of California Press, 1984).
12. For instance, Filipinos held a modified form of citizenship that allowed them to move to the US as workers between 1900 and 1934, but severely restricted their rights within the country in line with national and regional codes of racial segregation. After 1934 and nominal independence from the US, most Filipinos were prohibited from migrating to the US under existing "National Origins" restrictions as part of the Immigration Act of 1924. See "The Immigration Act of 1924 (The Johnson-Reed Act)," Office of the Historian, history.state.gov/milestones/1921-1936/immigration-act#
13. For an in-depth discussion of this period and process, see Justin Akers Chacón, introduction and part 2 in *Radicals in the Barrio: Magonistas, Socialists, Wobblies, and Communists in the Mexican-American Working Class* (Chicago: Haymarket Books, 2018).
14. Marx, "The General Law of Capital Accumulation," chapter 25 in *Capital*, vol. 1, www.marxists.org/archive/marx/works/1867-c1/ch25.htm.
15. See Kelly Lytle Hernandez, *Migra!: A History of the US Border Patrol* (Berkeley: University of California Press, 2010).

16. Ana Alicia Peña López, *Migración internacional y superexplotación del trabajo* (Mexico: Itaca, 2012), 33 (my translation).
17. Peña López, *Migración internacional,* 36.
18. Citizenship restrictions have been based on different and often overlapping factors, including race, class, nationality, sexual orientation, or physical capacities. See Kevin Johnson, *The Huddled Masses Myth: Immigration and Civil Rights* (Philadelphia: Temple University Press, 2003).
19. Centro de Estudios Puertorriqueños, *Labor Migration under Capitalism: The Puerto Rican Experience* (New York: Monthly Review Press, 1979), 94–95.
20. Miles Eugene Galvin, *The Organized Labor Movement in Puerto Rico* (Cranbury: Associated University Presses, 1979), 44.
21. Centro de Estudios Puertorriqueños, *Labor Migration under Capitalism, 94–5*
22. For a full discussion, see Galvin, *Organized Labor Movement in Puerto Rico,* especially chapter 3.
23. For an in-depth overview of this period, see Art Preis, *Labor's Giant Step: The First Twenty Years of the CIO, 1936-1955* (New York: Pathfinder Press, 1972).
24. James L. Dietz, *Economic History of Puerto Rico: Institutional Change and Capitalist Development* (Princeton: Princeton University Press, 1986), 209–10.
25. Centro de Estudios Puertorriqueños, *Labor Migration under Capitalism,* 127. Minimum wage exemptions for Puerto Rico were written into the Fair Labor Standards Act in 1940, see 129.
26. Eliezer Curet Cuevas, *Economía política de Puerto Rico: 1950 a 2000.* San Juan, (PR: Ediciones M.A.C., 2004), 70 (my translation).
27. Centro de Estudios Puertorriqueños, *Labor Migration under Capitalism,* 132, 138.
28. "Operation Bootstrap," Lehman College, http://lcw.lehman.edu/lehman/depts/latinampuertorican/latinoweb/PuertoRico/Bootstrap.htm.
29. Centro de Estudios Puertorriqueños, *Labor Migration Under Capitalism,* 103–4.
30. Data taken from United States Census Bureau, "QuickFacts," www.census.gov/quickfacts/PR; https://www.census.gov/quickfacts/fact/table/US/SEX255219.
31. Data taken from Federal Reserve Bank of New York, "Report on the Competitiveness of Puerto Rico's Economy" 2012, www.newyorkfed.org/medialibrary/media/regional/PuertoRico/report.pdf; see also St. Louis Federal Reserve Bank, "Youth Unemployment Rate for Puerto Rico," https://fred.stlouisfed.org/series/SLUEM1524ZSPRI.
32. See Marie T. Mora and Alberto Dávila, "The Hispanic-white Wage Gap Has Remained Wide and Relatively Steady," Economic Policy Institute, July 2, 2018, www.epi.org/publication/the-hispanic-white-wage-gap-has-remained-wide-and-relatively-steady-examining-hispanic-white-gaps-in-wages-unemployment-labor-force-participation-and-education-by-gender-immigrant/; see also, Federal Reserve Bank of St. Louis, "Real Disposable Personal Income: Per Capita" https://fred.stlouisfed.org/series/A229RX0.

33. See Mora and Dávila, "Hispanic-white Wage Gap."
34. For an overview and current analysis of this process, see Council of Foreign Relations, "Puerto Rico: A US Territory in Crisis," November 25, 2020, www.cfr.org/backgrounder/puerto-rico-us-territory-crisis.

## Chapter 2

1. For an overview of this historical period, see Friedrich Katz, *The Secret War in Mexico: Europe, the United States and the Mexican Revolution* (Chicago: University of Chicago Press, 1981); see also Gastón García Cantú, *Las invasiones norteamericanas en México* (Mexico: Consejo Nacional de Fomento Educativo, 1986).
2. For an overview of this historical process, see John Mason Hart, *Anarchism & the Mexican Working Class, 1860–1931* (Austin: University of Texas Press, 1987), especially chapters 9 and 10.
3. For a comprehensive study of the postrevolutionary ruling class see Adolfo Gilly, *The Mexican Revolution* (New York: New Press, 2006).
4. The party was first named the Partido Nacional Revolucionario (National Revolutionary Party) in 1929, then the Partido de la Revolución Mexicana (Mexican Revolutionary Party) in 1936, and then the Partido Institucional Revolucionaria (Institutional Revolutionary Party) in 1946.
5. Some historians have described this stage in postrevolutionary Mexico using the Marxist concept of "Bonapartism." This phenomenon generally refers to the idea of how middle-class, petty-bourgeois elements, especially coming from the military, seize power and navigate control in a revolutionary period where neither the capitalist class nor proletariat are strong enough to take power themselves. For examples, see Karl Marx, *The Eighteenth Brumaire of Louis Bonaparte* (New York: International Publishers, 1994); as applied to Mexico see Dan La Botz, *Mask of Democracy: Labor Suppression in Mexico Today* (Boston: South End Press, 1999).
6. See Donald Hodges and Ross Gandy, *Mexico 1910–1982: Reform or Revolution?* (London: Zed Books, 1983).
7. Sylvia Maxfield, *Governing Capital: International Finance and Mexican Politics* (Ithaca: Cornell University Press, 1990), 39–47.
8. Maxfield, *Governing Capital*, 39.
9. Maxfield, *Governing Capital*, 65.
10. For an overview of this period and process, see Mary Kay Vaughan and Stephen Lewis, *The Eagle and the Virgin: Nation and Cultural Revolution in Mexico, 1920–194* (Durham: Duke University Press, 2006.)
11. For a discussion on the nature and class character of bourgeois revolutions, see Neil Davidson, *How Revolutionary Were the Bourgeois Revolutions?* (Chicago: Haymarket Books, 2012).
12. Baird and McCaughan, *Beyond the Border: Mexico and the US Today* (New York: North American Congress on Latin America, 1979), 29.

13. Peter Baird and Ed McCaughan, *Beyond the Border,* 29.
14. See John J. Dwyer, *The Agrarian Dispute: The Expropriation of America-Owned Rural Land in Prorevolutionary Mexico* (Durham: Duke University Press, 2008).
15. This coincided with the height of urban labor militancy and growth of a strike movement, the influence of the Mexican Communist Party, and the state's attempt to prevent radicalism from growing beyond its control.
16. Roger Bartra, *Agrarian Structure and Political Power in Mexico* (Baltimore: Johns Hopkins University Press, 1993), 90.
17. Roger Bartra, *Agrarian Structure,* 93–4.
18. Maxfield, *Governing Capital,* 62.
19. Michel Gutelman, *Capitalismo y reforma agraria en México* (Mexico: Ediciones Era, 1974), 181.
20. Francisco Alba and Joseph E. Potter, "Population and Development in Mexico since 1940: An Interpretation" *Population and Development Review* 12, no. 1 (March, 1986): 51–2.
21. For a comprehensive analysis, see Rodolfo Stavenhagen, "Collective Agriculture and Capitalism in Mexico: A Way Out or a Dead End?" *Latin American Perspectives* 2, no. 2, (Summer, 1975):146–63; see also Gutelman, *Capitalismo y reforma agraria,* 191–4.
22. Gutelman, *Capitalismo y reforma agraria,* 188.
23. Bartra, *Agrarian Structure,* 93–94.
24. Gutelman, *Capitalismo y Reforma,* 196.
25. Discussed in more detail in the next chapter. Data is from: Gutelman, *Capitalismo y reforma agraria,* 197–201.
26. Baird and McCaughan, *Beyond the Border,* 205.
27. For a full historical overview and analysis, see Rocío Guadarrama, *Los sindicatos y la política en Mexico: La CROM, 1918–1929* (Mexico: Era Ediciones), 1984.
28. See Barry Carr, *Marxism & Communism in Twentieth-Century Mexico* (Lincoln: University of Nebraska Press, 1992).
29. For a full discussion of these strikes and others similar in nature, see Rodolfo F. Peña, *Insurgencia obrera y nacionalismo revolucionario* (Coyoacán, México: Ediciones Ell Caballito, 1973).
30. For a discussion of how this notion of class harmony is embedded in Article 123, see Teresa Healy, *Gendered Struggles against Globalisation in Mexico* (Hampshire, UK: Ashgate Publishing, 2008), 28–29.
31. Healy, *Gendered Struggles against Globalisation,* 31.
32. See Carr, *Marxism & Communism.*
33. Luis H. Mendez Berrueta, ed., *Modernidad productivida y sindicatos en México: 1983–2010* (Mexico: Universidad Autónomo Metropolitana, 2011), 65.

34. For an overview of this process, see Carr, *Marxism & Communism.*
35. For a comprehensive study of this process, see Dan La Botz, *Mask of Democracy: Labor Suppression in Mexico Today* (Boston: South End Press, 1992).
36. Maxfield, *Governing Capital*, 82.
37. Mendez Berrueta, ed., *Modernidad productivida y sindicatos*, 65–66.
38. Demetrio Vallejo, *Las Luchas Ferrocarrileras que Conmovieron a México* (self-produced historical account, in pamphlet form, written by Vallejo while he was in prison, published in Mexico City in 1967), 39.
39. Maximino Ortega Aguirre, "La lucha contra el 'charrismo,' en el STFRM. Las jornadas de junio de 1958" *Iztapalapa* (July–December 1981): 125.
40. Ortega Aguirre, "La lucha contra el 'charrismo,'" 131.
41. Vallejo, *Las Luchas Ferrocarrileras*, 27–28.
42. Ortega Aguirre, "La lucha contra el 'charrismo,'" 131.
43. La Botz, *Mask of Democracy*, 70.
44. La Botz, *Mask of Democracy*, 71.
45. Vallejo, *Las Luchas Ferrocarrileras*, 43.
46. Julio Moreno, *Yankee Don't Go Home: Mexican Nationalism, American Business Culture, and the Shaping of Modern Mexico, 1920–50* (Chapel Hill: University of North Carolina Press, 2003), 17.
47. For a theoretical overview, see Héctor Guillén Romo, *Orígenes de la Crisis en México.* (Mexico: Ediciones Era, 2005).
48. Lionel Morgan Summers, "The Calvo Clause," *Virginia Law Review* 19, no. 5 (March 1933), 459.
49. Rogelio Hernández Rodríguez, "La conducta empresarial en el gobierno de Miguel de la Madrid," *Foro Internacional* 30, no. 4 (April–June 1990): 737.
50. Elvira Concheiro Bórquez, *El gran acuerdo: gobierno y empresarios en la modernización salinista* (Mexico: Universidad Nacional Autónoma de México, Instituto de Investigaciones Económicas, 1996), 73–75.
51. Francisco Alba and Joseph E. Potter, "Population and Development in Mexico since 1940: An Interpretation," *Population and Development Review* 12, no. 1 (March 1986): 47–48.

## Chapter 3

1. For a thorough description of this historic process, see Norman A. Graebner, *Empire of the Pacific: A Study in American Commercial Power* (Claremont: Regina Books, 1983).
2. For a good theoretical analysis of this period of US-centric imperialist expansion, see Michael Kidron, *Capitalism and Theory: Selected Writings of Michael Kidron* (Chicago: Haymarket Books, 2018), especially chapters 2, 3, and 4.

3. For a detailed, exhaustive study of US economic imperialism in Mexico, see *Empire and Revolution: The Americans in Mexico since the Civil War* (Berkeley: University of California Press, 2006).
4. See Josefina Zoraida Vásquez y Lorenzo Meyer, "La guerra civil y la intervención norteamericana," chapter 6 in *México frente a Estados Unidos: Un ensayo histórico, 1776–2000.* (Mexico: Fondo de Cultura Económica, 2013).
5. This economic reorganization of global capitalism was followed by an attempt to create a new international political and military order with the US at the center, which transpired one year later with the launch of the United Nations Convention in San Francisco.
6. Harry Magdoff, *The Age of Imperialism: The Economics of US Foreign Policy* (New York, Monthly Review Press, 1969), 42, 56, 58.
7. For a critical analysis of the character of the Soviet Union from this perspective, see Tony Cliff, *State Capitalism in Russia* (Chicago: Haymarket Books, 2019).
8. Klaus Knorr, "The Bretton Woods Institutions in Transition" *International Organization* 2, no. 1 (February 1948): 19–20.
9. Robert Brenner, *The Economics of Global Turbulence* (New York: Verso Books, 2006), 66.
10. Mike Patton, "US Role in Global Economy Declines Nearly 50%," *Forbes,* February 29, 2016, www.forbes.com/sites/mikepatton/2016/02/29/u-s-role-in-global-economy-declines-nearly-50/.
11. See Odd Arne Westad, *Global Cold War: Third World Interventions and the Making of Our Times* (Cambridge: Cambridge University Press, 2011).
12. Magdoff, *Age of Imperialism,* 42.
13. Brenner, "Descent into Crisis," chapter 8 in *Economics of Global Turbulence.*
14. See Kim Moody, "The Roots of Change," chapter 1 in *On New Terrain: How Capital is Reshaping the Battleground of Class War* (Chicago: Haymarket Books, 2017).
15. For a fuller theoretical discussion of this phase of capitalist accumulation, see Brenner, *Economics of Global Turbulence.*
16. US capital traditionally dominated the thirty-three other nations comprising the Americas through military force, economic dependencies, and political subservience, facilitating exports and extraction of raw materials. Countries such as Mexico were determined to construct a path toward economic development through state-managed capitalism to overcome perpetual underdevelopment.
17. For an analysis of US-Mexico international policy in this period, see Robert Freeman Smith, *The United States and Revolutionary Nationalism in Mexico, 1916–1932* (Chicago: University of Chicago Press, 1972); see also Stephen D. Krasner, *Defending the National Interest: Raw Materials Investments and US Foreign Policy* (Princeton: Princeton University Press, 1978), 155–78.
18. Stephen R. Niblo, *War, Diplomacy, and Development: The United States and Mexico, 1938–54* (Wilmington: Scholarly Resources, 1995), 93–94.

19. Niblo, *War, Diplomacy, and Development*, 106.
20. Sylvia Maxfield, *Governing Capital: International Finance and Mexican Politics* (Ithaca: Cornell University Press, 1990), 74.
21. Niblo, *War, Diplomacy, and Development*, 109.
22. Barkin, "Mexico's Albatross," 70.
23. Peter Baird and Ed McCaughan, *Beyond the Border: Mexico and the US Today* (New York: North American Congress on Latin America, 1979), 6.
24. David Barkin, "Mexico's Albatross: The United States Economy" in *Latin American Perspectives* 2, no 2 (Summer 1975): 72.
25. See George Moss, *Moving On: The American People Since 1945* (London: Pearson, 2012), 3.
26. For a comprehensive study of the Bracero Program from a union organizer's point of view, see Ernesto Galarza, *Merchants of Labor: The Mexican Bracero Story: An Account of the Managed Migration of Mexican Farm Workers in California 1942–1960* (McNally and Loftin Publishing, 1964).
27. Linda C. Majka and Theo J. Majka, *Farm Workers, Agribusiness, and the State* (Philadelphia: Temple University Press, 1982), 141–42.
28. Deborah Cohen, *Braceros: Migrant Citizens and Transnational Subjects in the Postwar United States and Mexico* (Chapel Hill: University of North Carolina Press, 2011), 28–31.
29. Cohen, *Braceros: Migrant Citizens* , 24.
30. See Pam Belluck, "Settlement Will Allow Thousands of Mexican Laborers in US to Collect Back Pay," *New York Times,* October 15, 2008, www.nytimes.com/2008/10/16/us/16settle.html.
31. For an extensive study of this historical process see Ernesto Galarza, *Farm Workers and Agri-Business in California, 1947–1960* (Notre Dame, IN: University of Notre Dame Press, 1977).
32. For a description of how bracero wages were used, see Ronald L. Mize, "The Bracero Working Day and the Contested Terrain of Class Relations," chapter 3 in *The Invisible Workers of the US–Mexico Bracero Program: Obreros Olvidados* (Lanham, MD: Lexington Books, 2016).
33. John Lewis Gaddis, *Strategies of Containment: A Critical Appraisal of Postwar American National Security Policy* (New York: Oxford University Press, 1982), 4.
34. Gaddis, *Strategies of Containment,* 58.
35. That same year Senator Pat McCarran, a Democratic senator and vocal anticommunist and immigration restrictionist, justified his crusade for border enforcement by alleging that Communist agents were among the "wetbacks" who crossed the Rio Grande. In response to this purported threat, Eisenhower's attorney general Herbert Brownell applied containment ideology to border militarization when he initiated "Operation Wetback," a policy for border enforcement and unauthorized immigrant removal. Brownell's initial abortive immigration plans

included the placement of a thousand troops on the border and the construction of a one-hundred-and-fifty-mile border wall. His aggressive stance was illustrated by a notorious comment made at a meeting with labor unions that "one way of discouraging wetbacks would be to allow the border patrol to shoot some of them." See See Juan Ramon García, *Operation Wetback: The Mass Deportation of Mexican Undocumented Workers in 1954* (Westport, CT: Greenhaven Press, 1980).

36. Steven Schlesinger and Stephen Kinzer, *Bitter Fruit: The Untold Story of an American Coup in Guatemala* (Garden City, NY: Anchor Books, 1982), 11.
37. Diana Tussie, *Multilateral Development Banks: Inter-American Development Bank* (Warwickshire, UK: Practical Action Publishing, 1995), 20.
38. Harry M. Cleaver Jr., "The Contradictions of the Green Revolution," *American Economic Review* 62, no. 1/2 (March 1, 1972): 179.
39. Cristina Puga, *México: Empresarios y poder* (Mexico: Facultad de Ciencias Políticas y Sociales, UNAM, 1993), 38.
40. Baird and McCaughan, *Beyond the Border*, 4.
41. For a historical overview of this process, see Thomas O'Brien, "Globalization and Its Discontents," chapter 10 in *Making the Americas: The United States and Latin America from the Age of Revolutions to the Era of Globalization* (Albuquerque: University of New Mexico Press, 2007); Henry Veltmeyer, James Petras, and Steve Vieux, "Neoliberalism and Capitalism in Mexico 1983–95: Model of Structural Adjustment?" chapter 7 in *Neoliberalism and Class Conflict in Latin America: A Comparative Perspective on the Political Economy of Structural Adjustment* (London: Palgrave Macmillan, 1997).
42. For an exhaustive analysis of this process in the 1960s, see Frank Bardacke, *Trampling Out the Vintage: Cesar Chavez and the Two Souls of the United Farm Workers* (London: Verso Books, 2012).

## Chapter 4

1. Teresa Healy, *Gendered Struggles against Globalisation in Mexico* (Hampshire, UK: Ashgate Publishing, 2008), 72.
2. Sylvia Maxfield, *Governing Capital: International Finance and Mexican Politics* (Ithaca: Cornell University Press, 1990).
3. See Juan Mora-Torres, *The Making of the Mexican Border: The State, Capitalism, and Society in Nuevo León, 1848–1910* (Austin: University of Texas Press, 2001).
4. Katherine G. Morrissey and John-Michael H. Warner, *Border Spaces: Visualizing the US-Mexico Frontera* (Tucson: University of Arizona Press, 2018), 87.
5. Cristina Puga, *México: Empresarios y poder* (Mexico: Facultad de Ciencias Políticas y Sociales, UNAM, 1993), 47.
6. Brookings Institution, *Annual Report*, 1983.
7. María Patricia Fernández-Kelly, *For We Are Sold: Women and Industry in Mexico's Frontier* (Albany, State University of New York Press, 1983), 27.

8. Fernández-Kelly, *For We Are Sold*, 27–28.
9. Fernández-Kelly, "The Maquila Women: Characteristics of the Workforce in Ciudad Juarez's Assembly Plants," chapter 3 in *For We are Sold*, Chapter 3.
10. Rachael Kamel, "'This Is How It Starts': Women Maquila Workers in Mexico," *Labor Research Review* 1, no. 11 (April 1988): 16.
11. Juan Carlos Moreno-Brid, "Economic Development and Industrial Performance in Mexico post-NAFTA" (lecture at Taller Nacional sobre "Migración interna y desarrollo en México: Diagnóstico, perspectivas y políticas," organizado por la Comisión Económica para América Latina y el Caribe, CELADE-División de Población, con el apoyo y auspicio del Banco Interamericano de Desarrollo [BID]), Ciudad de México, México, April 16, 2007, www.cepal.org/sites/default/files/courses/files/jcmorenop.pdf.
12. Healy, *Gendered Struggles against Globalisation*, 41.
13. David Barkin, "Mexico's Albatross: The United States Economy," *Latin American Perspectives* 2, no. 2 (Summer 1975): 72.
14. Fernández-Kelly, *For We Are Sold*, 1983, 34.
15. Barkin, "Mexico's Albatross," 71.
16. Peter Baird and Ed McCaughan, *Beyond the Border: Mexico and the US Today* (New York: North American Congress on Latin America, 1979), 5.
17. Healy, *Gendered Struggles against Globalization*, 40.
18. Barkin, "Mexico's Albatross," 72.
19. John A. Adams Jr., *Mexican Banking and Investment in Transition* (Westport, CT: Quorum Books, 1997), 36.
20. Bert R. Pena, Amy Henderson, Eduardo Robles-Elias, James F. Smith, "US-Mexico Agricultural Trade and Investment after NAFTA," *United States-Mexico Law Journal* 1, no. 1 (1993): 262–63.
21. Pena, Henderson, Robles-Elias, and Smith, "US-Mexico Agricultural Trade," 262–63.
22. Eric Perramond, "The Rise, Fall, and Reconfiguration of the Mexican 'Ejido'," *Geographical Review* 98, no. 3 (July, 2008): 359. While the state cancelled the ejido, other forms of communal land persist.
23. USGAO, NSAID-87-77BR (1987), 12, www.gao.gov/assts/nsaid-87-77br.pdf.
24. Michael W. Goldman, Michael C. McClintock, James J. Tallaksen, and Richard J. Wolkowitz, "An Introduction to Direct Foreign Investment in Mexico: A Contemporary and Historical Legal Analysis of Mexican Direct Foreign Investment Laws and Policies and their Relation to the North American Free Trade Agreement," *Indiana International & Comparative Law Review* 5, no. 1 (1994): 106–9.
25. United States International Trade Commission, "Imports Under Items 806.30 And 807.00 of the Tariff Schedules of the United States, 1984–87," December 1988, 11.
26. Maxfield, *Governing Capital*, 116.
27. Adams, *Mexican Banking and Investment*, 55.

28. Moreno-Brid, "Economic Development and Industrial Performance."
29. See Justin Akers Chacón and Mike Davis, *No One Is Illegal: Fighting Racism and State Repression on the U.S.-Mexico Border* (Chicago: Haymarket Books, 2018), 121–22.

## Chapter 5

1. See Michael Roberts, "The Profitability Crisis and the Neoliberal Response," chapter 4 in *The Long Depression: Marxism and the Global Crisis of Capitalism* (Chicago: Haymarket Books, 2016).
2. For a comprehensive analysis of US imperialist interventions in Latin America, see Stephen G. Rabe, *The Killing Zone: The United States Wages Cold War in Latin America* (Oxford: Oxford University Press, 2016).
3. For a historical overview of this process, see David Harvey, *A Brief History of Neoliberalism* (Oxford: Oxford University Press, 2007).
4. For a thorough analysis of this historical process, see Michael C. Dreiling and Derek Y. Darves, *Agents of Neoliberal Globalization: Corporate Networks, State Structures, and Trade Policy* (Cambridge: Cambridge University Press, 2016).
5. For a thorough explanation of the Volker Shock and its significance, see Leo Panitch and Martijn Konings, "Constructing the Pillars of Imperial Finance," part 2 in *American Empire and the Political Economy of Global Finance* (New York: Palgrave Macmillan).
6. *Mexican Oil and Technology Transfer, Hearings before the Subcommittee on Investigations and Oversight of the Committee on Science and Technology,* US House of Representatives, 96th Cong. (US Government Printing Office Washington, DC, 1979), 52.
7. *Mexican Oil and Technology Transfer, Hearings*, 231.
8. *Mexican Oil and Technology Transfer, Hearings*, 230.
9. *Mexican Oil and Technology Transfer, Hearings*, 233.
10. *Mexican Oil and Technology Transfer, Hearings*, 235.
11. Paul V. Kershaw, "Averting a Global Financial Crisis: The US, the IMF, and the Mexican Debt Crisis of 1976," *International History Review* 40, no. 2 (2018): 292–314, https://doi.org/10.1080/07075332.2017.1326966.
12. Sylvia Maxfield, *Governing Capital: International Finance and Mexican Politics* (Ithaca: Cornell University Press, 1990), 124.
13. One example of this is the Foro Empresarial IberoAmerica, an annual hemispheric gathering of representatives of Latin American and North American capitalist groups that combines dialogue about relevant political issues affecting business interests with discourse about prospects for economic collaboration.
14. Cristina Puga, *México: empresarios y poder* (Mexico: Facultad de Ciencias Políticas y Sociales, UNAM, 1993), 46.
15. David Barkin, "Mexico's Albatross: The United States Economy" in *Latin American Perspectives* 2, no. 2 (Summer 1975): 67.

16. Maxfield, *Governing Capital*, 97.
17. Maxfield, *Governing Capital*, 97.
18. For an analysis of the decline of social democracy through the embrace of neoliberalism, see Ashley Lavelle, "Social Democracy and Neo-liberalism," chapter 2 in *The Death of Social Democracy: Political Consequences in the Twenty-First Century* (New York: Routledge, 2016).
19. Héctor Guillén Romo, *México Frente a la Mundialización Neoliberal* (Mexico: Ediciones Era, 2005), 32.
20. See Ed Lee Stacy, *Mexico and the United States* (New York: Marshall Cavendish, 2002), 39; see also Jeffrey F. Taffet, *Foreign Aid as Foreign Policy: The Alliance for Progress in Latin America* (New York: Routledge), 2011.
21. Jorge Mendoza García, "Reconstructing the Collective Memory of Mexico's Dirty War: Ideologization, Clandestine Detention, and Torture," *Latin American Perspectives* 43, no. 6 (September 2016): 124–40.
22. Vijay Prashad, *The Darker Nations: A People's History of the Third World* (New York: New Press, 2007), 257–58.
23. Strom C. Thacker, *Big Business, the State, and Free Trade: Constructing Coalitions in Mexico* (Cambridge, UK: Cambridge University Press, 2006), 67.
24. Elvira Concheiro Bórquez, *El gran acuerdo: Gobierno y empresarios en la modernización salinista* (Mexico: Instituto de Investigaciones Económicas, UNAM, 1996), 27.
25. Cristina Puga, *México: Empresarios y poder* (Mexico: Facultad de Ciencias Políticas y Sociales, UNAM, 1993), 55.
26. Concheiro Bórquez, *El gran acuerdo*, 60.
27. See Alex M. Saragoza, *The Monterrey Elite and the Mexican State, 1880–1940* (Austin: University of Texas Press, 1988).
28. David Harvey, *A Brief History of Neoliberalism* (Oxford: Oxford University Press, 2007), 103.
29. Thacker, *Big Business*, 17.
30. Maxfield, *Governing Capital*, 111.
31. John A. Adams Jr., *Mexican Banking and Investment in Transition* (Westport, CT: Quorum Books, 1997), 4.
32. Dale Story, *Industry, the State, and Public Policy in Mexico* (Austin: University of Texas Press), 101.
33. See Rogelio Hernández Rodríguez, "Los hombres del Presidente de la Madrid," *Foro Internacional* 28, no. 2 (July–September 1987): 5–38.
34. Rogelio Hernández Rodríguez, "La política y los empresarios después de la nacionalización bancaria," *Foro Internacional* 27, no. 2 (October–December 1984): 251–52.
35. Maxfield, *Governing Capital*, 160.
36. Hernández Rodríguez, "La política y los empresarios," 252.

37. Rogelio Hernández Rodríguez, "La conducta empresarial en el gobierno de Miguel de la Madrid," *Foro Internacional* 300, no. 4 (April–June 1990), 750.
38. Hernández Rodríguez, "La política y los empresarios," 252.
39. Thacker, *Big Business*, 72.
40. Concheiro Bórquez, *El gran acuerdo*, 28.
41. Quoted in Hernández Rodríguez, "La conducta empresarial," 742.
42. Hernández Rodríguez, "La conducta empresarial," 756, 759.
43. These included: The Pact for Stability and Economic Growth (PECE); followed by Pact for Stability, Competitiveness, and Employment (PECE); Pact of Economic Solidarity (PSE); and others.

## Chapter 6

1. Flavia Rodriguez, "The Mexican Privatization Programme: An Economic Analysis," *Social and Economic Studies* 41, no. 4(December 1992): 156.
2. Elvira Concheiro Bórquez, *El gran acuerdo: Gobierno y empresarios en la modernización salinista* (Mexico: Instituto de Investigaciones Económicas, UNAM, 1996), 73–79.
3. Concheiro Bórquez, *El gran acuerdo*, 79.
4. Dulce Olvera, "Las empresas públicas (63%) que remató Carlos Salinas hicieron a 23 familias súper ricas hasta hoy," elmanifesto.com.mx, Febrero 28, 2019, www.elmanifesto.com.mx/27-02-2019/3541993.
5. Simona Yagenova and Rodrigo J. Véliz, *Capital y luchas: Breve análisis de la protesta y el conflicto social actual* (Guatemala City: FLACSO, 2009), 44.
6. Elvira Concheiro Bórquez, *El gran acuerdo: Gobierno y empresarios en la modernización salinista* (Mexico: Instituto de Investigaciones Económicas, UNAM, 1996), 27.
7. Concheiro Bórquez, *El gran acuerdo*, 20.
8. Concheiro Bórquez, *El gran acuerdo*, 80.
9. Strom C. Thacker, *Big Business, the State, and Free Trade: Constructing Coalitions in Mexico* (Cambridge, UK: Cambridge University Press, 2006), 66.
10. Sylvia Maxfield, *Governing Capital: International Finance and Mexican Politics* (Ithaca: Cornell University Press, 1990), 139.
11. Thacker, *Big Business*, 60.
12. Thacker, *Big Business*, 51.
13. Concheiro Bórquez, *El gran acuerdo*, 23–24
14. Thacker, *Big Business*, 56. (Dollar-indexed T-bills; 57).
15. Concheiro Bórquez, *El gran acuerdo*, 36.
16. Concheiro Bórquez, *El gran acuerdo*, 35
17. James M. Cypher and Raúl Delgado Wise, *Mexico's Economic Dilemma: The*

*Developmental Failure of Neoliberalism* (Lanham: Rowman and Littlefield, 2010), 48.

18. John A. Adams Jr., *Mexican Banking and Investment in Transition* (Westport, CT: Quorum Books, 1997), 73, 93, 114.
19. See US Department of State, "2019 Investment Climate Statements: Mexico," www.state.gov/reports/2019-investment-climate-statements/mexico/.
20. Concheiro Bórquez, *El gran acuerdo*, 94–96.
21. Adams, *Mexican Banking and Investment*, 21.
22. Adams, *Mexican Banking and Investment*, 66.
23. The Economist Intelligence Unit, *Country Commerce: Mexico* (New York: EIU, 2018), 18. This maximum limit was realized with the passage of the USMCA in 2019.
24. Adams, *Mexican Banking and Investment*, 95.
25. Adams, *Mexican Banking and Investment*, 96–114.
26. Roy E. Allen, *Financial Crises and Recession in the Global Economy* (Northampton: Edward Elgar Publishing, Inc., 1999), 133,
27. It was also referred to colloquially as the "Tequila Crisis," as it impacted the economies of other countries in Latin America with trade relations with Mexico and its effects were compared to that of a hangover.
28. Adams, *Mexican Banking and Investment*, 118.
29. Adams, *Mexican Banking and Investment*, 120.
30. Mark Fineman, "Mexico Uses $4 Billion From US Bailout to Pay Investors," *Los Angeles Times*, April 5, 1995, www.latimes.com/archives/la-xpm-1995-04-05-mn-51117-story.html.
31. For a historical overview, see Jesus Cañas, Roberto Coronado, and Pia M. Orrenius, "Explaining the Increase in Remittances to Mexico" *Southwest Economy*, July/August 2007, www.dallasfed.org/~/media/documents/research/swe/2007/swe0704b.pdf.
32. The Federal Reserve Board, "Directo a México Frequently Asked Questions," www.frbservices.org/resources/financial-services/ach/faq/directo-a-mexico.html.
33. Stephen Haber, Aldo Musacchio, and Liliana Rojas-Suarez, "Foreign Entry and the Mexican Banking System, 1997–2007" *Economía* 13, no. 1 (Fall 2012): 15.
34. Rubén Hernández-Murillo, "Experiments in Financial Liberalization: The Mexican Banking Sector," *Federal Reserve Bank of St. Louis Review* (September/October 2007), 429, https://files.stlouisfed.org/files/htdocs/publications/review/07/09/HernandezMurillo.pdf.
35. Cypher and Delgado Wise, *Mexico's Economic Dilemma*, 48.
36. These include: the Asian-Pacific Economic Cooperation forum in 1993; the North American Free Trade Agreement, the Organization for Economic Cooperation and Development, and the Mexico–Colombia Free Trade Agreement in 1994; Chile–Mexico Free Trade Agreement in 1998; The European Free Trade Association (EFTA) and the Mexico–Israel Free Trade Agreement in 2000;

the Mexico–Uruguay Free Trade Agreement and the Japan-Mexico Economic Partnership Agreement in 2004; the Mexico-Bolivia Economic Complementation Agreement in 2010; the Mexico-Peru Trade Integration Agreement and the Pacific Alliance in 2011; the Mexico–Central America Free Trade Agreement in 2013; the Mexico–Panama Free Trade Agreement in 2015; the Trans-Pacific Partnership in 2017; the EU–Mexico Trade Agreement (replacing the EFTA) in 2018; and the United States–Mexico–Canada Agreement in 2019 (expanding NAFTA).

37. Tetakawi Group, *Mexico's Top Free Trade Agreements and their Impact*, May 22, 2020, https://insights.tetakawi.com/top-free-trade-agreements-with-mexico.

38. For some perspectives on this, see Alejandro Colas, Richard Saull, *The War on Terrorism and the American "Empire" After the Cold War* (Oxfordshire: Taylor & Francis, 2007).

39. The perspective of the Communist International was that it was impossible for semicolonial countries to achieve substantive development and industrialization, and to transform property relations without a socialist and democratic revolution. This required the overthrow of the semicolonial ruling class by the workers and peasants, national liberation of the country from its client relationship with foreign powers, and the formation of a revolutionary worker and peasant government in the mold of the Russian Revolution. In this particular case, I am using this model to describe the condition of Mexico in relation to the US, both before the Mexican Revolution of 1910 and after the dismantling of state-managed capitalism at the end of the twentieth century. For a historical analysis of this theory, see Ian Birchall, "The Communist International and Imperialism," *Viewpoint*, February 1, 2018, https://viewpointmag.com/2018/02/01/communist-international-imperialism/. See also Vladimir Ilyich Lenin, *Imperialism, the Highest Stage of Capitalism*, in *Lenin's Selected Works*, vol. 1 (Moscow: Progress Publishers, 1963), 667–766, www.marxists.org/archive/lenin/works/1916/imp-hsc/; another approach to this phenomenon, especially in the former colonized countries, has been referred to as "neo-colonialism," see Kwame Nkrumah, *Neo-Colonialism: The Last Stage of Imperialism* (New York: International Publishers, 1965).

40. See Ashley Smith and Kevin Lin, "China and the United States: A New Cold War," *New Politics* 18, no. 1 (Summer 2020), https://newpol.org/issue_post/china-and-the-united-states-a-new-cold-war/.

41. For example, see Nicholas Cunningham, "López Obrador Pivots on NAFTA" *NACLA*, October 25, 2018. https://nacla.org/news/2018/10/25/l%C3%B3pez-obrador-pivots-nafta.

42. See Kim Moody, *On New Terrain: How Capital Is Reshaping the Battleground of Class War* (Chicago: Haymarket Books, 2017), Part 1.

43. Andrew Keshner, "America's 1% Hasn't Had This Much Wealth Since Just before the Great Depression," *Market Watch*, February 24, 2019, www.marketwatch.com/story/its-been-almost-a-100-years-since-the-americas-1-had-so-much-wealth-2019-02-11.

44. Moody, *On New Terrain*, 30.

45. Ruchir Sharma, "The Billionaire Boom: How the Super-Rich Soaked up Covid Cash," *Financial Times*, May 13, 2021, www.ft.com/content/747a76dd-f018-4d0d-a9f3-4069bf2f5a93

46. Kerry A. Dolan, "Mexico's Richest Billionaires 2021," *Forbes*, April 6, 2021, www.forbes.com/sites/kerryadolan/2021/04/06/mexicos-richest-billionaires-2021/?sh=163683565265.

47. For a description of different stages in this process, see BBVA Research, *Handbook of Mexican Financial Instruments*, February 20, 2011, www.bbvaresearch.com/en/publicaciones/handbook-of-mexican-financial-instruments/.

48. Adams, *Mexican Banking and Investment*, 6.

49. Roberto Gonzalez Amador and David Brooks, "México, el mayor expulsor de migrantes del planeta, dice el BM," *La Jornada*, April 16, 2007.

50. For an international comparative case study, see Eduardo Silva, "The Import-Substitution Model: Chile in Comparative Perspective," *Latin American Perspectives* 34, no. 3 (May 2007): 67–90.

51. James M. Boughton, *Tearing Down Walls: The International Monetary Fund 1990–1999* (International Monetary Fund, 2012), 189, www.imf.org/external/pubs/ft/history/2012/.

52. Osvaldo Martínez and Luis Fierro, "Debt and Foreign Capital: The Origin of the Crisis," *Latin American Perspectives* 20, no. (Winter 1993): 69.

53. Robert Solomon, "The Debt of Developing Countries: Another Look," Brookings Papers on Economic Activity 2, 1981, 593–607, www.brookings.edu/wp-content/uploads/1981/06/1981b_bpea_solomon_sachs.pdf.

54. Dora Villanueva, "En poco más de 11 años la deuda externa de México creció 749 por ciento," *La Jornada*, April 13, 2020, www.jornada.com.mx/2020/04/13/economia/025n1eco. As ofSeptember 2020, according to data posted by the Banco de Mexico (Banxico), "Gross external debt position. By residence criteria. (CE101), www.banxico.org.mx/SieInternet/consultarDirectorioInternetAction.do?accion=consultarCuadro&idCuadro=CE101§orDescripcion=Balanza%20de%20pagos&locale=en.

55. Alejandro Alvarez Bejar, Gabriel Mendoza Pichardo, and John F. Uggen, "Mexico 1988–1991: A Successful Economic Adjustment Program?" *Latin American Perspectives* 20, no. 3 (Summer, 1993): 139.

56. International Monetary Fund, "Mexico: Arrangement Under the Flexible Credit Line and Cancellation of Current Arrangement—Press Release; and Staff Report," (IMF Country Report No. 19/354, November 2019).

57. See Rudiger Dornbusch and Stanley Fischer, "Third World Debt," *Science* 234, no. 4778 (November 14, 1986): 837; G. C. da Costa, "External Debt of Developing Countries Crisis of Growth," *Economic and Political Weekly* 26, no. 8 (February 23, 1991): 433.

58. World Bank, "Debt Stocks of Developing Countries Rose to $7.8 Trillion in 2018: World Bank International Debt Statistics," Press Release, October 2, 2019, www

.worldbank.org/en/news/press-release/2019/10/02/debt-stocks-of-developing-countries-rose-to-78-trillion-in-2018-world-bank-international-debt-statistics.

59. See Delphine Strauss and Jonathan Wheatley, "Developing countries scramble for funds to stave off virus impact," *Financial Times,* March 31 2020, www.ft.com/content/756d85fa-6fad-412f-9aaf-c3f476415ae1.

60. Luis Alberto Moreno, "Latin America's Lost Decades: The Toll of Inequality in the Age of COVID-19" *Foreign Affairs,* January/February 2021, www.foreignaffairs.com/articles/south-america/2020-12-08/latin-americas-lost-decades.

61. David de Ferranti, Guillermo E. Perry, Francisco H. G. Ferreira, Michael Walton, *Inequality in Latin America: Breaking with History?* (Washington, DC: World Bank, 2004), 1–5.

62. Moreno, "Latin America's Lost Decades."

63. Erica Belcher "Inequality in Mexico and How to Address It," LSE Government (blog), March 24, 2017, https://blogs.lse.ac.uk/government/2017/03/24/inequality-in-mexico-and-how-to-address-it/.

64. Belcher, "Inequality in Mexico and How to Address It."

65. "United States Corporate Profits," data collated from a US Bureau of Economic Analysis, published at Trading Economics, https://tradingeconomics.com/united-states/corporate-profits.

66. Congressional Research Service, *US–Mexico Economic Relations: Trends, Issues, and Implications,* December 6, 2018, 6, www.everycrsreport.com/files/20181206_RL32934_48c8185925caff74f542c3d28efe2b39717ae4af.pdf.

67. United States Department of Transportation, Bureau of Transportation Statistics, "US Trade with Canada and Mexico," www.bts.gov/archive/publications/north_american_trade_and_travel_trends/trade_can_mex.

68. Alan M. Field, "NAFTA at 20: A Transformational Force That Continues to Evolve," *Journal of Commerce,* January 24, 2014, joc.com; *Mexico: US–Mexico Trade Facts,* Office of the United States Trade Representative, available online at https://ustr.gov/countries-regions/americas/mexico.

69. United Nations Conference on Trade and Development, *World Investment Report 2018,* https://unctad.org/en/PublicationsLibrary/wir2018_en.pdf.

70. Gordon H. Hanson, "Globalization, Labor Income, and Poverty in Mexico" (working paper, National Bureau of Economic Research, 2004).

71. Economist Intelligence Unit, *Country Commerce: Mexico* (New York: EIU, 2009).

72. Dev Kar, "Mexico: Illicit Financial Flows, Macroeconomic Imbalances, and the Underground Economy" *SSRN Electronic Journal,* January 30, 2012, https://gfintegrity.org/report/mexico-illicit-financial-flows-macroeconomic-imbalances-and-the-underground-economy/.

## Chapter 7

1. James M. Cypher and Raúl Delgado Wise, *Mexico's Economic Dilemma: The*

*Developmental Failure of Neoliberalism* (Lanham: Rowman and Littlefield, 2010), 31.

2. Michael C. Dreiling, "The Class Embeddedness of Corporate Political Action: Leadership in Defense of the NAFTA," *Social Problems* 47, no. 1 (February 2000): 25.
3. Alfredo Corchado and Jasmine Aguilera, "The New Border: Mexico and US Join in Educating Students 'To Compete with the World,'" *Dallas Morning News,* 2015, http://res.dallasnews.com/interactives/mexico-students/.
4. Institute of International Education, *Open Doors Report on International Educational Exchange* (2020), www.opendoorsdata.org.
5. All records of the initiative were scrubbed from the US State Department's home page.
6. Uriel Naum, "Las empresas donde los universitarios mexicanos quieren trabajar," *Forbes México,* Jun 18, 2019, www.forbes.com.mx/las-empresas-donde-los-universitarios-mexicanos-quieren-trabajar/.
7. UBS/PwC, *New Visionaries and the Chinese Century: Billionaires Insights 2018* (Zurich, October 26, 2018), 24.
8. Nina Lakhani, "Honduras Elites Blamed for Violence against Environmental Activists," *Guardian,* January 31, 2017, www.theguardian.com/world/2017/jan/31/honduras-environmental-activists-global-witness-violence-berta-caceres.
9. Arturo Wallace, "¿Quiénes son los hombres más ricos de América Central y por qué es tan difícil saber a cuánto ascienden sus fortunas?" *BBC Mundo,* October 19, 2017, www.bbc.com/mundo/noticias-america-latina-41085699.
10. Wallace, "¿Quienes son los hombres más ricos?"
11. Blake Schmidt, "Carlos Slim Bested by Mobile Billionaire in Guatemala," *Bloomberg,* August 4, 2014, www.bloomberg.com/news/articles/2014-08-04/richest-guatemalan-lopez-emerges-with-tigo-cell-service.
12. See "Who Are the Richest Men in Central America an Why," Qcostarica, October 24, 2017, https://qcostarica.com/who-are-the-richest-men-in-central-america-and-why/; "The World Bank in El Salvador," worldbank.org, October 9, 2000, www.worldbank.org/en/country/elsalvador/overview.
13. Erica Belcher, "Inequality in Mexico and How to Address It," *LSE Government* (blog), March 24, 2017, https://blogs.lse.ac.uk/government/2017/03/24/inequality-in-mexico-and-how-to-address-it/
14. Lilia González, "México tendrá 70 millones de pobres si gobierno no se apoya en la IP para la reactivación," *El Economista,* June 4, 2020, www.eleconomista.com.mx/empresas/Mexico-tendra-70-millones-de-pobres-si-gobierno-no-se-apoya-en-la-IP-para-la-reactivacion-20200604-0072.html..
15. Hilary Klein, "A Spark of Hop: The Ongoing Lessons of the Zapatista Revolution 25 Years On," *NACLA,* January 18, 2019, https://nacla.org/news/2019/01/18/spark-hope-ongoing-lessons-zapatista-revolution-25-years.
16. David Bacon, "The Rebirth of Mexico's Electrical Workers," *NACLA,* February 7, 2019, https://nacla.org/news/2019/02/07/rebirth-mexico%E2%80%99s

-electrical-workers.

17. For an overview, see María Eugenia De la O and Christian Zlolniski, "At the Crossroads: Challenges and Opportunities of Union Organizing in the Mexico-US Border," *Dialectical Anthropology* 44 (2020), 187–204.
18. David Barkin, "Mexico's Albatross: The United States Economy," *Latin American Perspectives* 2, no. 2 (Summer 1975): 77.
19. Stephen R. Niblo, "Progress and the Standard of Living in Mexico," *Latin American Perspectives* 2, no. 2 (Summer 1975): 113.
20. *Mexican Oil and Technology Transfer: Hearings Before the Subcommittee on Investigations and Oversight of the Committee on Science and Technology*, 96th Cong. (1979), 233.
21. Cypher and Delgado Wise, *Mexico's Economic Dilemma*, 49
22. John A. Adams Jr., *Mexican Banking and Investment in Transition* (Westport, CT: Quorum Books, 1997), 160.
23. Luis H. Mendez Berrueta, ed., *Modernidad Productivida y sindicatos en México: 1983–2010* (Mexico: Universidad Autónomo Metropolitana, 2011), 168–73.
24. Gordon H. Hanson, "Globalization, Labor Income, and Poverty in Mexico," in *Globalization and Poverty*, ed. Ann Harrison (University of Chicago Press, 2007), 422.
25. Martha Ojeda and Rosemary Hennessy, eds., NAFTA from Below: Maquiladora Workers, Farmers and Indigenous Communities Speak Out on the Impact of Free Trade in Mexico (San Antonio: Coalition for Justice in the Maquiladoras, 2006).
26. Mark Eric Williams, "Learning the Limits of Power: Privatization and State-Labor Interactions in Mexico," *Latin American Politics and Society* 43, no. 4 (Winter 2001): 93.
27. Mendez Berrueta, ed., *Modernidad Productivida y sindicatos*, 47.
28. Mendez Berrueta, ed., *Modernidad Productivida y sindicatos*, 133.
29. Cypher and Delgado Wise, *Mexico's Economic Dilemma*, 58.
30. Mendez Berrueta, ed., *Modernidad Productivida y sindicatos*, 155.
31. Mendez Berrueta, ed., *Modernidad Productivida y sindicatos*, 155.
32. Raúl Madrid, "The Politics and Economics of Pension Privatization in Latin America," *Latin American Research Review* 37, no. 2 (2002): 166.
33. Oscar Rico, "The Privatisation of Mexican Airports," *Journal of Air Transport Management* 14, no. 6 (November 2008): 321.
34. Forbes staff, "México, el pais con l salario mínimo más bajo en el OCDE," *Forbes Mexico*, August 3, 2015, www.forbes.com.mx/mexico-el-pais-con-el-salario-minimo-mas-bajo-en-la-ocde/.
35. Stratfor, "Mexico's Manufacturing Sector Continues to Grow," *Forbes*, April 8, 2015, www.forbes.com/sites/stratfor/2015/04/08/mexicos-manufacturing-sector-continues-to-grow/#1bf2b6f85764.

36. George Friedman, "The PC16: Identifying China's Successors," *Stratfor*, July 30, 2013, https://worldview.stratfor.com/article/pc16-identifying-chinas-successors.
37. Duncan Wood, *Mexico's New Energy Reform*, Wilson Center, October 2018, www.wilsoncenter.org/sites/default/files/media/documents/publication/mexicos_new_energy_reform.pdf.
38. *Prospectiva del Sector Eléctrico: 2015–2020*, Secretary of Energy, Mexico, 2015, www.gob.mx/cms/uploads/attachment/file/44328/Prospectiva_del_Sector_Electrico.pdf.
39. Marta Tienda and Susana Sanchez, "Latin American Immigration to the United States," Daedalus 142, no. 3 (Summer 2013): 48–64, www.ncbi.nlm.nih.gov/pmc/articles/PMC4638184/.
40. Jie Zong and Jeanne Batalova, "Mexican Immigrants in the United States in 2017," *Migration Policy Institute*, October 11, 2018, www.migrationpolicy.org/article/mexican-immigrants-united-states.
41. *Hearings before Committee on Homeland Security*, House of Representatives, 111th Cong. (2009, statement of Richard Stana, Director of Homeland Security).
42. Charlotte Edmond, "Global Migration, by the Numbers: Who Migrates, Where They Go and Why," *World Economic Forum*, January 10, 2020, www.weforum.org/agenda/2020/01/iom-global-migration-report-international-migrants-2020/.
43. See Greg Grandin, "The Militarization of the Southern Border Is a Long-Standing American Tradition," *NACLA*, January 17, 2019, https://nacla.org/blog/2019/01/17/militarization-southern-border-long-standing-american-tradition.

## Part II

Quoted in David Bacon, "Los jornaleros del Valle de San Quintín quieren dejar de ser invisibles," *Equal Times*, January 20, 2016, www.equaltimes.org/los-jornaleros-del-valle-de-san#.YBipE-hKiUk (my translation).

## Chapter 8

1. See David Harvey, "Introduction" in *The Limits to Capital* (London: Verso, 2018).
2. Joseph Grunwald, "Restructuring Industry Offshore: The US–Mexico Connection," *Brookings Review* vol. 1, no. 3 (Spring 1983): 24.
3. William B. Cassidy, "Warehousing, Logistics Demand Rising on US–Mexico Border," *Journal of Commerce*, December 9, 2016, joc.com/regulation-policy/trade-agreements/warehousing-logistics-demand-rising-US-mexico-border_20161209.html.
4. Based on the research of Maria Xelhuantzi Lopez, a political science professor at National Autonomous University of Mexico cited in John Otis, "How Mexico's Pro-Industry Unions Undermine Workers' Rights," Agence France-Presse, March 21, 2012, www.pri.org/stories/2012-03-21/how-mexicos-pro-industry-unions-undermine-workers-rights.
5. There are various ways federal and state governments prevent and suppress strikes.

The most obvious way is by withholding legal recognition. See Aminetth Sánchez, "Un país sin huelgas," *Expansión*, November 5, 2018, https://expansion.mx/economia/2018/11/05/un-pais-sin-huelgas.

6. See William Guillermo Jímenez, Juan Pablo Turizo, "Militarización de la policía y policización de las fuerzas militares: Revisión del fenómenoa nivel internacional y nacional," *Revista Logos, Ciencia & Tecnología* vol. 3, no. 1, July–December, 2011, 112–26, www.redalyc.org/pdf/5177/517751801010.pdf.
7. Congressional Research Service, "Mexico: Evolution of the Mérida Initiative, 2007–2020," crsreports.congress.gov, February 19, 2020, http://fas.org/sgp/crs/row/IF10578.pdf.
8. For example, see Efrén Flores, "Líderes 'charros' violentan a los que migran a otros movimientos, acusan en Correos, Metro, IMSS," *Sinembargo*, September 6, 2019, www.sinembargo.mx/06-09-2019/3638954.
9. Dr. Arturo Fernández Arras, *Huelga y libertad sindical en el umbral del siglo XXI*, Comisión Organizadora de Festejos del Bicentenario de la Independencia y Centenario de la Revolución Mexicana, 233, 240, www.derecho.unam.mx/investigacion/publicaciones/librosfac/pdf/pub05/07DrFERNANDEZ.pdf (my translation).

## Chapter 9

1. For an excellent overview of independent union movements in the maquiladoras see Teresa Healy, "Nissan Workers, *Caudillismo*, and Social Unionism," chapter 3, and "The *Maquilisation* of Ford de México," chapter 4 in *Gendered Struggles against Globalisation in Mexico*, (Hampshire, UK: Ashgate Publishing, 2008); see also, David Bacon, *Children of NAFTA: Labor Wars on the US/Mexico Border* (Berkeley: University of California Press, 2004).
2. Pablo Ruiz Nápoles and Eduardo Moreno Reyes, "Los Eeuu son los ganadores del tlcan, pero no quieren enterarse," *El Heraldo de Mexico* 1, no. 2 (June 8, 2018).
3. Estimates vary based on definitions. For an overview of the complex and varied designations of Maquiladora production, see "IMMEX in Mexico: What Is It and How It Works," *TECMA Communications* (blog), https://borderassembly.com/immex-in-mexico/.
4. "The Manufacturing Industry Represents Almost 90% of Mexican Exports during 2018" *Mexico Now*, September 29, 2018.
5. Christine Murray, "Mexico Manufacturing Surge Hides Low-Wage Drag on Economy," Reuters, June 2, 2014, www.reuters.com/article/us-mexico-economy-analysis/mexico-manufacturing-surge-hides-low-wage-drag-on-economy-idUSKBN0ED20H20140602.
6. Julieta Martinez, "Sube 16% salario mínimo; se duplica en frontera norte," *La Jornada*, December 17, 2018, www.jornada.com.mx/ultimas/politica/2018/12/17/sube-16-salario-minimo-se-duplica-en-frontera-norte-7066.html.
7. Mary Beth Sheridan, "Mexico is Giving Millions of Workers a Historic Pay

Increase, but Will It Have Much Effect?" *Washington Post*, January 2, 2020, www.washingtonpost.com/world/the_americas/mexico-is-giving-millions-of-workers-a-historic-pay-increase-but-will-it-have-much-effect/2020/01/01/9f18db56-28d4-11ea-9cc9-e19cfbc87e51_story.html.

8. Alma E. Muñoz and Enrique Méndez, "Empresarios de Monterrey apoyarán a AMLO," *La Jornada*, July 27, 2018, www.jornada.com.mx/2018/07/27/politica/007n1pol.

9. López Obrador made this clear when he authorized the full reopening of the maquiladoras in the early phase of the coronavirus pandemic in May 2020, even amid a deadly outbreak spreading across the northern border states, largely attributed to the fact that many US owners of the maquilas never shut down operations and refused to provide their workers with adequate personal protective equipment or safety measures. See Ana Lilia Ramírez, "Maquilas no esenciales no han parado ni tienen protección, acusan empleados," *La Jornada*, April 2, 2020, www.jornadabc.mx/tijuana/02-04-2020/maquilas-no-esenciales-no-han-parado-ni-tienen-proteccion-acusan-empleados; María Encarnación López, "The Lives of Mexico's Maquiladora Workers Are Being Put at Risk by Lax COVID-19 Rules and the Demands of International Trade," *LSE* (blog), May 25, 2020, https://blogs.lse.ac.uk/latamcaribbean/2020/05/25/the-lives-of-mexicos-maquiladora-workers-are-being-put-at-risk-by-lax-covid-19-rules-and-the-demands-of-international-trade/.

10. Editoras OEM, "Por aumento al salario, maquilas amenazan recortes de nómina" *El Sol de México*, January 14, 2019, www.elsoldemexico.com.mx/finanzas/por-aumento-al-salario-maquilas-amenazan-recortes-de-nomina-empresarios-buscan-reducir-costos-2919464.html.

11. Juan Tolentino Morales, "La industria maquiladora dice que hay 1,500 despidos por la huelga en Matamoros," *Expansión*, February 7, 2019, https://expansion.mx/empresas/2019/02/07/maquiladora-dice-1-500-despidos-por-la-huelga-en-matamoros.

12. For a retrospective overview, see Sergio Abraham Méndez Moissen, "20-32 Testimonios de la resistencia obrera en Matamoros," *La Izquierda Diario*, October 3, 2019, www.laizquierdadiario.com/20-32-Testimonios-de-la-resistencia-obrera-en-Matamoros.

13. Claudia Velázquez, "Llaman al diálogo para evitar paros en maquiladoras," *Periódico Contacto*, January 12, 2019.

14. "Llega nueva empresa a Matamoros" *Mexico Industry*, April 2017, http://mexicoindustry.com/noticia/llega-nueva-empresa-a-matamoros.

15. César Peralta, "Obreros protestan en Matamoros y piden huelga," *Milenio*, January 12, 2019, www.milenio.com/politica/comunidad/piden-huelga-obreros-de-maquiladoras-en-matamoros.

16. Peralta, "Obreros protestan en Matamoros."

17. Julia Antonieta Le Duc "Se van a huelga obreros de 45 maquiladoras de

Matamoros," *La Jornada,* January 13, 2019, www.jornada.com.mx/2019/01/13/estados/023n2est.

18. Raul Espinosa S. "Busca Ejército mantener la paz que se vive en estos momentos en Matamoros," EnLineaDirecta.info, January 25, 2019, www.enlineadirecta.info/noticia.php?article=345573.
19. "Envía gobierno de AMLO, a abogados que buscarán conciliación obrero-patronal: Alcalde Mario López,"*El Bravo,* January 23, 2019, www.elbravo.mx/envia-gobierno-de-amlo-a-abogados-que-buscaran-conciliacion-obrero-patronal-alcalde-mario-lopez/.
20. Julia Le Duc y Martín Sánchez Treviño, "Segundo día de huelga en maquiladoras de Matamoros," *La Jornada,* Jnauary 27, 2019, www.jornada.com.mx/ultimas/estados/2019/01/27/segundo-dia-de-huelga-en-maquiladoras-de-matamoros-3731.html (my translation).
21. Julia Le Duc, "Han aceptado 19 empresas las exigencias de los obreros," *La Jornada,* January 29, 2019, www.jornada.com.mx/2019/01/29/estados/026n3est; Marco Rodríguez, "Termina huelga en enpresa Varel en Matamoros," *Hoy Tamaulipas,* February 6, 2019, www.hoytamaulipas.net/notas/371236/Termina-huelga-en-empresa-Varel-de-Matamoros.html.
22. See Julian Resendiz, "Juarez Labor Lawyer Freed from Tamaulipas Jail, but Told Not to Come Back," *Border Report,* July 2, 2020, www.border-report/juarez-labor-lawyer-freed-from-tamaulipas-jail-but-told-not-to-come-back/.

## Chapter 10

1. Debra Menk and Bernard Swiecki, *The Growing Role of Mexico in the North American Automotive Industry: Trends, Drivers and Forecasts,* (Ann Arbor: Center for Automotive Research, 2016), 2.
2. Asociación Mexicana de la Industria Automotriz, "Boletín de Prensa: Cifras De Noviembre Y Acumulado 2019." Bulletins can be accessed online at www.amia.com.mx/descargarb.html.
3. Menk and Swiecki, *Growing Role of Mexico,* 2.
4. Stratfor, "Mexico's Manufactoring Sector Continues to Grow," Forbes, April 8, 2015, www.forbes.com/sites/stratfor/2015/04/08/mexicos-manufacturing-sector-continues-to-grow/#1bf2b6f85764.
5. Brad Plumer, "How Mexico Is Upending the US Auto Industry," *Washington Post,* October 13, 2013, www.washingtonpost.com/news/wonk/wp/2013/10/18/how-mexico-is-upending-the-u-s-auto-industry/.
6. Swiecki and Menk, *Growing Role of Mexico,* 26–7.
7. Thomas H. Klier and James Rubenstein, "Mexico's Growing Role in the Auto Industry under NAFTA," Economic Perspectives 41, no. 6 (2017), www.chicagofed.org/publications/economic-perspectives/2017/6; "Auto Manufacturing Industry in Mexico, NAPS, https://napsintl.com/manufacturing-in-mexico/industries-in-mexico/automotive-manufacturing-in-mexico/.

8. Klier and Rubenstein, "Mexico's Growing Role."
9. Statistics taken from the Mexican National Institute of Statistics and Geography (known as INEGI by its Spanish acronym), available at https://www.inegi.org.mx/sistemas/bie/; "Mexico Will End 2018 as Fifth Biggest Auto Parts Manufacturer Worldwide: INA," *MexicoNow*, July 16, 2018, https://mexico-now.com/mexico-consolidates-as-the-fifth-biggest-auto-parts-manufacturer-worldwide-ina/; "Number of U.S. Automotive Industry Employees between August 2010 and 2020, by Sector," *Statistica*, 2020, www.statista.com/statistics/276474/automotive-industry-employees-in-the-united-states-by-sector/; *Update on Auto and NAFTA*, Unifor, www.unifor.org/sites/default/files/documents/document/2017-02-update_on_auto_and_nafta-en.pdf.
10. Klier and Rubenstein, "Mexico's Growing Role ."
11. David Welch and Nacha Cattan, "How Mexico's Unions Sell Out Autoworkers," *Bloomberg News*, May 5, 2017, www.bloomberg.com/news/articles/2017-05-05/how-mexico-s-unions-sell-out-autoworkers.
12. Sharay Angulo, Daina Beth Solomon, and Sandra Tovar, "Factories in Matamoros Losing USD $50 Million a Day Amid Strikes," *El Universal*, January 31, 2019.
13. Lisa Schencker, "The GM Strike Is Now Affecting the Automaker's Suppliers—and Illinois Companies Are Increasingly Feeling the Pressure," *Chicago Tribune*, October 15, 2019, www.chicagotribune.com/business/ct-biz-illinois-suppliers-general-motors-strike-20191015-qvmye2gxangmpmbcuduznmbeuu-story.html.
14. Neal E. Boudette, "Strike Will Cost G.M. Nearly $3 Billion in 2019 Earnings, Company Says," New York Times, October 29, 2019, www.nytimes.com/2019/10/29/business/gm-earnings.html.
15. See Teresa Healy, "Nissan Workers, *Caudillismo*, and Social Unionism," chapter 3 and "The *Maquilisation* of Ford de México," chapter 4 in *Gendered Struggles against Globalisation in Mexico* (Hampshire, UK: Ashgate Publishing, 2008); see also, Kevin J. Middlebrook, "Union Democratization in the Mexican Automobile Industry: A Reappraisal," *Latin American Research Review* 24, no. 2 (1989): 69–93.
16. Michael Wayland, "GM to Invest $1 Billion in Mexico for Electric Vehicle Production, Angering UAW Members," CNBC, April 29, 2021, www.cnbc.com/2021/04/29/gm-to-invest-1-billion-in-mexico-for-electric-vehicle-production.html.
17. Karla Silva, "Despide GM Silao a obreros que apoyan huelga mundial" *Periódico Correo*, September 23, 2019, https://periodicocorreo.com.mx/despide-gm-silao-a-obreros-que-apoyan-huelga-mundial/.
18. Keith Laing and Ian Thibodeau, "UAW Membership Dropped by 35,000 in 2018," *Detroit News*, March 29, 2019, www.detroitnews.com/story/business/autos/2019/03/29/uaw-membership-dropped-last-year/3314861002/; https://www.autonews.com/manufacturing/instead-national-strike-uaw-could-target-key-plants-ripple-effect.
19. Hannah Lutz, "For GM, Deal May Be a Labor-Cost Setback," *Automotive News*,

October 27, 2019, www.autonews.com/manufacturing/gm-deal-may-be-labor-cost-setback; Chris Brooks and Jane Slaughter, "GM Workers Ratify Contract Though 'Mixed at Best,'" October 25, 2019, https://labornotes.org/2019/10/gm-workers-ratify-contract-though-mixed-best

## Chapter 11

1. Antonio Sosa, "Trabajadores de Soriana y Chedraui se suman a la huelga en Matamoros," *El Sol de México*, February 7, 2019, www.elsoldemexico.com.mx/republica/sociedad/se-suman-empleados-de-chedraui-a-paros-en-matamoros-huelga-coca-cola-maquiladora-3021303.html.
2. Zenyazen Flores, "Trabajadores de Walmart México anuncian que si no les aumentan el salario se irán a huelga," *El Financiero*, February 26, 2019, www.elfinanciero.com.mx/empresas/trabajadores-de-walmart-mexico-amenazan-con-irse-a-huelga-por-salarios.
3. Elías Medina P., "Emplazan a huelga a Walmart, Super Center y Aurrera," *El Sudcaliforniano*, February 16, 2019, www.elsudcaliforniano.com.mx/local/emplazan-a-huelga-a-walmart-super-center-y-aurrera-3066895.html; see also Juan Carlos Flores, "Paro en tiendas de Grupo Walmart y Soriana en Colima," *La Jornada*, February 14, 2019, www.jornada.com.mx/2019/02/14/estados/027n1est.
4. See María del Pilar Martínez, "Sindicatos desafían a Walmart y la emplazan a huelga," *El Economista*, February 27, 2019, www.eleconomista.com.mx/empresas/Sindicatos-desafian-a-Walmart-y-la-emplazan-a-huelga-20190227-0043.html;
5. For example, see united4respect.org.
6. The Economist Intelligence Unit, *Country Commerce: Mexico* (New York: EIU, 2018), 13.
7. Jose Luis Gonzalez and Lizbeth Diaz, "Truckers gridlocked at US-Mexico line as border agents moved," Reuters, April 2, 2019, www.reuters.com/article/us-usa-immigration-mexico/truckers-gridlocked-at-us-mexico-line-as-border-agents-moved-idUSKCN1RE2GQ; see also Office of the United States Trade Representative, "Mexico: US-Mexico Trade Facts," https://ustr.gov/countries-regions/americas/mexico.
8. See Office of the United States Trade Representative, "Mexico: US-Mexico Trade Facts," https://ustr.gov/countries-regions/americas/mexico.
9. Jennifer Smith, "Logistics Spending Jumped 11.4% on Strong Economic Growth," *Wall Street Journal*, June 18, 2019, www.wsj.com/articles/logistics-spending-jumped-11-4-on-strong-economic-growth-11560862800.
10. Lizbeth Diaz, "Mexico Sees $300 Billion in Infrastructure Spending through 2018," Reuters, July 15, 2013, www.reuters.com/article/us-mexico-infrastructure/mexico-sees-300-billion-in-infrastructure-spending-through-2018-idUSBRE96E0SA20130715.
11. Hugh R. Morley, "Ryder Expands Mexican Warehousing as Cargo Demand Rises,"

*Journal of Commerce*, April 5, 2019, www.joc.com/international-logistics/industrial-real-estate/ryder-xpands-mexican-warehousing-cargo-demand-rises_20190405.html.

12. Tim Wang, Julia Laumont, and Pedro Niño, "The US Warehouse Boom," Legg Mason Global Asset Management, January 30, 2019, www.leggmason.com/en-us/insights/investment-insights/us-warehouse-boom.html.

13. Statistics from the Mexican National Chamber of Freight Transport (Cámara Nacional de Autotransporte de Carga) and published at: "Políticas públicas Inseguridad y jornadas largas dejan déficit de 80 mil traileros en carreteras," Arena Pública, July 24, 2018, www.arenapublica.com/articulo/2018/07/24/12678/inseguridad-y-jornadas-largas-dejan-deficit-de-80-mil-traileros-en-carreteras.

14. William B. Cassidy "Mexican Trucking Past US Border in Crosshairs," *Journal of Commerce*, February 13, 2017, www.joc.com/trucking-logistics/truckload-freight/politics-economis-collide-us-mexico-truck-crossings_20170213.html.

15. Dan Ronan, "Trucking Industry Revenue Topped $700 Billion in 2017, ATA Report Shows," *Transport Topic News*, August 20, 2018, www.ttnews.com/articles/trucking-industry-revenue-topped-700-billion-2017-ata-report-shows.

16. William B. Cassidy "US-Mexico Cargo Delays Spur New Transport Approaches," *Journal of Commerce*, April 20, 2019, www.joc.com/trucking-logistics/us-mexico-cargo-delays-spur-new-transport-approaches_20190420.html; see also "2019 JOC Directory of Trucking Companies," *Journal of Commerce*, April 20, 2019, www.joc.com/trucking-logistics/2019-joc-directory-trucking-companies_20190816.html.

17. Cassidy "Mexican Trucking Past US Border."

18. Micol Seigel, "Privatization in Mexico Is a Road to Nowhere," *Quartz*, August 9, 2013, https://qz.com/113017/privatization-in-mexico-is-a-road-to-nowhere/.

19. "Camioneros y trabajadores de puertos de Los Ángeles y Long Beach protestan con paro por la contratación," *Univisión*, June 18, 2017, www.univision.com/local/los-angeles-kmex/camioneros-y-trabajadores-de-puertos-de-los-angeles-y-long-beach-protestan-con-paro-por-la-contratacion.

20. Hugh R. Morley, "Top Mexican Ports Lead Modernization Charge," *Journal of Commerce*, January 10, 2017, www.joc.com/port-news/international-ports/port-lázaro-cárdenas/top-mexican-ports-take-modernization-lead_20170110.html.

21. The Economist Intelligence Unit, *Country Commerce: Mexico* (New York: EIU, 2018), 12–13.

22. Andrew Khouri, "Backlog of Cargo Ships at L.A., Long Beach Ports Grows Amid Labor Dispute," *Los Angeles Times*, February 16, 2015, www.latimes.com/business/la-fi-port-dispute-20150217-story.html.

23. *Morning Edition*, "Learning More About Longshoremen and Their Powerful Union," National Public Radio, February 20, 2015, www.npr.org/2015/02/20/387685093/learning-more-about-longshoremen-and-their-powerful-union.

24. Cassidy, "US–Mexico Cargo Delays"; see also "2019 JOC Directory of Trucking

Companies."

25. Alan M.Field, "NAFTA at 20: A Transformational Force That Continues to Evolve," *Journal of Commerce*, January 24, 2014.
26. "Anuario Estadístico Ferroviario 2018," Gobierno de México, www.gob.mx/artf/acciones-y-programas/anuario-estadistico-ferroviario-2018.
27. See "What Do We Transport?— Automotive," Ferromex, www.ferromex.com.mx/ferromex-lo-mueve-eng/automotriz.jsp.
28. Omar Magaña, "Modernization on Track," *Negocios ProMéxico* (December 2013–January 2014), 33.
29. Lynn Adler, "US Transport Companies Cash in on Mexico Trade Boom," Reuters, December 3, 2012, www.reuters.com/article/us-usa-transports-mexico/u-s-transport-companies-cash-in-on-mexico-trade-boom-idUSBRE8B307020121204?feedType=RSS&feedName=businessNews.
30. See their website at www.progressrail.com/en/locations/americas/mexico.html.
31. "Railroad Workers," Occupational Outlook Handbook, Bureau of Labor Statistics, www.bls.gov/ooh/transportation-and-material-moving/railroad-occupations.htm. The number of Mexican railroad workers is according to the union, Sindicato de Trabajadores Ferrocarrileros de la Republica Mexicana (STFRM). Their website is http://www.sindicatoferrocarrilero.org.mx/home.html.
32. See Néstor Jiménez, "Llama AMLO a la CNTE a levantar bloqueo en Michoacán," *La Jornada*, January 28, 2019. https://www.jornada.com.mx/ultimas/estados/2019/01/28/llama-amlo-a-la-cnte-a-levantar-bloqueo-en-michoacan-7044.html; Expansion Política, "En Michoacán, la CNTE mantiene bloqueos y el gobierno federal llama al diálogo," Januray 27, 2019, https://politica.expansion.mx/mexico/2019/01/27/en-michoacan-la-cnte-mantiene-bloqueos-y-el-gobierno-federal-llama-al-dialogo?fbclid=IwAR1UbZGhuGuvO3_7oUungLrDSKumfrQMJrD8Jq-CKR4OIWMtm2nXpuxx4B8; El Economista, "Jiménez Espriú y Silvano Aureoles enfrentan posiciones por los bloqueos de la CNTE en Michoacán," January 27, 2019, www.eleconomista.com.mx/politica/Jimenez-Espriu-y-Silvano-Aureoles-enfrentan-posiciones-por-los-bloqueos-de-la-CNTE-en-Michoacan-20190127-0044.htmlBloqueos%20de%20la%20CNTE.
33. Jesse Wheeler, Francesco Menonna, and Aleksei Vjazinkin, *Latin America Monitor: Mexico* (London: Fitch Solutions, 2019), 3.

## Chapter 12

1. For instance the Immigration Act of 1917 first introduced the legalized importation of Mexican contract labor into agriculture, where the workers were not offered naturalization and were expected to return to Mexico seasonally.
2. "Apples in Washington State" *Washington State University*, https://extension.wsu.edu/chelan-douglas/agriculture/treefruit/horticulture/apples_in_washington_state/
3. Dana Goodyear, "How Driscoll's Reinvented the Strawberry," *New Yorker*,

August 14, 2017, www.newyorker.com/magazine/2017/08/21/how-driscolls-reinvented-the-strawberry/amp.

4. James F. Smith, "United States-Mexico Agricultural Trade," *U.C. Davis Law Review* 23, no. 3 (Spring 1990): 435–36.

5. Christian Zlolniski, *Made in Baja: The Lives of Farmworkers and Growers behind Mexico's Transnational Agricultural Boom*, (Berkeley, University of California Press, 2019) 37–38, 67.

6. Julia Preston, "US Farmers Go Where Workers Are: Mexico," *New York Times*, September 4, 2007, www.nytimes.com/2007/09/04/world/americas/04iht-export.4.7380436.html

7. Agustin Escobar, Philip Martin, and Omar Stabridis, *Farm Labor and Mexico's Export Produce Industry*, Wilson Center, October 2019, 55–56, www.wilsoncenter.org/sites/default/files/media/uploads/documents/mexico%20farm%20book_V2.pdf.

8. United States Department of Agriculture, *Opportunities for U.S. Agricultural Exports in Mexico*, October 29, 2019, www.fas.usda.gov/data/opportunities-us-agricultural-exports-mexico.

9. Escobar, Martin, and Stabridis, "Farm Labor and Mexico's Export ."

10. See Justin Akers Chacón, *Radicals in the Barrio: Magonistas, Socialists, Wobblies, and Communists in the Mexican-American Working Class* (Chicago: Haymarket, 2018), especially chapters 4, 17, 18, 21, 22, and 23.

11. Zlolniski, *Made in Baja*, 152.

12. For more information, see Silvia Giagnoni, *Fields of Resistance: The Struggle of Florida's Farmworkers for Justice* (Chicago: Haymarket Books, 2011).

13. For a detailed overview of the strike and aftermath, see Graciela Bensusán Areous, and Elena Jaloma Cruz, "Representación sindical y redistribución: el caso de los jornaleros del valle de San Quintín," *Perfiles latinoamericanos* 27, no. 53 (June 2019), www.scielo.org.mx/scielo.php?script=sci_arttext&pid=S0188-76532019000100009.

14. Noémie Taylor-Rosner, "De los campos de San Quintín a los supermercados de EEUU: Los trabajadores agrícolas mexicanos piden solidaridad," *Equal Times*, December 11, 2018, www.equaltimes.org/de-los-campos-de-san-quintin-a-los?lang=en#.X_uYXNhKiUk.

15. Ross Courtney, "Fresh Fruit Sales Driving Record Exports for Yakima County," *Yakima Herald*, July 12, 2015, www.yakimaherald.com/news/business/local/fresh-fruit-sales-driving-record-exports-for-yakima-county/article_41bf70dc-291f-11e5-9054-6f498af1b438.html.

16. Mia Hoang, "Farmworker Advocates, Agriculture Industry at Odds on Bill in Washington Legislature," *Yakima Herald*, March 28, 2019, www.yakimaherald.com/news/business/local/farmworker-advocates-agriculture-industry-at-odds-on-bill-in-washington-legislature/article_7fe21cc4-51e4-11e9-b6d8-5b4d0ec0e18b.html.

17. Mai Hoang and Lex Talamo, "Increasing Number of Yakima Valley Farmworkers

Are Walking Out to Protest Conditions during COVID-19 Pandemic," *Seattle Times,* May 14, 2020, www.seattletimes.com/seattle-news/health/increasing-number-of-yakima-valley-farmworkers-are-walking-out-to-protest-conditions-during-covid-19-pandemic/.

18. Robert Narai, "The US Migrant Workers on Strike during the Pandemic," *Red Flag,* August 30, 2020, https://redflag.org.au/node/7345
19. Narai, "US Migrant Workers on Strike."
20. David Bacon, "Apple Shed Strikes Win Recognition, But the Fight Goes On," *Labor Notes,* June 2, 2020, https://labornotes.org/2020/06/apple-shed-strikes-win-recognition-fight-goes.

## Part III

Patrick Mcdonnell, "New Outlook in the Fields: Amnesty Stirring Move to Unionize" *Los Angeles Times,* May 28, 1989, p. J1A.

## Chapter 13

1. *The Impact of Increased United States with Mexico trade on Southwest Border Development: Report to the Senate Committee on Finance on Investigation,* 98th Cong. (1986), 31.
2. David Rogers, "The Latino Tide: Curbs on Illegal Aliens, Due for a House Vote, Split Texas Delegation," *Wall Street Journal,* June 11, 1984, 1.
3. Rogers, "Latino Tide."
4. Bob Baker, "Unions Try Bilingual Recruiting," *Los Angeles Times,* March 25, 1991, VYA1.
5. Baker, "Unions Try Bilingual Recruiting," VYAI.
6. The US issued over a million border-crossing cards, allowing people to cross for up to seventy-two hours (but not to work). Many worked anyway or stayed permanently. The "openness" of the border at this time shows how workers were allowed to cross with less restriction and closure enforcement, leading a natural progression toward working-class formation. Data is from: *The Impact of Increased United States with Mexico Trade on Southwest Border Development: Report to the Senate Committee on Finance on Investigation,* 98th Cong. (1986), 29–30.
7. Baker, "Unions Try Bilingual Recruiting."
8. Bob Baker, "Immigrants OK Union; Largest Action in Years," *Los Angeles Times,* December 21, 1990, VYB1.
9. Robert Scheer, "Law Part of Problem: Illegal Aliens' Half-Life: Hard Work, Few Benefits," *Los Angeles Times,* November 12, 1979, B1.
10. For a description of "business unionism," which essentially replaces class-conscious politics with trade-conscious politics and prioritizes collaboration with employers over militancy and workplace actions, see Kim Moody, "Contextualizing Organized Labor in Expansion and Crisis: The Case of the United States," chapter 3 in *In Solidarity: Essays on Working-Class Organization in the United States*

(Chicago: Haymarket Books, 2014).

11. Baker, "Unions Try Bilingual Recruiting."
12. Karen Tumulty, "Foes Hope to Block Immigration Bill: House Confrontation Over Illegal Aliens Due Monday," *Los Angeles Times*, June 10, 1984, A1.
13. "Amnesty: Do It Right," *Los Angeles Times*, May 3, 1987, E4.
14. Henry Weinstein, "Union to Advise Illegal Aliens on Amnesty," *Los Angeles Times*, November 21, 1986, OCA6.
15. Henry Weinstein, "Unions Will Open 6 Centers to Assist Aliens with Amnesty," *Los Angeles Times*, May 2, 1987, 34.
16. Harry Bernstein, "Unions Trying New Sales Tactics to Stimulate Growth," *Los Angeles Times*, September 27, 1988, E1.
17. Harry Bernstein, "Labor: Unions Expected to Support Immigration Bill, Despite Recent Hostility Labor," *Los Angeles Times*, June 25, 1984, E1.
18. David Holloway and Bob Schwartz, "INS Considers Ways of Smoothing Enforcement of Employer Sanctions," *Los Angeles Times*, February 28, 1987, OCA6.
19. Marita Hernandez, "Fraud Found in Farm Worker Amnesty Papers: Incomplete Source," *Los Angeles Times*, November 30, 1988, 16.
20. Bob Baker, "Union Targets L.A. Sweatshop Operators," *Los Angeles Times*, April 29, 1990, VCB19.
21. David Reyes, "Union Efforts Focus on Organizing Hotel Industry in County," *Los Angeles Times*, April 28, 1986, E1.
22. David Reyes, "Dry Wallers Take Pay Protest to Job Sites: Immigration Law Is Factor in Unrest Among Mostly Latino Workers," *Los Angeles Times*, July 1, 1987, OCA1.
23. Mary Helen Berg, "Labor Leaders Aim Efforts at Immigrants," *Los Angeles Times*, October 30, 1994, H3.
24. Stuart Silverstein and Josh Meyer, "Fast-Growing Union Hits Obstacles in L.A.," *Los Angeles Times*, September 18, 1995, A1.
25. Debora Vrana, "Union Vote Is Friday at O.C. Vans Plant: Labor: Election May Presage Wider Organizing Efforts, Especially among Immigrant Workers," *Los Angeles Times*, April 7, 1994, OCA1.
26. For an overview of research, see Justin Akers Chacón and Mike Davis, *No One Is Illegal: Fighting Racism and State Repression on the U.S.-Mexico Border* (Chicago: Haymarket Books, 2018), especially chapters 19, 30, 32, and 33.
27. Michael Bernabè Aguilera, "The Effect of Legalization on the Labor Markets of Latin American Immigrants: A Gendered Comparison," *Sociological Focus* 37, no. 4 (November 2004): 349–69.
28. Katharine M. Donato, Jorge Durand, and Douglas S. Massey, "Changing Conditions in the US Labor Market: Effects of the Immigration Reform and Control Act of 1986," *Population Research and Policy Review* 11, no. 2 (1992): 96.
29. Abby Budiman, "Key Findings about US Immigrants," *Pew Research Center*,

August 20, 2020, www.pewresearch.org/fact-tank/2020/08/20/key-findings-about-u-s-immigrants/.

30. See Jeffrey S. Passel and D'Vera Cohn, "20 Metro Areas Are Home to Six-in-Ten Unauthorized Immigrants in US," *Pew Research Center*, March 11, 2019, www.pewresearch.org/fact-tank/2019/03/11/us-metro-areas-unauthorized-immigrants/.

## Chapter 14

1. William Langewiesche, "The Border," *Atlantic Monthly*, May 1992, www.theatlantic.com/past/docs/issues/92may/border.htm.
2. William E. Colby, "Food Stamps for International Neighbors," *Worldview* 21, no. 1–2 (February 1978), 26.
3. Stewart Russell, "Former CIA Director William Colby Believes the Greatest Threat Stability Over the Next Decade Is Not the Soviet Union," Reuters, September 30, 1983, www.cia.gov/library/readingroom/docs/CIA-RDP90-00806R000201180099-1.pdf
4. *Hearing before the Subcommittee on Immigration and Refugee Policy of the Committee on the Judiciary*, United States Senate, 97th Cong., Second Session, March 29, 1982 (Washington: U.S. Government Printing Office, 1982.)
5. Robert E. Fenton, *Illegal Immigration to The United States: A Growing Problem for Law Enforcement* (Newport, RI: United States Naval War College, Center for Advanced Research, 1983), V–VII.
6. See Austin T. Fragomen Jr., "President Carter's Amnesty and Sanctions Proposal," *International Migration Review* 11, no. 4 (Winter 1977): 524–32.
7. This data is taken from Alberto Dávila, José A. Pagán, and Montserrat Viladrich Grau, "Immigration Reform, the INS, and the Distribution of Interior and Border Enforcement Resources," *Public Choice* 99, no. 3 (1999): 329. The authors of this report exemplify a body of researchers who can't quite understand why there is a major difference between the rhetoric and practice of immigration enforcement.
8. John Burnett, "Employers Struggle with Hiring Undocumented Workers: 'You Cannot Hire American Here,'" NPR August 21, 2019, www.npr.org/2019/08/21/752336132/employers-struggle-with-hiring-undocumented-workers-you-cannot-hire-american-her.
9. Migrant repression produced a profitable growth industry, both in terms of lower wages through labor criminalization and the ensuing privatization of the means of repression. This includes for the arms industry, the detention industry, information and technology, etc.
10. Katharine M. Donato and Douglas S. Massey, "Effect of the Immigration Reform and Control Act on the Wages of Mexican Migrants," *Social Science Quarterly* 74, no. 3 (September 1993): 539.
11. Although growers preference for undocumented labor returned them to the fields in the ensuing years, especially as the United Farm Workers union largely disappeared.

12. Cynthia Bansak and Steven Raphael, "Immigration Reform and the Earnings of Latino Workers: Do Employer Sanctions Cause Discrimination?" *Industrial and Labor Relations Review* 54, no. 2 (January 2001): 291–93.
13. David Holley, "Aliens, Employers Share Confusion on New Amnesty Law," *Los Angeles Times,* December 7, 1986, A3.
14. Dawn Garcia, "Rulings Broaden Rights of Alien Workers / Court Decisions Protect Employees, Make It Easier to Gain Legal Status," *San Francisco Chronicle,* March 25, 1991, A7.
15. Muzaffar A. Chishti, "The Impact of IRCA's Employer Sanctions Provision on Workers and Workplace," *In Defense of the Alien* 12 (1989): 190.
16. Alfredo Corchado, and Dianna Solis, "Immigration Law Creates a Subclass of Illegals Bound to Their Bosses and Vulnerable to Abuses," *Wall Street Journal,* September 2, 1987, 44.
17. The growth in transborder migration over this period was a direct result of economic displacement associated with structural adjustment programs, NAFTA-associated reductions in tariffs and investment restrictions, and the subsequent influx of foreign capital (discussed in chapter 1).
18. Ramon G. McLeod, "Illegal Immigration Reported Down a Bit—Study Credits the Federal Amnesty Law," *San Francisco Chronicle,* May 4, 1990, A2.
19. Tammany J. Mulder, Frederick W. Hollmann, Lisa R. Lollock, Rachel C. Cassidy, Joseph M. Costanzo, and Josephine D. Baker, "US Census Bureau Measurement of Net International Migration to the United States: 1990 to 2000" working paper number 51, US Census Bureau, December 2001, www.census.gov/library/working-papers/2001/demo/POP-twps0051.html#unauth
20. Pia M. Orrenius and Madeline Zavodny, "Do Amnesty Programs Reduce Undocumented Immigration? Evidence from IRCA," *Demography* 40, no. 3 (August, 2003): 438.
21. Julie A. Phillips and Douglas S. Massey, "The New Labor Market: Immigrants and Wages after IRCA," *Demography* 36, no. 2 (May, 1999): 243.
22. Katharine M. Donato, Jorge Durand, and Douglas S. Massey, "Changing Conditions in the US Labor Market: Effects of the Immigration Reform and Control Act of 1986," *Population Research and Policy Review* 11, no. 2 (1992): 104.
23. In 1952, Congress passed the Texas Proviso, which makes "harboring an illegal entrant" a felony but excludes from punishment those who hire them.
24. See Kerstin Gentsch and Douglas S. Massey, "Labor Market Outcomes for Legal Mexican Immigrants under the New Regime of Immigration Enforcement," *Social Science Quarterly* 92, no. 3 (September 2011): 875–93; Timothy J. Dunn, *The Militarization of the US–Mexico Border, 1978–1992: Low-Intensity Conflict Doctrine Comes Home* (Austin: University of Texas at Austin Center for Mexican-American Studies, 1997).
25. See Gordon H. Hanson, Raymond Robertson, Antonio Spilimbergo, "Does Border Enforcement Protect US Workers from Illegal Immigration?" (working

paper 7054, National Bureau of Economic Research, March 1999).

26. Gordon H. Hanson and Antonio Spilimbergo, Political Economy, Sectoral Shocks, and Border Enforcement" *National Bureau of Economic Research*, Working Paper 7315, August 1999.

27. For an analysis of violence against migrant people, see Justin Akers Chacón and Mike Davis, *No One Is Illegal Fighting Racism and State Violence on the U.S.-Mexico Border* (Chicago: Haymarket Books, 2018).

28. "Mandatory Detention Fact Sheet," Detention Watch Network, www.detentionwatchnetwork.org/sites/default/files/Mandatory%20Detention%20Fact%20Sheet.pdf.

29. Douglas S. Massey, *Immigration and the Great Recession* (The Russell Sage Foundation and The Stanford Center on Poverty and Inequality, 2012), http://inequality.stanford.edu/sites/default/files/Immigration_fact_sheet.pdf.

30. Jeffrey S. Passel, D'vera Cohn, and Ana Gonzalez-Barrera, "Net Migration from Mexico Falls to Zero—and Perhaps Less," Pew Research Center, April 23, 2012, www.pewresearch.org/hispanic/2012/04/23/net-migration-from-mexico-falls-to-zero-and-perhaps-less/

31. Douglas S. Massey and Kerstin Gentsch, "Undocumented Migration to the United States and the Wages of Mexican Immigrants," *International Migration Review* 48, no. 2 (Summer 2014): 483.

32. Massey and Gentsch, "Undocumented Migration," 483.

33. Giovanni Peri, "The Effect of Immigration on Productivity: Evidence from US States" (working paper no. 15507, National Bureau of Economic Research, November 2009).

34. Elizabeth Fussell, "The Deportation Threat Dynamic and Victimization of Latino Migrants: Wage Theft and Robbery," *Sociological Quarterly* 52, no. 4 (Fall 2011): 595.

35. Stephen Lee, "Private Immigration Screening in the Workplace," *Stanford Law Review*, 61 (2009): 1128.

36. Cynthia Bansak, "The Differential Wage Impact of the Immigration Reform and Control Act on Latino Ethnic Subgroups," *Social Science Quarterly* 86 (December 2005):1295.

37. Elaine Sorensen and Frank D. Bean, "The Immigration Reform and Control Act and the Wages of Mexican Origin Workers: Evidence from Current Population Surveys," *Social Science Quarterly* 75, no. 1 (March 1994): 1–17.

38. For example, see Caitlin Webber, "Business Groups Lobby Congress for Immigration Rewrite," *Bloomberg News*, August 2, 2013, www.bloomberg.com/news/articles/2013-08-02/business-groups-lobby-congress-for-immigration-rewrite.

39. See Travis Putnam Hill, "Big Employers No Strangers to Benefits of Cheap, Illegal Labor," *Texas Tribune*, December 19, 2016, www.texastribune.org/2016/12/19/big-name-businesses-exploit-immigrant-labor/.

40. Wayne A. Cornelius, "Impacts of the 1986 US Immigration Law on Emigration from Rural Mexican Sending Communities," *Population and Development Review* 15, no. 4 (December, 1989): 702.
41. Jorge Durand, Douglas S. Massey, and Fernando Charvet "The Changing Geography of Mexican Immigration to the United States: 1910–1996," *Social Science Quarterly* 81, no. 1 (March 2000): 15.
42. Leah Haus, "Openings in the Wall: Transnational Migrants, Labor Unions, and US Immigration Policy," *International Organization* 49, no. 2 (Spring 1995): 204.

## Chapter 15

1. An example of this liberal anguish is captured in this editorial published by the *LA Times*' labor editor nine years after IRCA, in which employer sanctions failed to stop migration. The author calls for another amnesty, while urging even more border enforcement and harsher restrictions and penalties for those who come after. See Harry Bernstein, "A New Card Could Help Border Control: Grant Another Amnesty for Those Here Illegally Then Bolster and Enforce the 1986 Law," *Los Angeles Times*, January 3, 1995, WVB7.
2. "AFL-CIO Calls for Amnesty For Illegal Immigrants," *Wall Street Journal*, February 17, 2000, C18.
3. Eduardo Porter, "Illegal Immigrants May Total 8.5 Million," *Wall Street Journal*, August 14, 2001, A4.
4. This shift is reflected in the editorial pages of the Wall Street Journal. For instance, see "Amnesty Shootout," *Wall Street Journal*, July 30, 2001, A-18.
5. Marjorie Valbrun, "Congress Backs Limited Amnesty Plan, Other Measures for Many Immigrants," *Wall Street Journal*, December 18, 2000, B4.
6. Jim VandeHei and Gary Fields, "Bush Faces Tough Job Selling Amnesty to His Own Party," *Wall Street Journal*, July 17, 2001.
7. Joel Millman and Will Pinkston, "Mexicans Transform a Town in Georgia—And an Entire Industry," *Wall Street Journal*, August 30, 2001, A1.
8. For a good overview of this period of repression, see Deepa Fernandes, *Targeted: Homeland Security and the Business of Immigration* (New York: Seven Stories Press, 2007).
9. Discussed in detail in Justin Akers Chacón and Mike Davis, *No One Is Illegal: Fighting Racism and State Violence on the U.S.-Mexico Border* (Chicago: Haymarket Books, 2018), especially chapters 32–34.
10. Todd Miller, *More Than A Wall: Corporate Profiteering and the Militarization of US Borders*, Transnational Institute, September 16, 2019, www.tni.org/en/morethanawall.
11. Michelle Chen, The US Border Security Industry Could Be Worth $740 Billion by 2023," *Truthout*, October 6, 2019, http://truthout.org/articles/the-us-border-security-industry-could-be-worth-740-billion-by-2023/.
12. US Customs and Border Enforcement, *A Summary of CBP Facts and Figures*, May

2019, www.cbp.gov/sites/default/files/assets/documents/2019-May/cbp-snapshot-05162019.pdf; "Fusion Centers" Department of Homeland Security, September 19, 2019, www.dhs.gov/fusion-centers; and "Who We Are," Immigration and Customs Enforcement, January 8, 2020, www.ice.gov/about.

13. "National Map of 287(g) Agreements," Immigrant Legal Resource Center, www.ilrc.org/national-map-287g-agreements.
14. "New Data on 637 Detention Facilities Used by ICE in FY 2015," Transactional Records Access Clearinghouse (TRAC), April 12, 2016, https://trac.syr.edu/immigration/reports/422/; Mike Ludwig, "Asylum Seekers Are Being 'Disappeared' in Private Louisiana Jails," *Truthout,* May 17, 2019, https://truthout.org/articles/asylum-seekers-are-being-disappeared-in-private-louisiana-jails/.
15. Daniel Costa, "Immigration Enforcement Is Funded at a Much Higher Rate Than Labor Standards Enforcement—and the Gap Is Widening," *Economic Policy Institute,* June 20, 2019, www.epi.org/blog/immigration-enforcement-is-funded-at-a-much-higher-rate-than-labor-standards-enforcement-and-the-gap-is-widening/.
16. Muzaffar Chishti and Claire Bergeron, "Post-9/11 Policies Dramatically Alter the US Immigration Landscape," *Migration Policy Institute,* September 8, 2011, www.migrationpolicy.org/article/post-911-policies-dramatically-alter-us-immigration-landscape
17. Rani Molla, "Microsoft, Dell, Concur: Here Are All the Tech Companies Doing Business with ICE and How Much They're Getting Paid," *Vox,* July 30, 2019, www.vox.com/recode/2019/7/30/20728147/tech-company-ice-contracts-foia-microsoft-palantir-concur-dell; Karen Hao, "Amazon Is the Invisible Backbone of ICE's Immigration Crackdown," *Technology Review,* October 22, 2018, www.technologyreview.com/s/612335/amazon-is-the-invisible-backbone-behind-ices-immigration-crackdown/
18. "Who Supplies the Data, Analysis, and Tech Infrastructure to US Immigration Authorities?" Privacy International, August 9, 2018, https://privacyinternational.org/feature/2216/who-supplies-data-analysis-and-tech-infrastructure-us-immigration-authorities.
19. Edward Ongweso Jr, "Palantir's CEO Finally Admits to Helping ICE Deport Undocumented Immigrants," *Vice News,* January 24 2020, www.vice.com/en_us/article/pkeg99/palantirs-ceo-finally-admits-to-helping-ice-deport-undocumented-immigrants.
20. Alex Kotch, "Who Is Making Money from CBP in Your State?" *American Prospect,* June 28, 2019, https://prospect.org/civil-rights/making-money-cbp-state/.

## Part IV

Arturo Santamaria Gómez, *La izquierda norteamericana y los trabajadores indocumentados,* (Universidad Autónoma de Sinaloa: Ediciones de Cultura Popular, 1988), 15.

## Chapter 16

1. For some examples, see Caitlin Dickerson, Seth Freed Wessler, and Miriam Jordan, "Immigrants Say They Were Pressured into Unneeded Surgeries," *New York Times* September 29, 2020, www.nytimes.com/2020/09/29/us/ice-hysterectomies-surgeries-georgia.html. See also Julian Borger, "US ICE Officers 'Used Torture to Make Africans Sign Own Deportation Orders,'" *Guardian*, Octboer 22, 2020, www.theguardian.com/us-news/2020/oct/22/us-ice-officers-allegedly-used-torture-to-make-africans-sign-own-deportation-orders.
2. For some harrowing examples, see Ryan Devereaux, "Ice Has Conducted Hundreds of Raids in New York Since Trump Came to Power. Here's What those Operations Look Like," *Intercept*, July 23, 2018, https://theintercept.com/2018/07/23/ice-raids-in-new-york/.
3. For a historical analysis of this concept, see Alex Henderson, "7 Fascist Regimes America Enthusiastically Supported," *Salon*, February 10, 2015, www.salon.com/2015/02/10/7_fascist_regimes_america_enthusiastically_supported_partner/.
4. Thomas P. McDonough, Howard M. Bloom, and Richard F. Vitarelli, "Union Membership Rates Continue to Decline," *National Law Review* 10, no. 31 (January 2021), www.natlawreview.com/article/union-membership-rates-continue-to-decline.
5. See Daniel Costa, "Employers Increase Their Profits and Put Downward Pressure on Wages and Labor Standards by Exploiting Migrant Workers," *Economic Policy Institute*, August 27, 2019, www.epi.org/publication/labor-day-2019-immigration-policy/
6. For a theoretical analysis of the state bureaucracy under capitalism, see Göran Therborn, *What Does the Ruling Class Do When It Rules? State Apparatuses and State Power Under Feudalism, Capitalism and Socialism* (London: Verso Books, 2016), especially chapters 3, 4, and 5.
7. A. Naomi Paik "Abolishing Police Includes Abolishing ICE and Border Protection," *Truthout*, July 13, 2020, https://truthout.org/articles/abolishing-police-includes-abolishing-ice-and-border-protection/.
8. Neta C. Crawford, *United States Budgetary Costs of Post-911 Wars Through FY2018* (Providence: Brown University Watson Institute, 2017), https://open.bu.edu/ds2/stream/?#/documents/224991/page/1.
9. See Tanvi Misra, "Immigration Agencies to Assist Law Enforcement Amid Unrest," *Roll Call*, June 1, 2020, www.rollcall.com/2020/06/01/immigration-agencies-to-assist-law-enforcement-amid-unrest/.
10. See Justin Akers Chacón, "Migrant Workers: Casualties of Neoliberalism," *International Socialist Review*, Issue 54 (July–August 2007), https://isreview.org/issues/54/casualties.shtml.
11. See Justin Akers Chacón and Mike Davis, "State Repression of Immigrant Workers," chapter 34 in *No One Is Illegal: Fighting Racism and State Violence in U.S.-Mexico Border* (Chicago: Haymarket Books, 2018).

12. Ari Shapiro, "Months After Massive ICE Raid, Residents of a Mississippi Town Wait and Worry," NPR, November 17, 2019, www.npr.org/2019/11/17/778611834/months-after-massive-ice-raid-residents-of-a-mississippi-town-wait-and-worry.

13. Mica Rosenberg and Kristina Cooke, "Allegations of Labor Abuses Dogged Mississippi Plant Years Before Immigration Raids," Reuters, August 9, 2019, www.reuters.com/article/us-usa-immigration-koch-foods/allegations-of-labor-abuses-dogged-mississippi-plant-years-before-immigration-raids-idUSKCN1UZ1OV.

14. See Miriam J. Wells, "The Political Construction of the Farm Labor Market," chapter 3 in *Strawberry Fields: Politics, Class, and Work in California Agriculture* (Ithaca: Cornell University Press, 1996).

15. John Burnett, "See the 20+ Immigration Activists Arrested Under Trump," NPR, March 16, 2018, www.npr.org/2018/03/16/591879718/see-the-20-immigration-activists-arrested-under-trump.

16. See "Fusion Center Locations and Contact Information," Department of Homeland Security, www.dhs.gov/fusion-center-locations-and-contact-information/.

17. Michelle Mittelstadt, "US Spends More on Immigration Enforcement than on FBI, DEA, Secret Service & All Other Federal Criminal Law Enforcement Agencies Combined," *Migration Policy Institute*, January 7, 2013, www.migrationpolicy.org/news/us-spends-more-immigration-enforcement-fbi-dea-secret-service-all-other-federal-criminal-law.

18. "Who We Are," Immigration and Customs Enforcement, www.ice.gov/about.

19. For an in-depth analysis of the convergence between counterinsurgency policy and immigration enforcement, see Timothy J. Dunn, *The Militarization of the US–Mexico Border, 1978–1992: Low-Intensity Conflict Doctrine Comes Home* (Austin: University of Texas Press, 1996).

20. See Justin Akers Chacón, "ICE: The Making of an American Gestapo," *Socialist Worker*, July 17, 2018, https://socialistworker.org/2018/07/17/ice-the-making-of-an-american-gestapo. See also Franklin Foer, "How Trump Radicalized ICE," *Atlantic*, September 2018, www.theatlantic.com/magazine/archive/2018/09/trump-ice/565772/; Eric Kerl, "Four Theses on American Fascism," *Rampant Magazine*, November 2, 2020, http://rampantmag.com/2020/11/02/four-theses-on-american-fascism/.

21. See Margot Mendelson, Shayna Strom, and Michael Wishnie, "Collateral Damage: An Examination of ICE's Fugitive Operations Program," *Migration Policy Institute*, February 2009, www.migrationpolicy.org/pubs/NFOP_Feb09.pdf.

22. Discussed in detail in Fernanda Echeverri and Noam Hassenfeld, "Obama Leaves Office As 'Deporter-In-Chief'" *Latino USA*, NPR, January 20, 2017, www.npr.org/2017/01/20/510799842/obama-leaves-office-as-deporter-in-chief.

23. To understand how the Trump regime cooked the numbers to show an absurdly distorted picture of 92 percent criminality, see *FY 2017 ICE Enforcement and*

*Removal Operators Report* (Washington: Immigration and Customs Reform, 2017), www.ice.gov/removal-statistics/2017..

24. Tal Kopan, "How Trump Changed the Rules to Arrest More Non-Criminal Immigrants," CNN, March 2, 2018, www.cnn.com/2018/03/02/politics /ice-immigration-deportations/index.html.
25. His attempt was ultimately thwarted by his own stacked Supreme Court, most likely because the ruling occurred during the Black Lives Matter uprising in June 2020. See Brent Kendall, Jess Bravin, and Michelle Hackman, "Trump's Bid to End DACA Blocked by Supreme Court" *Wall Street Journal*, June 18, 2020, www.wsj.com/articles/supreme-court-blocks-trump-cancellation-of-daca -immigration-program-11592489280.
26. Alan Maass, "The Pro-Immigrant Majority in the Streets," *Socialist Worker*, July 2, 2018, https://socialistworker.org/2018/07/02/the-pro-immigrant -majority-in-the-streets.
27. "Growing the Resistance: How Sanctuary Laws and Policies Have Flourished During the Trump Administration," Immigrant Legal Resource Center, December 17, 2019, www.ilrc.org/growing-resistance-how-sanctuary-laws-and -policies-have-flourished-during-trump-administration.
28. ACLU, "Enforceable Standards and Community-Based Alternatives To Detention Still Needed, Says ACLU," (press release) August 6, 2009, www.aclu.org/press-releases/dhs-plan-improve-immigration-detention -and-close-hutto-facility-good-first-step.
29. For a full analysis, see Muzaffar Chishti and Sarah Pierce, "Despite Trump Invitation to Stop Taking Refugees, Red and Blue States Alike Endorse Resettlement," *Migration Policy Institute*, January 29, 2020, www.migrationpolicy.org/article/despite-trump-invitation-stop-taking -refugees-red-and-blue-states-alike-endorse-resettlement.
30. See Congressional Research Service, "The Trump Administration's 'Zero Tolerance' Immigration Enforcement Policy," February 26, 2019, https://fas.org /sgp/crs/homesec/R45266.pdf; Caitlin Dickerson, "Parents of 545 Children Separated at the Border Cannot Be Found," *New York Times*, October 21, 2020, www.nytimes.com/2020/10/21/us /migrant-children-separated.html.
31. Hunt Palmquist, "Flight Attendant: I Won't Work Flights That Separate Immigrant Kids from Families," *Houston Chronicle*, June 20, 2018, www.houstonchronicle.com/local/gray-matters/article/Flight-attendant-I -won-t-work-flights-that-13008372.php.
32. See Association of Flight Attendants-CWA, "Separated Families Intersecting with Aviation," June 20, 2018, www.afacwa.org/separated_families_intersecting _with_aviation. See also Amy Pollard, "Flight Attendants Want No Part in Separating Immigrant Children From Parents," *Slate*, June 20, 2018, https://slate.com/news-and-politics/2018/06/flight-attendants-oppose -trump-administrations-family-separation-policy.html; Anthony Zurcher,

"Trump Backs Down on Migrant Family Separations Policy," BBC, June 21, 2018, www.bbc.com/news/world-us-canada-44552852.

33. "Statement on Recent Reports of Separated Families"American Airlines Newsroom, June 20, 2018, http://news.aa.com/news/news-details/2018/Statement-on-Recent-Reports-of-Separated-Families/default.aspx.

34. See Anthony Cuthbertson, "Amazon Workers 'Refuse' To Build Tech For US Immigration, Warning Jeff Bezos of IBM's Nazi Legacy," *Independent*, June 22, 2018, www.independent.co.uk/life-style/gadgets-and-tech/news/amazon-workers-immigration-jeff-bezos-ibm-nazi-protest-a8411601.html. For the text of the letter, go to www.scribd.com/document/382334740/Dear-Jeff.

35. Sheera Frenkel, "Microsoft Employees Protest Work with ICE, as Tech Industry Mobilizes over Immigration," *New York Times*, June 19, 2018, www.nytimes.com/2018/06/19/technology/tech-companies-immigration-border.html.

36. Johana Bhuiyan, "Employees of Microsoft's GitHub Demand Company Cancel its Contract with ICE," *Los Angeles Times*, October 9, 2019, www.latimes.com/business/technology/story/2019-10-09/github-ice-contract-employee-oppose.

37. Meg Wagner, Veronica Rocha, Brian Ries, and Amanda Wills, "What's Happening at the US Border," CNN, June 22, 2018, www.cnn.com/politics/live-news/immigration-border-children-separation/h_d746f2f137474c2d6257449c16a697ba.

38. Miles Parks, Scott Detrow, Kelsey Snell, "Trump Signs Order to End Family Separations," NPR, June 20, 2018, www.npr.org/2018/06/20/621798823/speaker-ryan-plans-immigration-votes-amid-doubts-that-bills-can-pass.

39. Michael D. Shear, Eileen Sullivan and Zolan Kanno-Youngs, "What Will Trump's Tough New Asylum Policy Mean for Migrants on the Border?" *New York Times*, April 17, 2019, www.nytimes.com/2019/04/17/us/politics/asylum-facts-seekers-laws.html.

40. Caitlin Dickerson, "Border at 'Breaking Point' as More Than 76,000 Unauthorized Migrants Cross in a Month," *New York Times*, March 5, 2019, www.nytimes.com/2019/03/05/us/border-crossing-increase.html.

41. TRAC Immigration, "Immigrant Detention Numbers Fall under Biden, but Border Book-Ins Rise," TRAC is a nonpartisan, nonprofit data research center affiliated with the Newhouse School of Public Communications and the Whitman School of Management, both at Syracuse University, https://trac.syr.edu/immigration/reports/640/ and Jaden Urbi, "This Is How Much It Costs to Detain an Immigrant in the US," *CNBC.com*, July 5, 2020, https://www.cnbc.com/2018/06/20/cost-us-immigrant-detention-trump-zero-tolerance-tents-cages.html.

42. Bea Bischoff, "Immigrant Detention Conditions Were Atrocious Under Obama. Here's Why They're So Much Worse Under Trump," *Slate*, June 25, 2019, https://slate.com/news-and-politics/2019/06/trump-child-immigrant-detention-no-toothpaste-obama.html.

43. Data can be found at "Southwest Border Migration FY 2019," US Customs and

Border Protection, www.cbp.gov/newsroom/stats/sw-border-migration/fy-2019.

44. Ryan Baugh, "Refugees and Asylees: 2019," Office of Immigration Statistics, Department of Homeland Security, September 2020, https://www.dhs.gov/sites/default/files/publications/immigration-statistics/yearbook/2019/refugee_and_asylee_2019.pdf.

45. Caitlin Dickerson, "'There Is a Stench': Soiled Clothes and No Baths for Migrant Children at a Texas Center," *New York Times*, June 21, 2019, www.nytimes.com/2019/06/21/us/migrant-children-border-soap.html.

46. Robert Moore, "In El Paso, Border Patrol Is Detaining Migrants in 'a Human Dog Pound,'" *Texas Monthly*, June 11, 2019, www.texasmonthly.com/news/border-patrol-outdoor-detention-migrants-el-paso/.

47. Moore, "In El Paso, Border Patrol."

48. Nicole Acevedo, "Why Are Migrant Children Dying in US Custody?" NBC News, May 29, 2019, www.nbcnews.com/news/latino/why-are-migrant-children-dying-u-s-custody-n1010316.

49. Robert Moore, "Six Children Died in Border Patrol Care. Democrats in Congress Want to Know Why," *ProPublica*, January 13, 2020, www.propublica.org/article/six-children-died-in-border-patrol-care-democrats-in-congress-want-to-know-why.

50. Harriet Sinclair, "Border Agent Jokes as Kids Cry After Being Separated from Parents, Audio Recording Reveals," *Newsweek*, June 19, 2018, www.newsweek.com/border-agent-jokes-kids-cry-after-being-separated-parents-audio-983199.

51. A. C. Thompson, "Inside the Secret Border Patrol Facebook Group Where Agents Joke About Migrant Deaths and Post Sexist Memes," *ProPublica*, July 1, 2019, www.propublica.org/article/secret-border-patrol-facebook-group-agents-joke-about-migrant-deaths-post-sexist-memes.

52. See a continuing compilation of deaths at the border at the hands of immigration agents at "Deaths by Border Patrol Since 2010," Southern Border Communities Coalition, www.southernborder.org/deaths_by_border_patrol.

53. Guillermo Cantor and Walter Ewing, "Still No Action Taken: Complaints against Border Patrol Agents Continue to Go Unanswered," *American Immigration Council*, August 2, 2017, www.americanimmigrationcouncil.org/research/still-no-action-taken-complaints-against-border-patrol-agents-continue-go-unanswered.

54. Shibley Telhami and Stella M. Rouse, "New Poll: Despite Partisan Divides on Immigration, Americans Oppose Family Separation," *Lawfare*, April 10, 2019, www.lawfareblog.com/new-poll-despite-partisan-divides-immigration-americans-oppose-family-separation.

55. Vanessa Romo, "US Supreme Court Allows 'Remain in Mexico' Program to Continue," NPR, March 11, 2020, www.npr.org/2020/03/11/814582798/u-s-supreme-court-allows-remain-in-mexico-program-to-continue.

56. Peniel Ibe, "How Trump Is Making It Harder for Asylum Seekers" *American Friends Service Committee* (blog), November 2, 2020, https://www.afsc.org/blogs/news-and-commentary/how-trump-making-it-harder-asylum-seekers.

57. Jose Cabezas, "Mexico Says National Guard Deployment to Southern Border Starts on Wednesday," Reuters, June 12, 2019, www.reuters.com/article/us-usa-trade-mexico-border/mexico-says-national-guard-deployment-to-southern-border-starts-on-wednesday-idUSKCN1TD1UI; Dave Graham, "Mexico Says It Has Deployed 15,000 Forces in the North to Halt U.S.-Bound Migration," Reuters, June 24, 2019, www.reuters.com/article/us-usa-trade-mexico-immigration/mexico-says-it-has-deployed-15000-forces-in-the-north-to-halt-u-s-bound-migration-idUSKCN1TP2YN.
58. Kristina Cooke, Mica Rosenberg, Reade Levinson, "Exclusive: US Migrant Policy Sends Thousands of Children, Including Babies, Back to Mexico," Reuters, October 11, 2019, www.reuters.com/article/us-usa-immigration-babies-exclusive/exclusive-u-s-migrant-policy-sends-thousands-of-children-including-babies-back-to-mexico-idUSKBN1WQ1H1.
59. See *A Year of Horrors: The Trump Administration's Illegal Returns of Asylum Seekers to Danger in Mexico*, Human Rights First, January 2020 ,www.humanrightsfirst.org/sites/default/files/MPP-aYearofHorrors-UPDATED.pdf.
60. Robert Schroeder, "Trump Today: President Says Migrants Are Coming to US Like It's Disneyland and escalates trade fight with Europe," *Market Watch,* April 9, 2019, www.marketwatch.com/story/trump-today-president-says-migrants-are-coming-to-us-like-its-disneyland-and-escalates-trade-fight-with-europe-2019-04-09.
61. For more information see their webpage at https://www.swkey.org/.
62. "Mr. Obama's Dubious Detention Centers," editorial, *New York Times*, July 18, 2016, www.nytimes.com/2016/07/18/opinion/mr-obamas-dubious-detention-centers.html.
63. Kim Barker, Nicholas Kulish, and Rebecca R. Ruiz, "He's Built an Empire, with Detained Migrant Children as the Bricks," *New York Times*, December 2, 2018, www.nytimes.com/2018/12/02/us/southwest-key-migrant-children.html.
64. Barker, Kulish, and Ruiz, "He's Built an Empire."
65. Barker, Kulish, and Ruiz, "He's Built an Empire."
66. See David Boddiger, "Videos Show Southwest Key Employees Dragging and Shoving Migrant Kids," *Splinter News,* December 30, 2018, https://splinternews.com/videos-show-southwest-key-employees-dragging-and-shovin-1831388383. See also Melissa Adan and Tom Jones, "Former Employees Allege Immigrant Youth Shelters Would Not Properly Report Cases of Sexual Abuse and Misconduct," NBC San Diego, December 5, 2018, www.nbcsandiego.com/investigations/Former-Employees-Allege-Immigrant-Youth-Shelters-Would-Not-Properly-Report-Cases-of-Sexual-Abuse-and-Misconduct-501906191.html; Bree Burkitt, "Jury Finds Southwest Key Employee Guilty of Molesting Unaccompanied Minors at Mesa Shelter," *Arizona Republic*, www.azcentral.com/story/news/politics/immigration/2018/09/10/southwest-key-worker-convicted-abusing-minors-arizona-migrant-shelter/1258594002/.
67. Laura Gómez, "State Inspectors Visited Six Southwest Key Facilities. Here's

What They Found," *AZ Mirror,* May 16, 2019, www.azmirror.com/2019/05/16/state-inspectors-visited-six-southwest-key-facilities-heres-what-they-found/.

68. Priscilla Alvarez, "HHS Cutting Activities for Unaccompanied Children in Shelters," CNN, June 5, 2019, www.cnn.com/2019/06/05/politics/hhs-activities-unaccompanied-children/index.html.

69. Garance Burke, Juliet Linderman, and Martha Mendoza, "Revealed: Biden Administration Holding Tens of Thousands of Migrant Children," *Guardian,* May 11, 2021, www.theguardian.com/us-news/2021/may/11/us-migrant-children-opaque-network-facilities.

70. See "Detention Management," Immigration and Customs Enforcement, www.ice.gov/detention-management.

71. For a complete map and list of GEO Group operations, go to their webpage at www.geogroup.com/LOCATIONS. For CoreCivic, see "CoreCivic, Inc." American Friends Service Committee, July 19, 2019, https://investigate.afsc.org/company/corecivic.

72. Perla Trevizo, "COVID-19 Cases at a Texas Immigration Detention Center Soared. Now, Town Leaders Want Answers," *Texas Tribune,* May 11, 2020, www.texastribune.org/2020/05/11/covid-19-cases-soar-texas-immigrant-detention-center-town-wants-answer/.

73. See *Lives in Peril: How Ineffective Inspections Make ICE Complicit in Immigration Detention Abuse,* Immigration Detention Transparency and Human Rights Project, October 2015, http://immigrantjustice.org/sites/immigrantjustice.org/files/THR-Inspections-FOIA-Report-EXECUTIVE-SUMMARY-October-2015.pdf.

74. Ron Nixon, "Is ICE's Help-Wanted Sign a Welcome Mat for Rogue Applicants, Too?" *New York Times,* March 12, 2017, www.nytimes.com/2017/03/12/us/politics/trump-ice-agents-deportations-immigrants.html.

75. Hannah Rappleye and Lisa Riordan Seville, "24 Immigrants Have Died in ICE Custody During the Trump Administration," NBC News, June 9, 2019, www.nbcnews.com/politics/immigration/24-immigrants-have-died-ice-custody-during-trump-administration-n1015291.

76. See *Widespread Sexual Assault,* Freedom for Immigrants, www.freedomforimmigrants.org/sexual-assault.

77. John Burnett, "Big Money as Private Immigrant Jails Boom," NPR, November 21, 2017, www.npr.org/2017/11/21/565318778/big-money-as-private-immigrant-jails-boom.

78. Aimee Picchi, "Working for Peanuts: Detained Immigrants Paid $1 a Day," CBS News, September 22, 2017. https://www.cbsnews.com/news/working-for-peanuts-detained-immigrants-paid-1-a-day/. See also Michele Chen, "ICE's Captive Immigrant Labor Force," *Nation,* October 11, 2017, www.thenation.com/article/ices-captive-immigrant-labor-force/.

79. Kate Duguid, "U.S. Private Prison Revenue under Pressure from New Biden

Rules," Reuters, January 27, 2021, www.reuters.com/article/us-usa-companies-biden-prisons/u-s-private-prison-revenue-under-pressure-from-new-biden-rules-idUSKBN29W14Z.

80. Alan Gomez, "Trump Plans Massive Increase in Federal Immigration Jails," *USA Today*, October 17, 2017, www.usatoday.com/story/news/world/2017/10/17/trump-plans-massive-increase-federal-immigration-jails/771414001/.
81. Gomez, "Trump Plans Massive Increase in Federal Immigration Jails."
82. See the list of "GEO managers" at www.geogroup.com/management_team.
83. Lisa Olsen, "Private Prisons Boom in Texas and across America under Trump's Immigration Crackdown," *Houston Chronicle*, August 19, 2017, www.houstonchronicle.com/news/houston-texas/houston/article/Private-prisons-boom-in-Texas-and-across-America-11944652.php; see also Natalie J. Pierson, "ICE Boss to Take Private Prison Gig," *Daily Beast*, May 9, 2017, www.thedailybeast.com/ice-boss-to-take-private-prison-gig; Betsy Swan, "ICE Boss to Take Private Prison Gig," Daily Beast May 09, 2017, www.thedailybeast.com/ice-boss-to-take-private-prison-gig..
84. Noah Lanard, "ICE's Revolving Door: Top Official Goes to Work for Private Prison Company," *Mother Jones*, November 25, 2019, www.motherjones.com/politics/2019/11/ices-revolving-door-top-official-goes-to-work-for-private-prison-company/.
85. See her profile on the George Washington University Center for Cyber and Homeland Security website at https://web.archive.org/web/20170907080357/https:/cchs.gwu.edu/kirstjen-nielsen.
86. See their website at http://pangiam.com/index.html.
87. Julia Ainsley, Katy Tur, and Laura Strickler, "Trump Admin Considering Chad Wolf, an Author of Family Separation Policy, for DHS Chief," NBC News, October 22, 2019, www.nbcnews.com/politics/immigration/trump-admin-considering-chad-wolf-architect-family-separation-dhs-chief-n1070006.
88. Justin Elliott, Al Shaw, and Derek Kravitz, "Meet the Hundreds of Officials Trump Has Quietly Installed Across the Government," *ProPublica*, March 8, 2017, www.propublica.org/article/meet-hundreds-of-officials-trump-has-quietly-installed-across-government.
89. Justin Rohrlich and Heather Timmons, "ICE Plans to Transport 225,000 Immigrant Kids to Shelters over the Next Five Years," *Quartz* May 16, 2019, https://qz.com/1620064/ice-plans-to-transport-225000-immigrant-kids/.
90. The action can be seen at www.youtube.com/watch?v=S7l1jga_R3o.
91. Find more information at www.neveragainaction.com/; and here: John Nichols, "ICE Is Everywhere, So Is Never Again Action," *Nation*, December 13, 2019, www.thenation.com/article/archive/ice-activism-never-again-action/.
92. Find more information about these groups at www.facebook.com/CoalitiontoClosetheCamps; http://nomorecamps.org/; http://act.moveon.org/event/close-camps-now_attend/search/; www.lightsforliberty.org/.

93. Natalie Shure, "Wayfair Workers Walk Out," *Nation*, Jun 28, 2019, www.thenation.com/article/archive/wayfair-workers-walk-out/.

94. Jorge L. Ortiz, "Wayfair Walkout: Employees Stage Protest over Company Selling Goods to Detention Camps," *USA Today*, June 26, 2019, www.usatoday.com/story/news/nation/2019/06/25/wayfair-walkout-employees-protest-retailer-selling-detention-camps-border-children-immigration/1566160001/

95. Nick Statt, "Whole Foods Employees Demand Amazon Break All Ties with ICE and Palantir," *Verge*, August 12, 2019, www.theverge.com/2019/8/12/20802893/whole-foods-employees-amazon-ice-protest-palantir-facial-recognition.

96. Bhuiyan, "Employees of Microsoft's GitHub."

97. Rosalie Chan, "The Microsoft-Owned GitHub Is under Pressure for Its Work with ICE, as Employees Resign and Activists Protest Its Biggest Event of the Year," *Business Insider*, November 13, 2019. Available online at www.businessinsider.com/github-employees-ice-contracts-protest-microsoft-2019-11.

98. Alia Wong, "The Unique Racial Dynamics of the L.A. Teachers' Strike," *Atlantic*, January 14, 2019, www.theatlantic.com/education/archive/2019/01/why-los-angeles-teachers-are-striking/580360/.

99. "What We Won," United Teachers of Los Angeles, https://www.utla.net/sites/default/files/What%20We%20Won%20Side-by-Side%20032919.pdf.

100. "Exclusive Poll: LA Public Supports Striking Teachers," ABC7.com. https://abc7.com/lausd-teachers-strike-la-poll-surveyusa/5077986/.

101. "Ocasio-Cortez wants to abolish ICE," CNN, June 27, 2018, www.cnn.com/videos/politics/2018/06/27/alexandria-ocasio-cortez-abolish-ice-newsroom-sot-vpx.cnn.

102. Libby Torres, "Cynthia Nixon Calls ICE a 'Terrorist Organization,'" *Gothamist*, June 22, 2018, https://gothamist.com/news/cynthia-nixon-calls-ice-a-terrorist-organization.

103. Establishing a Humane Immigration Enforcement System Act, H. R. 6361, 115th Cong. www.congress.gov/bill/115th-congress/house-bill/6361.

104. Lee Harris, "Progressive Democrats Introduce Bill to Abolish ICE," ABC News, July 12, 2018, https://abcnews.go.com/Politics/progressive-democrats-introduce-bill-abolish-ice/story?id=56537797.

105. Juliegrace Brufke, "Dems Say They'll Vote 'No' on Their 'Abolish ICE' Legislation," *The Hill*, July 12, 2018, https://thehill.com/homenews/house/396818-dems-say-theyll-vote-no-on-their-abolish-ice-legislation.

106. Kevin Urlacher, Kevin Shaul, and Michael Scherer, "Where 2020 Democrats Stand on Immigration," *Washington Post*, April 18, 2020, www.washingtonpost.com/graphics/politics/policy-2020/immigration/.

107. For a fuller description of the first months of the Biden administration and Democratic congressional majority, see Justin Akers Chacón, "A Path to Nowhere," *Rampant Magazine*, March 3, 2021, rampantmag.com

/2021/03/a-path-to-nowhere/.

108. Bernie Sanders, "A Welcoming and Safe America for All," https://berniesanders.com/issues/welcoming-and-safe-america-all/.

109. There are various examples to examine as part of engaging in this work. For international examples, see Kate Bronfenbrenner, ed., *Global Unions: Challenging Transnational Capital through Cross-border Campaigns* (Ithaca: Cornell University Press, 2007). For North American examples, see Richard Roman and Edur Velasco Arreguí, *Continental Crucible: Big Business, Workers and Unions in the Transformation of North America* (Nova Scotia: PM Press, 2015). For an example from Mexico, see Dale Hathaway, *Allies Across the Border: Mexico's Authentic Labor Front and Global Solidarity* (Boston: South End Press, 2000).

110. David Dayen, "Meet the Militant Flight Attendant Leader Who Threatened a Strike—And Helped Stop Trump's Shutdown," *In These Times*, February 8, 2019, https://inthesetimes.com/working/entry/21735/flight-attendant-union-labor-trump-shutdown-sara-nelson-strike.

111. Kim Kelly, "Sara Nelson's Art of War," *New Republic*, May 13, 2019, https://newrepublic.com/article/153797/sara-nelsons-art-war.

112. Liza Featherstone, "How Flight Attendants Grounded Trump's Shutdown," *Jacobin*, February 8, 2019, http://jacobinmag.com/2019/02/flight-attendants-union-sara-nelson-shutdown.

113. Ben Beckett, "Sickouts and Strike Threats Stopped the Government Shutdown," *Jacobin*, January 25, 2019, http://jacobinmag.com/2019/01/government-shutdown-collective-action-strikes-unions.

114. Jim Norman, "Solid Majority Still Opposes New Construction on Border Wall," *Gallup*, February 4, 2019, https://news.gallup.com/poll/246455/solid-majority-opposes-new-construction-border-wall.aspx.

115. Nicole Narea, "How "Abolish ICE" Helped Bring Abolitionist Ideas into the Mainstream," *Vox*, July 9, 2020, www.vox.com/policy-and-politics/2020/7/9/21307137/abolish-ice-police-immigrant-black-lives-matter.

116. See Joseph Zeballos-Roig, "GOP Senator Calls on Trump to Reopen Parts of the Coronavirus-Stricken Economy Because 'Death Is an Unavoidable Part of Life,'" *Business Insider*, March 31, 2020, www.businessinsider.com/gop-senator-open-economy-coronavirus-death-unavoidable-part-johnson-life-2020-3. See also Abigail Censky, "Heavily Armed Protesters Gather Again at Michigan Capitol to Decry Stay-at-Home Order," NPR May 14, 2020, www.npr.org/2020/05/14/855918852/heavily-armed-protesters-gather-again-at-michigans-capitol-denouncing-home-order.

# Index

"Passim" (literally "scattered") indicates intermittent discussion of a topic over a cluster of pages.